1918

1918

The Decisive Year
in Soldiers' own
Words and Photographs

Richard van Emden

Pen & Sword
MILITARY
AN IMPRINT OF PEN & SWORD BOOKS LTD.
YORKSHIRE – PHILADELPHIA

First published in Great Britain in 2018 by
Pen & Sword Military
an imprint of
Pen & Sword Books Ltd
Yorkshire – Philadelphia

ISBN 978 1 52675 232 1

Typeset in Ehrhardt by
Mac Style
Printed and bound in the UK by CPI Group (UK) Ltd, Croydon, CR0 4YY

Pen & Sword Books Ltd incorporates the imprints of Pen & Sword Archaeology, Atlas,
Aviation, Battleground, Discovery, Family History, History, Maritime, Military, Naval, Politics,
Railways, Select, Transport, True Crime, Fiction, Frontline Books, Leo Cooper, Praetorian
Press, Seaforth Publishing, Wharncliffe and White Owl.

For a complete list of Pen & Sword titles please contact

PEN & SWORD BOOKS LIMITED
47 Church Street, Barnsley, South Yorkshire, S70 2AS, England
E-mail: enquiries@pen-and-sword.co.uk
Website: www.pen-and-sword.co.uk

or

PEN AND SWORD BOOKS
1950 Lawrence Rd, Havertown, PA 19083, USA
E-mail: uspen-and-sword@casematepublishers.com
Website: www.penandswordbooks.com

The National Archives logo device is a trade mark of The National Archives
and issued under licence.

The National Archives logo © Crown Copyright 2018.

The National Archives is the official archives and publisher for the UK Government,
and for England and Wales. We work to bring together and secure the future of the public
record, both digital and physical, for future generations.

The National Archives is open to all, offering a range of activities and spaces to enjoy,
as well as our reading rooms for research. Many of our most popular records are also
available online. For more information, visit nationalarchives.gov.uk

Title Page: *Opposing sides but the same idea: soldiers with chalk-decorated dud artillery shells.*

Frontispiece: *A German observation balloon takes to the air, February 1918.*

To

Richard Comstive

CONTENTS

Opposite: *An officer of an anti-aircraft battery, summer 1918. He is wearing the small box respirator on his chest.*

Introduction

'Suddenly a nearby battery of long-range guns cracked out an ear-splitting salvo. And before the desolating rush of the shells had faded from the ear a nightingale hidden among the trees burst into song. That also was part of the war.'

**Captain George Nicholls, C Battery,
2nd Brigade, Royal Field Artillery**

The Western Front finally 'unblocked' in 1918. The trench stalemate, which came to define popular memory of the Great War, could not last forever, although at times it appeared as if it might. After three and a half years of fighting, the tide of the war was moving slowly and resolutely in favour of the Allies, leaving Germany little option but to launch a frenzied all-out assault to win or resign itself to defeat.

In March 1918 that assault came, smashing through Allied lines, threatening to push the British back over vital transport hubs and supply lines and ultimately to the Channel ports; the French were simultaneously driven south to defend Paris. It was one of the most dramatic moments of the war and yet today it is an event almost forgotten by the public – revisited only, perhaps, in R.C. Sherriff's theatrical masterpiece *Journey's End*, a stifling, claustrophobic story of British infantry officers waiting for the German storm to break.

The enemy offensive of March 1918 quickly enveloped the Somme battlefield, but today, for the British at least, the Somme is emotionally the preserve of 1916, that hugely destructive set piece and oft-repeated first day's casualties. In April 1918, the Germans attacked at Ypres, but the name of that Belgian town is largely synonymous with 1917 and the suffering there amidst the German pillboxes and torrential rain. In May 1918, the Germans pushed on the Aisne, and in July along the Marne. But

Opposite: A damaged crucifix at the battered village of Violaines, 6 miles east of Béthune.

if either the Aisne or the Marne is spoken of, it is usually with reference to the fighting there in 1914, at the end of the epic 200-mile retreat from Mons.

Quite simply, the German March Offensive does not have the cachet of the 1916 Somme or the Battle of Passchendaele, as the 1917 assault at Ypres is best remembered. The March Offensive, or its alternative names, the Spring Offensive, the Kaiserschlacht, has never attained and will never attain a corresponding resonance, even though the fighting was every bit as hard and the casualties comparable.

And in the second half of 1918, what of the great final Allied counterstroke, the so-called 100 days to victory? The Germans were forced to give up their gains of the spring, retreating until the only recourse open to Berlin was unreserved capitulation and, in the Kaiser's case, a swift abdication and exit to Holland. This great Allied victory, utilizing everything that had been learnt in the previous years, skilfully combining the military technologies of land and air at Field Marshal Haig's disposal: what names have we for that litany of victories? The Battles of Amiens, Épehy, the Hindenburg Line, the Sambre – all names officially awarded for these successful actions, amongst others, but they hardly trip off the public tongue.

That has been the fate of 1918: it is a year that is somehow ignored, shunted into a siding, perhaps because battles of significant movement, where great tracts of ground are gained by one side and then the other, are out of step with the Great War's established narrative of static trench warfare and lives lost for yards gained of muddy, blood-soaked ground. Perhaps, when the prevailing ethos is to remember that time as misery heaped on futility, the word 'victory' sounds hollow, and out of step with modern sentiment.

Yet in so many ways, 1918 can lay claim to be the most interesting year of all, because it has a little bit of everything and drama without parallel. The unblocking of the Western Front included stupefying bombardments reminiscent of the Somme and Ypres offensives and of conventional daily trench warfare too. There was a German offensive against the British, an event not experienced since 1915, and then there was open warfare akin to the 'war of movement' last seen in the late summer and early autumn of 1914.

Britain's fight in 1918 would be carried to the enemy by men of many nationalities, race and colour. Amongst Britain's troops were regular and territorial men from the early years of the conflict, and men of Kitchener's Army as well as Derby men recruited in late 1915 during the last spasms of voluntary enlistment. They were all there still, although the bulk of fighting men were of the conscript army called up after 1916. And then there were the young lads shipped over to France in their tens of thousands in the dire days of March and April 1918, the 'men of eighteen in 1918' as one of them referred to himself and his friends, drafted abroad to help save the British cause.

These, then, were the men involved, armed with the latest military technology, weapons employed and combined in so-called 'All Arms' offensives, the prototype for 'shock and awe'.

Exhausted men of the 4th (Royal Irish) Dragoon Guards occupy a makeshift trench, winter 1917/18.

This is the latest book in my series featuring the words of the men who fought and illustrated by their own photographs. It is dedicated to telling the soldiers' stories, understanding their motivations and fears as well as their humour – natural, funny, often dark. I am always aware that I am writing the soldiers' war, their experience, not a military history of the campaign. There is a clear difference. 'Campaign' historians will follow the fighting: the preparation, the execution and the aftermath. These authors are less interested in the minutiae of daily life, the small idiosyncrasies of service, the curious incidents that have no wider repercussions for a battle, or the whimsical observations by a soldier of his feelings and thoughts.

In reality, the soldier's life was rarely offensive in spirit or in action. Fighting may have been close by, but his attention was drawn to the here and now, the parochial life of the section, the platoon or, at most, the company, in and out of the trenches. If a man was not 'involved' in combat, then what happened ten or five miles, or even one mile away was of little importance. The fighting barely abated between March and November 1918. Britain's casualties – killed, wounded, missing and prisoners of war – were the greatest of any year of the war, but the intention here is not remorselessly to describe the fighting, but to balance the overall narrative of the broader chronological story with the narrative of the individual man, the soldier.

In recent years, I have become interested in both the home front and the Western Front, not in isolation from one another – most books focus exclusively on one side of the English Channel or the other – but bound together, one having an immediate and direct influence on the other. For this reason, and as a small departure from the other books in this series, I have included extracts from witnesses on the home front, brief impressionistic interludes at home in order to compare and contrast the thoughts and feelings expressed with those of the servicemen in France and Belgium. Equally, I have included the thoughts of men on the Western Front who sometimes fretted about the pessimism and thoughtlessness of people at home, especially at critical moments in the war when national unity was required. And, in another departure, I have sought to follow the stories of fewer characters in order that readers begin to feel a greater sympathy for the men quoted here and an understanding of who they were.

Many men were transformed during their service abroad, both mentally and spiritually, and not all for the better. That journey is important to our appreciation of what these men went through and therefore what they mean to us, one hundred years later.

The pictures featured here are, in the main, taken by soldiers on their own illegally held cameras. By 1918, the ban on cameras had been in place for three years. It had been issued just days before Christmas 1914 in response to the army's growing awareness of a trade in photographs between soldiers – primarily officers – and newspapers: cash in exchange for images of front-line life and, if at all possible, 'action' photographs. Huge sums were advertised for the best, most dramatic shots sent home, with press offers of free film development. In reality the vast majority of published images commanded small, only slightly better than nominal, fees.

This irregular communication between serving soldiers and the media back home was anathema to the army authorities, whose distaste for the press and ignorance of the use of pictures as propaganda had ensured that there were no journalists or photographers embedded with the forces in 1914. No official photographers appeared on the Western Front until 1916, when two were permitted to work under restrictions. By mid-1915, any soldier caught with a camera faced court martial and severe sanctions, sanctions repeated to all ranks prior to the Battle of Loos in September, when there was a widespread fear of spies infiltrating the British line. The vast majority of men sent their cameras home in 1915, albeit not without a grumble.

But those were the heady days when victory was still in sight, or so it seemed, and, broadly speaking, enthusiasm was high. The soldiers' appetite for taking images waned in any case as the war dragged on and fighting became increasingly businesslike and industrial. The bleak battlefields of 1916 and 1917 offered less in the way of photographic inspiration or variation to the individual soldier, except behind the lines.

Collectively, the images taken in the last year of the war give a fascinating insight, different from those of 1916 and 1917 in large part because open warfare resumed and because the location of the Germans' spring and summer assaults varied, from the wet Flanders plains down to the rolling lands of the Somme and further south still to the quaint

valleys and hills of the Marne near Paris. The soldiers who continued to keep hold of cameras tended to be either new to the front and still curious and keen to record what they saw, or individuals who were keen on both photography and war.

Once again, I have used German photographs in this book, in particular devoting one chapter – as I did in *The Somme* and *The Road to Passchendaele* – to images taken by enemy soldiers so as to reflect their perspective of the war. And as with my two previous books, I have also sought to cover the entire year, not just the months of fighting but also the winter 'downtime' before the German Spring Offensive, and the weeks after the Armistice and the Allied march to the Rhineland.

The battles of Verdun (for the French) and the Somme and Passchendaele (for the British) dominated commemorations in 2016 and 2017. By contrast, this year's national and international commemorations will not linger on any single offensive, but rather remembrance will be pointedly focused on the Armistice in November. Heartfelt tributes will be paid to the fallen on all sides. There will undoubtedly be analysis of the political and social lessons learnt or not learnt after peace, and identification of the conflict's 100-year-old ripples still felt around the globe. Thought will be given, too, to those who came back physically maimed and mentally wounded by war, as well as to the families who fought to survive at home while loved ones were away. It seems unlikely that there will be much discussion of the mechanics of Allied victory, the series of successful offensives that won the war and the extraordinary individual feats of arms. Nineteen eighteen will probably remain a neglected year. Whether that is the right decision, or, alternatively, an opportunity missed, I leave you to decide.

Richard van Emden
July 2018

Overleaf: 'Resting', according to the caption, in deep winter snow after a 'strafe'. The man referred to as 'me' appears to be an Artillery Observation Officer with binoculars in hand.

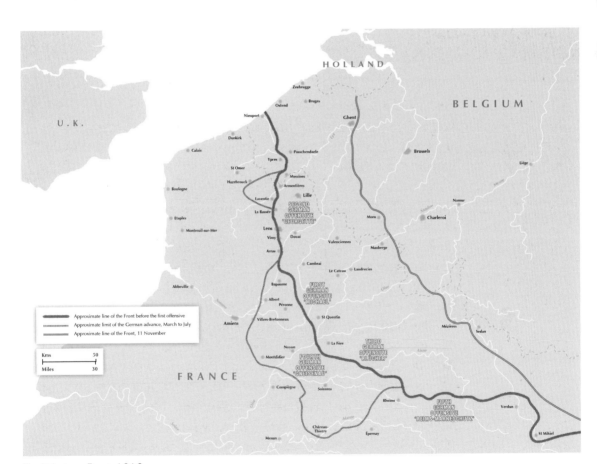

The Western Front, 1918.

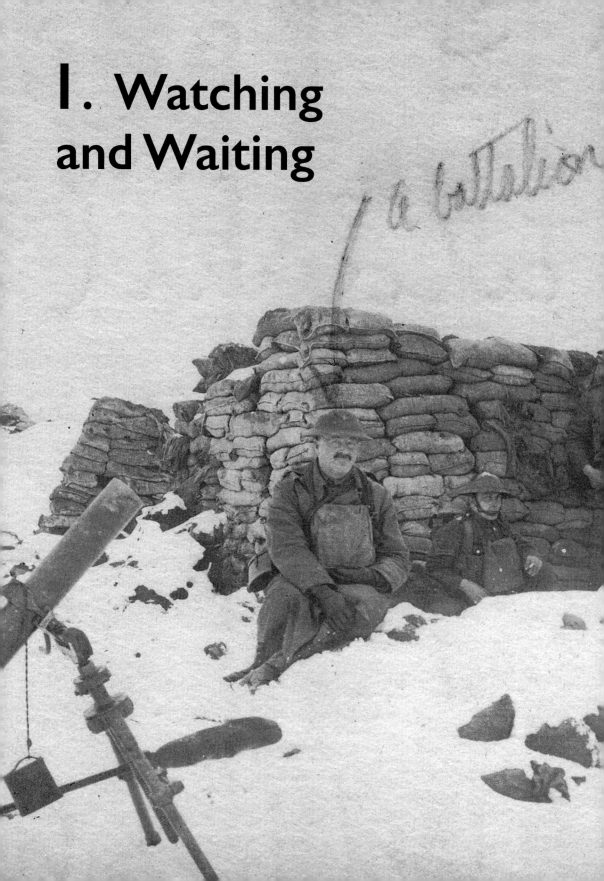

1. Watching and Waiting

'It is terribly slippery on the roads and in the trenches these days, but I am becoming a most accomplished tumbler. Even a backward full-length slip was safely and gracefully performed.'

Pioneer George Dewdney, Special Brigade, Royal Engineers

Two seismic events took place away from the battlefields in 1917 that would have huge repercussions for events upon it. America would enter the war on the Allied side, and Russia, in the wake of revolution, would exit, suing for peace with Germany. Losing one great ally in the east but gaining another deploying its troops in France and Belgium meant that the war – the world war – would be won or lost on the Western Front. But in 1918? Few Allied generals would be so gung-ho as to predict victory by Christmas after three years of brutal, draining conflict.

Owing to battlefield adversity, the German Army's High Command was best placed to appreciate that 1918 *had to be* the year of decision. In Berlin, the army, led by Field Marshal Paul von Hindenburg and Quartermaster General Erich Ludendorff, held all the key levers of power, the civilian government all but neutered. To the Kaiser and his military entourage what truly mattered was the prosecution of total war and final victory; civilian concerns came a distant second. This fixation was politically viable while Germany appeared to be winning and before the nation's economic lifeblood had drained away; problems multiplied once that scenario changed. As the war progressed, an Allied blockade on German ports became an ever more effective means of starving the enemy's economy of vital raw supplies. By 1917, Germany was suffering acute shortages of everything that was significant in prosecuting war, while leaving the civilian population begging for scraps, literally and metaphorically. The army's colossal job, supplying both Eastern and Western fronts, and the economic mismanagement that ensued, hastened the country's final plunge into the abyss. '*Ersatz*' (substitute) became a common word in spoken and written language and, as food rations were cut and cut again, social unrest grew: tens of thousands of Germans would die of malnourishment and associated illnesses by war's end.

Opposite:
The Somme battlefield near Martinpuich, early February. The battlefield was 20 miles behind the front line in early 1918 but would be overrun again in the months to come.

Russia's own descent into chaos, after the March and October revolutions and the ascent of the Bolshevik republic, handed Germany a brief window of opportunity. With peace in the east, a million battle-hardened men could be transferred to the Western Front, tipping the balance on the battlefield in favour of Germany. The High Command's aim was to drive a wedge between the British and the French, pushing the former north on to the Channel ports and the latter to hold or push back on Paris. German troops could win the war before American units arrived in enough numbers to tilt the balance irretrievably the other way. A series of offensives was planned and each given a name, including Michael, Mars, and George.

Field Marshal Haig, commanding British forces, was sombrely aware of German plans and prepared for the coming storm, though the Germans were not his only concern. In April 1917, the French Army mutinied after enduring colossal battlefield losses. To cover up the acute loss of morale in the French Army, the British forces shouldered a greater responsibility for fighting the Germans, launching offensive after offensive in part to keep the enemy occupied and ignorant of wider events. The high number of casualties suffered by British and Empire forces in 1917 led politicians at home to question Haig's handling of the war, ushering in a bitter breach of trust between Prime Minister David Lloyd George and his commander-in-chief. In order to curtail any thoughts Haig might have of a New Year offensive, Lloyd George, who believed the war could be won anywhere but the Western Front, consciously held back reinforcements in England. This decision seriously weakened the British Army's ability to defend itself when attacked by scores of reinvigorated German divisions.

In January 1918, that offensive was still three months away and, like every January before, most men battled not the enemy but the elements, keen simply to survive the freezing weather.

1st January: Although we had a large brazier in the barn, it took an enormous amount of fuel to keep it going, consequently we had to take it in turns in nightly raids on a neighbouring wood. Now, there had been so much damage done to this wood by troops, that the owners had already claimed several thousand francs from our battalion for damages, which had in turn been stopped from our pay, and our CO [commanding officer] had issued orders that no one was again to enter the wood.

However, we could not go cold, so we risked it and the wood was visited every night. From the owner of our barn, we borrowed a large sledge, and a cross-cut saw, and on reaching the wood, some would share in sawing down a tree, whilst others would be on the lookout, in case of unwelcome visitors. What a noise these trees made as they crashed to the ground. As soon as we had sawn them up into about 10-foot lengths, they were put on the sledge and pulled home – the sawdust and tracks in the wood we endeavoured to cover with snow, but in the darkness were not always successful.

The most trying times of these little stunts was in passing down the village street to our barn, with the heavily laden sledge, as we had a fear that we should be caught by an officer and reported to the CO. On one occasion, we bumped into one of our officers, we could not see who he was in the darkness; anyhow, his flash-lamp switched on to our load, but

Rifleman Frank Dunham, 7th (City of London Battalion) The London Regiment

Lieutenant John Sanderson, 4th (Royal Irish) Dragoon Guards, wrapped up against the cold. Photographed by fellow officer Lieutenant Gilbert Cattley.

in an instant, we had all vanished into the yards close by, leaving him by the sledge. He turned out to be a sport, for he walked off without endeavouring to find out who we were.

Pioneer George
Dewdney,
Special Brigade,
Royal Engineers

We left the [Arras] catacombs two days ago: I had had nearly enough of underground existence. The air was not exactly of the best and the lack of sunshine – we were there a month – was beginning to tell on us. All the same we were very comfy there and we could laugh at the cold and snow. We marched back to the old camp and here we are again in tents. We feel the difference, of course, and keep warm either by keeping a brazier going with fuel which we 'scrounge' – from solely legitimate sources of course! – or, if towards night and fuel is exhausted, by turning in. We cuddle up and keep quite warm there. It is a treat to breathe fresh air again and be within reach of YMCA huts and recreation rooms with amusements for leisure hours. Moreover, as the last place afforded none of these things, our wealth accumulated and we feel quite rich and now able to indulge our 'fresh air begotten' appetites. During dinner hour we made a wonderful meal. The menu of course was stew. The enamel plates provided were a bit of a novelty in this life, it is true, but the real success of the dinner lay in the cutlery – of which there was none!! Some of the fellows fashioned spoons out of biscuit tins and they really were works of art. I found the lid of a 6d tin of Oxo Cubes.

Living in a fetid, airless world in the labyrinth of Arras's medieval caves may have made re-emergence into the bitter cold seem inviting. However, that Christmas and New Year in 1917/18 was at times every bit as cold as the previous year and the ground proved extremely difficult to traverse. In early January, 379th Battery, Royal Field Artillery, was ordered to move to the village of Chuignolles, south of the Somme River. It was an excruciating journey, and the men and horses suffered every yard of the way.

Captain Arthur
Gibbs, 379th
Battery, Royal
Field Artillery

It is difficult to convey just what that march meant. It lasted four days, once the blizzard being so thick and blinding that the march was abandoned, the whole brigade remaining in temporary billets. The pace was a crawl. The [gun] team horses slid into each other and fell, the leads bringing the centres down, at every 20 yards or so. The least rise had to be navigated by improvising means of footholds – scattering a near manure heap, getting gunners up with picks and shovels and hacking at the road surface, assisting the horses with dragropes – and all the time the wind was like a razor on one's face and the drivers up on the staggering horses beat their chests with both arms and changed over with the gunners when all feeling had gone from their limbs. Hour after hour one trekked through the blinding white, silent country, stamping up and down at the halts with an anxious eye on the teams, chewing bully beef and biscuits and thanking God for coffee piping hot out of a thermos in the middle of the day. Then on again in the afternoon while the light grew less and dropped finally to an inky grey and the wind grew colder – hoping that the GS [general service] wagons, long since miles behind, would catch up. Hour after hour stiff in the saddle with icy hands and feet, one's neck cricked to dodge the wind, or sliding off stiffly to walk and get some warmth into one's aching limbs, the straps and weight of one's equipment becoming more and more irksome and heavy with every step forward that slipped two back. …

The British tank Hypatia, knocked out during the Cambrai Offensive in November 1917. The picture shows it being dismantled on 2 January 1918.

The snow came again and one went on the next day, blinded by the feathery touch of flakes that closed one's eyes so gently, crept down one's neck and pockets, lodged heavily in one's lap when mounted, clung in a frozen garment to one's coat when walking, hissed softly on one's pipe and made one giddy with the silent, whirling, endless pattern which blotted out the landscape.

Lieutenant Colonel Rowland Feilding, 6th The Connaught Rangers

8th January: Once more I have vowed that never again if I can help it will I travel by the 'leave' train. I had forgotten to bring a candle, so, the cold being bitter and the windows broken, I shivered in the darkness.

It is beyond my powers adequately to describe the horrors of the leave train, the scandal of which still continues after three and a half years of war. Though timed to arrive at [the] Divisional Railhead in the early morning we did not do so till the afternoon, and, after fifteen hours on the train, I reached my transport lines near Villers-Faucon at 2 pm in a blizzard having nothing to eat since last evening.

At the transport lines I found officers and men still under canvas, and as the ground was deep in snow the appearance of everything was very uninviting and conducive to nostalgia:- I believe that is the word.

The line is very quiet.

9th January: The terrible weather still holds. The frost having lasted practically since I left on 23rd December to go on leave. The blizzard continues, and the trenches are half full of snow. I have spent a good deal of today and tonight in them, and find that both officers and men retain their usual cheerfulness and patience in spite of their appalling hardships.

Company Quarter Master Sergeant Edward Lyons, Army Service Corps, 6th Division

10th January: We hold a rather curious and insecure line. There appears to be no proper trenches, chiefly a string of shell holes connected up. When we first took over the line here, it was quite easy to wander into the enemy lines by mistake. An officers' mess cart, a wagon and some men walked right into his lines one night and of course were taken prisoners, and it seems the Boche has a certain amount of humour still, for they sent one of the men back to thank us for our nice gift.

There had been some trouble with the Dublin Fusiliers and if what I'm told is true a party of six or seven gave themselves up to the enemy some nights ago, and again yesterday two more did likewise. It's a pity someone did not see them and speed them on the way with a couple of bombs.

We began to move at mid-day on Sunday, forty of us in a cattle truck: at midnight we reached a certain junction where the train was to stop a few hours – it was twenty-four hours as a matter of fact. We were glad to get out of the truck and stretch our legs, what with our cramped positions and the changing breezes – stifling hot from a brazier we had scrounged and icy cold from the various draughts – it was not always a joy ride. Repairing to a neighbouring canteen, we got busy with cocoa, and bread with sausages a foot long, which were certainly not intended for dining room consumption. At midnight the train made up its mind to move on, in which mind it continued more or less until the following (Tuesday) mid-day. After changing trains we finally got to this place [Fruges] about 1.30 pm.

Pioneer George Dewdney, Special Brigade, Royal Engineers

It was raining when we marched the 1½ miles to the billet. That was unpleasant but not too bad until the road disappeared under water and then our feelings which had been pretty well controlled, found relief! The wind, too, was blowing great guns, so that the rain came beneath the tiles of our barn billet.

The surrounding country is pleasant; not of striking beauty, but enough rolling hills high enough to make one want to climb them and see what is on the other side; some clumps of trees, and little streams and water-ways in the valley. And then there is the peace of everything. No guns here forever rumbling in the distance and no fear that the waxing moon will bring unwelcome visitors, for we are a long way from the war, and Fritz does not think this place worthy of his notice.

We are not here solely for a holiday, it's true. Rifle training is to occupy a considerable part of the time: we are giving up our revolvers – but the present is the only time to think of in army life, and just now it is all pleasant! Quiet, with little jobs to keep us fit and warm.

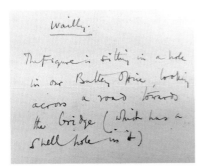

Wailly.

The figure is sitting in a hole in our Battery Office, looking across a road towards the bridge (which has a shell hole in it)

A poignant image of an artillery officer looking towards the shell-damaged bridge at Wailly, south-west of Arras.

Captain Arthur Behrend, 90th Brigade, Royal Garrison Artillery

During the past few months, despite the fact that we were barely 5,000 yards from the front line, the war had seemed so remote that we might have been 50 miles away from it. No shell had fallen within a thousand yards of us; our batteries had been living in comfort and luxury; visits to OPs [observation posts] or trips up the line were as devoid of incident as tramps over the Yorkshire Moors.

Since the Cambrai show [the previous November] the whole brigade had barely had a dozen casualties; in fact since Christmas life on the Bapaume front had been exceedingly pleasant – a succession of glorious canters across the overgrown downs to the batteries, joy-rides to Amiens through the snowy wastes of the Somme, early morning partridge shoots over the fields around our headquarters.

Captain Arthur Gibbs, 379th Battery, Royal Field Artillery

The village of Chuignolles, ice-bound, desolate, wood-patched, was our destination. The battles of the Somme had passed that way, wiping everything out. Old shell holes were softened with growing vegetation. Farm cottages were held together by bits of corrugated iron. The wind whistled through them, playing ghostly tunes on splintered trunks that once had been a wood.

Two prison camps full of Germans, who in some mysterious way knew that we had been in the Cambrai push and commented about it as we marched in, were the only human beings, save the village schoolmaster and his wife and child, in whose cottage we shared a billet with a Canadian forester. The schoolmaster was minus one arm, the wife had survived the German occupation and the child was a golden-haired boy full of laughter, with tiny teeth, blue eyes and chubby fingers that curled round his mother's heart. The men were lodged under bits of brick wall and felting that constituted at least shelter. … What kept them going? Was it that vague thing patriotism, the more vague because the war wasn't in their own country? Was it the ultimate hope of getting back to their Flos and Lucys, although leave, for them, was non-existent? What had they to look forward to but endless work in filth and danger, heaving guns, grooming horses, cleaning harness eternally?

It was hard for men to feel anything other than depressed. Fighting might be postponed in sub-zero winter weather, but the war had still to be won and the end appeared nowhere in sight. It was important that those at home were supportive and encouraging, not miserable.

You say many people at home are very depressed about the war. Now that is a very serious thing – it means that morale at home is bad. One of the first and most essential things about an army is that in order to fight well it must have good morale. You all at home are bearing the strain of the war just as much as we are out here, only in a different way – in fact I should think that most of you have got a bigger strain to bear than the underlings of an army GHQ! And if your morale is bad you won't be able to bear it, and you'll give way and want to make peace. This is apparently, and I gather from other sources besides your letter, somewhat the present state of affairs in England, and it seems to me to be very serious. There are many reasons why we should not make peace now. We went into this war because we believe our country to be the upholder of certain ideals and beliefs which we and our fathers before us have held for centuries. …

Captain Lancelot Spicer, 9th King's Own (Yorkshire Light Infantry) attd., 64th Brigade Headquarters, writing to his sister

Previous page:
*Passing through:
an unknown
artillery battery
wending its way
through a shell-
battered town.*

Both sides are now war-weary and it is merely a question of who can hold out longest. Owing to the collapse of Russia, Germany has temporarily got the better position. I say temporarily because I honestly do not think she will have it for long. …

What we want out here more than anything else is to feel that you at home are not only worrying about our individual safety, but are really keen to see us win, and not come back till we really have finished the war properly. If you possibly can, will you please read a book called *Christine* by Alice Cholmondeley. They are the genuine letters of 'Christine' who went to Germany in May 1914 and died of pneumonia in Stuttgart in August '14, and are written to her mother. If, having read those letters (which, mark you, were mostly written before war had been declared) and aren't keen to fight on until such time as we can definitely dictate to Germany the codes of life which she is going to observe in future – well, then thousands of lives have been wasted and we had better never have entered into the war. Unfortunately I have only read half the book, so would you ask Marion to forward me a copy?

All the above is I'm afraid a somewhat sententious and loquacious sermon! But I really do feel very strongly on the matter, and much as I loathe and hate war I am afraid we've got to fight on.

Captain Arthur
Gibbs, 379th
Battery, Royal
Field Artillery

The guns we drew from Ordnance at Chuignolles were not calibrated, but there was a range half a day's march distant and we were ordered to fire them in readiness for going back into the line. So one morning before dawn we set out to find the pin-point given us on the map. Dawn found us on a road which led through a worse hell than even Dante visited. Endless desolation spread away on every side, empty, flat, filled with an infinite melancholy. No part of the earth's surface remained intact. One shell hole merged into another in an endless pattern of pockmarks, unexploded duds lying in hundreds in every direction. Bits of wreckage lay scattered, shell baskets, vague shapes of iron and metal which bespoke the one-time presence of man. Here and there steamrollers, broken and riddled, stuck up like bones of camels in the desert. A few wooden crosses marked the wayside graces, very few. For the most part the dead had lain where they fell, trodden into the earth. Everywhere one almost saw a hand sticking up, a foot that had worked up to the surface again. The spirits of a million dead wailed over that ghastly graveyard, unconsecrated by the priests of God. In the grey light one could almost see the corpses sit up in their countless hundreds at the noise of the horses' feet and point with long fingers, screaming bitter ridicule through their shapeless gaping jaws. And when at last we found the range and the guns broke the eerie stillness the echo in the hills was like bursts of horrible laughter.

And on the edge of all this death was that little sturdy boy with the golden hair, bubbling with life, who played with the empty sleeve of his young father spewed out of the carnage.

Cavalry officers and men muffled up against the cold. Greatcoats were kept until the last day of March.

British troops would spend much of the winter months preparing for the German assault. As the men dug new defensive lines, intelligence was gathered from prisoners captured in raids.

Examination of Two Other Ranks (Deserters) of 12th Coy, 3rd Bn, 451 IR [Infantry Regiment]

<u>Ground of Desertion</u>
Both complained of ill-treatment from NCOs and from bad food. One is a Pole.

<u>The New Offensive</u> – The Pole's account is as follows.
On Jan. 14th the 451 Regt marched from Arleux to a training ground south of Lécluse where a half day's practice was held in the 'new' method of attack. This first practice was not a success and it was repeated in Coy training near Arleux every day until Jan 20th.

In explaining the Coy training, the Coy Commander told them they must get on with it as fast they can, for they hadn't any time to spare. The offensive would begin early in February – on what front was a secret of the higher command and must remain so to prevent leakage to the English. They had settled with the Russians and if the English wouldn't see it too, then they would show them what the Germans can do.

Driver Aubrey Smith, 1/5th The London Regiment (London Rifle Brigade)

On 20th January an old first battalion man named Gill, who had just come out again with a draft, walked down to the transport billets. We found him dubious as to the possibility of a German attack and very optimistic as to its outcome if it took place, being convinced that if the Germans couldn't break through at the Second Battle of Ypres [1915] they would never be able to do so now.

I may say at once that we shared this conviction and confidence, but to tease him we assumed an air of utter disbelief in anything, an attitude that was fast becoming the most fashionable feature of the British soldier's inevitable grouse.

'I'm sorry to see you're all fed up,' said he.

'Isn't it enough to make anyone fed up,' said Mac, 'when we're crying out for more men after four years of war, not to carry out an offensive, but to hold our own blessed line?'

The whole fact of the matter was that we could not yet swallow the bitter pill of acting on the defensive when our whole training and outlook for three years had been aggressive. Words fail to describe our feelings towards the Russians; we were impatient with the Italians and peevish with the French, who were forcing us to take over more of their line. No less was our resentment against the Government, whose fear of the workmen at home prevented strong action when it was needed. …

[Nevertheless] it was not likely that the enemy could make any real progress if we had failed to do so in 1916 and 1917 with our then superiority of guns and man-power. At the worst Fritz would only outnumber us on the whole of the Western Front and our people ought to be aware in good time of the portion that was likely to be attacked by overwhelming forces and take steps to meet them. From bitter experience we knew that barbed wire and trenches were terrible obstacles to the attack, and we were now at the right end of the machine gun. … The utmost we expected was a good hammering until the cream of the German Army, their storm troops, was destroyed.

In March the Germans would have an advantage of around forty divisions on the Western Front and Haig would have to deploy his troops accordingly. He had to protect vitally important parts of the line such as the Ypres Salient, where even a small German advance would make vulnerable the Channel ports upon which the entire British Army relied. At Arras there were similar considerations. On the Somme, the calculation was different. Haig kept fewer divisions, knowing that an orderly retreat would relinquish nothing of strategic importance until the enemy reached the railhead of Amiens 50 miles away. Here, his Fifth Army of just twelve infantry divisions, with two in reserve, would hold the ground, along with three cavalry divisions. The tough decisions Haig made in this avoidable crisis were calculated to make the best of a bad situation. Neither he nor the British Army had been on the defensive since 1915: the officers and men would need to learn a new style of fighting.

Lance Corporal
Archibald Davis,
419th Field
Company, Royal
Engineers

23rd January: In the evening I went with the OC to Mt Bernanchon and it was during this trip that he unfolded to me what he required me to do. It appeared that in order to keep the Germans back it was proposed to lay a barbed-wire entanglement all across the fields parallel with the main road to Béthune, through Locon and Lestrem. I was to have a party of infantry, and with some motor lorries we were to obtain, unload and deliver the material so that the work should proceed at great speed without any delay. I noted in my diary that there were to be three rows of barbed-wire entanglements with machine-gun emplacements.

I was now spending quite a lot of time on the barges in the [La Bassée] Canal, arranging for the delivery, unloading and transport of barbed wire

Preparing for the onslaught: men of the 4th Worcestershire Regiment improving defences in the Ypres Salient, early 1918.

… distributing it to the points where it was required. Coils of barbed wire are rotten things to handle, and it was not an easy task getting them from the barge to the Canal bank, and from there into the lorry. The infantry would not work as hard as I wanted. Then the lorry driver would argue with me as to the load he should take. As a matter of fact, whatever material it happened to be, I had it worked out as to how much a lorry could safely carry. Then there was always the question of getting it right to the spot required, across fields intersected by small canals. On one occasion, a driver refused to take a load down a road alongside of which ran a fairly big stream. After arguing for some time I insisted on him going, and before he had got very far the side of the bank gave way, and into the stream went the lorry. It was a much bigger job getting it out than getting it in.

27th January: Today is the Kaiser's birthday, and we half expected that things might happen, but there has been a thick fog, and all has been as silent as can be. I am afraid the troops are not so sorry as they ought to be.

Lieutenant Colonel Rowland Feilding, 6th The Connaught Rangers

'Am I offensive enough?' is one of the questions laid down in a pamphlet that reaches us from an Army School some 30 miles behind the line. It is for the Subaltern to ask himself each morning as he rises from his bed.

Most laudable! But, as the Lewis Gun Officer remarked today, it is one of the paradoxes of war that the further you get from the battle line the more 'offensive' are the people you meet!

The battalion is getting very weak, and something will have to be done before long.

28th January: We came up into the front line this evening, relieving the 1st Royal Munster Fusiliers, and this morning, in anticipation, I went round the trenches.

The change is remarkable. I left the trenches frozen like rock. I find them today, half full of sticky mud; twice as wide and half as deep owing to the caving of the sides; two layers of trench-boards buried 2 feet deep in glutinous mud. It is a labour to walk on them, and today being a clear, sunny day it was not an occasion for easy cuts across the open.

Even so, for long stretches of these trenches you are under full view of the enemy – about 500 yards away. But he does not shoot, which suggests that his trenches are no better than ours (which, no doubt, is the case), and that he does not want us to shoot at him.

Indeed, for a few days past I find that the officers on duty on both sides have been making it a practice to walk along the parapet, so as to avoid the quagmire of the trenches. This morning, however, when an officer on our side tried it, the enemy opened with machine-gun fire: so this highly irregular practice is now at an end, which is perhaps as well.

Driver Aubrey Smith, 1/5th The London Regiment (London Rifle Brigade)

Our numbers [in France] were so low that one battalion in every four was disbanded to provide drafts for the others and we thought at one time that we ourselves were to be treated like this; but it was our second battalion that was broken up, while in our brigade the poor QVRs [Queen Victoria Rifles] were selected for this treatment. ... It was a shame that old-established Territorial battalions like the Rangers, QVRs and others should be swept out of existence, considering all their traditions and the splendid esprit de corps that existed in them. The men were furious over it.

Owing to the shortage of men, each infantry division would be made up of three brigades, each of three rather than four battalions. The men of the disbanded battalion were distributed amongst other units, temporarily damaging efficiency and lowering morale at a crucial moment. Just as the Germans were planning their offensive, General Headquarters had to focus on slicing and dicing divisions to order: it was madness. From the 140th Brigade, the 1/7th London Regiment was broken up, just one of 134 battalions to suffer such a fate.

Rifleman Frank Dunham, 1/7th The London Regiment

We, of the rank and file, had no inkling of any untoward happening, until we received orders to prepare for a full battalion parade on the morrow, and this started tongues wagging, and rumours flew about galore.

At the parade, Colonel Green explained the position to us, and said he was heartbroken to know that he would command us no longer, but wished us all good luck wherever we might be sent.

We were all very sorrowful, as the break-up of the battalion meant a lot to us; we all had our pals, had confidence and respect for our officers, and knew that in Colonel Green we had a CO second to none in the army.

The Orderly Room staff had a very busy day sorting out officers and men as the arrangement was that fourteen officers and 350 other ranks would be transferred to the 1/19th Battalion London Regiment in the 141st Brigade of our 47th Division, whilst the remainder were to join the 2/7th London Regiment in the 58th Division. Naturally everyone hoped to be one of the party going to the 2/7th Londons as we preferred to keep in the same regiment, but the fairest course was adopted, and those who had seen the longest service were selected to go to this battalion, but I was not amongst their number.

To celebrate the parting of so many friends, our officers provided us with a farewell dinner. The officers' mess sergeant had been sent far back in the early morning to procure something by way of a treat for dinner, and a real good spread did we have. As a fitting end to the old battalion, a mock funeral was arranged and carried out; a grave was dug in the midst of our camp, and a wooden cross erected bearing the information, ornamented with an old tin hat.

The 19th Londons were at the moment holding the front line, but as the transfers had to be completed quickly, we had to move up the line the same evening. The other party for the 2/7th left in buses the next day.

As usual, we rode on the light railway for most of the distance; and as a send-off the band, which was going intact to the 2/7th, played us off, and I should always remember the strains of *Auld Lang Syne* floating through the air, as the train carrying us gradually moved away.

A general reorganization of the army had taken place, the exact object of which, being no tactician, I did not understand; but the effect was that the number of battalions forming a brigade, and the number of brigades forming a division, were reduced, thus – on paper – increasing the number of divisions at the front. In some esoteric fashion this was supposed to have increased the strength of the army! I presume the 'big wigs' of the High Command understood this; I confess I didn't.

Guardsman Frederick Noakes, 1st Coldstream Guards

From the end of January the weather improved and in the middle of February became glorious, with unseasonal warm temperatures lasting until the end of the month. In early March there was a cold snap and a hurricane of snow, but good weather returned again after a week, aiding work on defences, until differences of opinion undid some of the good work.

Lance Corporal Archibald Davis, 419th Field Company, Royal Engineers

19th February: It was very evident that there was great anxiety about the [Armentières] Sector. In addition to my ordinary work, I was busy preparing plans for reinforced concrete dugouts, getting out the quantities and getting the materials up to the British Line. The OC asked me ... to send in a graph showing exactly the number of loads of concreting materials I was getting up each night, and showing the increase from day to day. When I commenced the job I was getting twelve loads a night, and towards the end, eighty loads a night. There was much cursing and swearing and many objections raised at being ordered about by a lance corporal, but the work was done.

Captain Charles Miller, 2nd The Royal Inniskilling Fusiliers

Looking out of Headquarters dugout, 48th Battalion, Australian Imperial Force (AIF).

We had already started to dig the strongpoints in the sites selected by the colonels, when the Brigadier chose to inspect them, and of course, decided to alter the positions. We started all over again, but there were lots of other 'brass hats' who had to have their say in the matter, and time and time again the position of the strongpoints was changed. The appalling and crass stupidity of it all! Putting up barbed-wire entanglements at night-time is a hard enough job in itself, but we reached the point where we had to uproot the entanglements that we had previously erected on abandoned sites, cart them off and erect them on new sites, which is simply Herculean labour. And all this had to be done on the nights when we were supposed to be resting. The result was chaotic. In the first place, the men were tired to death; in the second place, since the position of the strongpoints was constantly being changed it was impossible to organize a regular drill by which every man knew his strongpoint and got there in the quickest possible time when ordered to do so; lastly, instead of being deeply dug, strongly revetted and wired, it was quite obvious that when the moment came to use them the strongpoints would hardly be strong enough to keep out a well-aimed snowball.

One of the chief occupations during the day was to make our huts and stables splinter-proof by building up banks of earth around them, according to a definite formula laid down by corps or division. The annoying part about this scheme was that the army's idea as to thickness, height, and so on, varied from day to day. A hut was made splinter-proof one day and next morning someone would come round with a new idea, so that another pattern had to be done.

Driver Aubrey Smith, 1/5th The London Regiment (London Rifle Brigade)

Fine weather had set in. For several months we had been working in a wood-yard and saw-mills. Our lives had become unspeakably monotonous, but the coming of warm days banished much of our dreariness. The hazy blue sky was an object of real delight. I often contrived to slip away from my work and lean idly against a wall in the mild sunshine. At times I was so filled with the sense of physical well-being, and so penetrated by the sensuous enjoyment of warmth and colour, that I even forgot the war.

Private Frederick Voigt, Labour Corps

At the bottom of the wood-yard was a little stream, and on the far bank clusters of oxlips were in bloom. Here we would lie down during the midday interval and surrender to the charm of the spring weather. It seemed unnatural and almost uncanny that we should be happy, but there were moments when we felt something very much like happiness.

Bagging up charcoal. Charcoal was widely used in water filtration, as well as cooking and heating.

Wood stacks awaiting transportation: the army's requirement for wood was voracious.

France: men of 366 Forestry Company, Royal Engineers, with German prisoners felling pine trees for loading onto a light railway.

Once a fortnight we paraded for our pay outside one of the bigger sheds of the yard. As a rule, I was filled with impatience and irritation at having to wait in a long queue and move forward step by step, but now it had become pleasant to tarry in the sunshine. One day, when we were lined up between two large huts, a deep Yellow Brimstone butterfly came floating idly past. It gave me inexpressible delight, a delight tempered by sadness and a longing for better times. I drew my pay and saluted perfunctorily.

In being unable and unwilling to think of anything but the beauty of the sky, the sun, and the wonderful insect, I held my three ten-franc notes in my hand and thought: 'I will enjoy this lovely day to the full. When we get back to camp I will do without the repulsive army fare, I will dine at the St Martin and buy a bottle of the best French wine, even if it costs me twenty francs. And then I'll walk to the little wood on the hill-slope and there I'll lie all the evening and dream or read a book.'

The whistle sounded. It was time to go back to work. But I cursed the work and decided to take the small risk and remain idle for an hour or two. I went to an outlying part of the yard and sat down on a patch of long grass and leant back against a shed.

All the talk on the way up was of the beautiful quietude of the area we were riding through: no weed-choked houses with the windows all blown in; no sound of guns, no line of filled-up ambulances; few lorries on the main thoroughfares; only the khaki-clad road-repairers and the 'Gas Alert' notice-boards to remind us we were in a British area. As we reached the quarry that was to become Brigade Headquarters, we marvelled still more. A veritable quarry de luxe. A mess fashioned out of stone-blocks hewn from the quarry, perfectly cut and perfectly laid. Six-inch girders to support the concrete roof, and an underground passage as a funk-hole from bombs, shells, and gas. Separate strong-room bedrooms for the officers; and someone had had time to paint on the doors, 'OC, RFA Brigade', 'Adjutant', 'Intelligence Officer, RFA', and 'Signal Officer, RFA', with proper professional skill. Electric light laid on to all these quarters, and to the brigade office and the signallers' underground chamber. Aladdin didn't enjoy a more gorgeous eye-opener on his first tour of his palace.

'Never seen such headquarters,' grinned the Adjutant. 'Wonder why there's no place for the Divisional Band.'

Captain George Nicholls, C Battery, 82nd Brigade, Royal Field Artillery

Private
Frederick Voigt,
Labour Corps

Some distance ahead was a farm of the usual Flemish type – a thatched roof, whitewashed walls, and green shutters. Nearby was a little pond with willows growing round it. In the field beyond, a cow was grazing peacefully. The sky seemed a deeper blue through the willow-branches. The tender green of the grass was wonderfully refreshing to the eyes. The cow had a beautiful coat of glossy brown that shone in the sunlight. I abandoned myself to the charm of the little idyll that was spread out before me and forgot the war once again.

And then all at once a gigantic, plume-shaped, sepia-coloured mass rose towering out of the ground. There was a rending, deafening, double thunder-clap that seemed to split my head. For a moment I was dazed and my ears sang. Then I looked up – the black mass was thinning and collapsing. The cow had disappeared.

I walked into the yard full of rage and bitterness. All the men had left the sheds and were flocking into the road. Some were strolling along in leisurely fashion, some were walking with hurried steps, some were running, some were laughing and talking, some looked startled, some looked anxious, and some were very pale.

We crossed the road and the railway. Then, traversing several fields, we came to a halt and waited. We waited for nearly an hour, but nothing happened and we gradually straggled back to the yard.

Some of us walked to the spot where the shell had burst. There was a huge hole, edged by a ring of heaped-up earth, and loose mould and grassy sods lay scattered all round. Here and there lay big lumps of bleeding flesh. The cow had been blown to bits. The larger pieces had already been collected by the farmer, who had covered them with a tarpaulin sheet from which a hoof protruded.

The next day, at about the same hour, the dark cloud again rose from the ground and the double explosion followed. We again abandoned the yard and waited in the field. But this time there were several further shell-bursts. No dull boom in the distance followed by a long-drawn whine, but only the earth and smoke thrown darkly up and then the deafening double detonation. The next day more shells came over, and the next day also.

The big holes with their earthen rims began to dot the fields in many places. No damage of 'military importance' had been done. Not even a soldier had been killed, but only a cow.

The way from Brigade HQ, past the batteries and up to the front line, was over a wide rolling country of ploughed and fallow lands, of the first wild flowers, of budding hedgerows, of woods in which birds lilted their spring songs. The atmosphere was fresh and redolent of clean earth; odd shell holes you came across were, miracle of miracles, grass-grown – a sight for eyes tired with the drab stinking desolation of Flanders. A more than spring warmth quickened growing things. White tendrils of fluff floated strangely in the air, and spread thousands of soft clinging threads over telephone wires, treetops, and across miles of growing fields – the curious output of myriads of spinning-spiders. There were quaintly restful visits to the front line. The Boche was a mile away at least; and when you were weary of staring through binoculars, trying to spot enemy movement, you could sit and lounge, and hum the rag-time *Wait and See the Ducks go by*, with a new and very thorough meaning.

Captain George Nicholls, C Battery, 82nd Brigade, Royal Field Artillery

German guns were waking from seasonal slumber, and feverish speculation abounded that the enemy would attack even before the end of February. The general nervousness was palpable.

Corporal Shelton and I took it in turns to have the telephone exactly by our ears, waiting for the code word to come through which meant the Germans were coming over and we must retire. …

We were supplied with a secret code word and also a book giving us the solution of secret code messages. This was very complicated, and both the word and the book were changed from time to time. In case we were captured, the book was always put carefully away where it would not be easily found. Secret messages so very rarely came through that the book was put away and never thought of again. One day, however, a code message really did come through, and I was the unfortunate individual who took the message down. We could not understand it and the codebook could not be found. The Major was near hairless. Everything in that Orderly Room was turned out dozens of times, but the book still remained hidden. I was instructed to have the messages repeated, which I did time after time, but with the same result, and we got in touch with every unit possible to try and find out if they had received a similar message. The codebook was not found, and the message remained a secret until several weeks after, when

Lance Corporal Archibald Davis, 419th Field Company, Royal Engineers

we learnt that it was merely notifying us of some infantry movements which did not directly concern us. …

On the 25th February we heard that Fritz was massing on our front and had been expected over the day before, but he did not come. On this day we were instructed to carry out work in the Back Area.

On the 26th and 27th Fritz was making things very lively for us, and 6-inch and 8-inch shells were falling in the yards and farms occupied by civilians, and bits were flying all around.

On the 28th I found that the civilians had been supplied with box respirators. We were standing-to at 4 am, waiting for the Germans to come over, but again they did not come. They however, knocked two large holes in cottages occupied by civilians.

We have captured a German deserter. He told us the Germans were going to attack us on the 1st March. We are again standing-to fully equipped at 4.30 am, but with the same results as before.

We are daily supplied with code words, and were every minute expecting to have the word which meant that we were to run away from the Germans as hard as we could go. The code words were frequently changed, in case Fritz got to know. One day it was 'Idle', then 'Idler', 'Ignite', 'Imitate', and so on.

Captain George Nicholls, C Battery, 82nd Brigade, Royal Field Artillery

Whether the Boche would attack in force on our part of the front was argued upon and considered from every point of view. There were certain natural features that made such an attempt exceedingly improbable. Nevertheless infantry and artillery kept hard at it, strengthening our means of defence. One day I did a tour with the Machine Gun commander in order to know the exact whereabouts of the machine-gun posts. They were superlatively well hidden, and the Major General himself had to laugh when one battalion commander, saying, 'There's one just about here, sir,' was startled by a corporal's voice near his very boot-toes calling out, 'Yes, sir, it's here, sir.'

Camouflaging is now, of course, a studied science, and our colonel, who issued special guiding notes to his batteries, had a few sharp words to say one afternoon. The British soldier, old and new, is always happy when he is demolishing something; and a sergeant, sent to prepare a pit for a forward gun, had collected wood and corrugated iron for it by pulling to

A morning wash and shave in newly constructed defences near Le Verguier, early March 1918. The officer on the right was wounded later that month.

pieces a near-by dummy gun, placed specially to draw enemy fire. 'Bad as some Pioneers I noticed yesterday,' said the Colonel tersely. 'They shifted a couple of trees to a place where there had been no trees before and thought that that was camouflage.'

Although we were well back from the front [Essigny], as a precautionary measure I decided to fix up an OP [observation post] in the nearest of three ash trees which were to the left of our guns. The tree branched 16 feet up so I sent to the wagon line for a dozen pointed horseshoes to make a ladder. I remember that as soon as they arrived I started hammering

Lieutenant William Carr, 377th Battery, 169th Brigade, Royal Field Artillery

them into the trunk and made my way up to 12 feet where my ascent was blocked by a nest of bees. Down I came, dismantled a shell, took out several sticks of cordite, climbed up the horseshoe ladder and rammed one or two sticks into the nest. Then I took out a match, lit it and threw it in. There was a minor explosion as slivers of burning cordite shot towards me. As I had more cordite in my pockets I came down mighty quickly. When it was safe to climb again I was surprised to find some honey, most unusual in March.

Acting Captain Kenneth Jones, 5th The Welsh Regiment

The sunsets have been very remarkable lately, and we have all turned out to view them. A few days ago I was watching a fine one, which suddenly struck me by its resemblance to something I had seen before. Looking carefully I saw it all clearly. By some freak of nature there lay before us a perfect image of the Severn as viewed from Doverow or Frocester, and one of our officers from Gloucestershire saw it too. There was a long bluish purple stratus cloud, just like the hills of the Forest of Dean, and then some light-coloured twisting clouds, touched with silver, made a perfect river, whilst the land in front of us was level and low. What more could one want, save the reality?

We have been having the most gorgeous summer weather for nearly a month now. In fact it is almost like August. The larks are singing their hearts out up above, and nature is bursting with pride and delight down below. The willow catkins light up the small copses, and the bees are working as hard as we are. Long may it last! No doubt 'big things' are in the air, but unless the Hun is quick, he won't get much chance. He is very quiet at present, although our guns are hammering away all day and every day with their eternal thunder. I often pity him! All the same, quiet on the Hun's part is not nice, and so we are all on the *qui vive*. Something will have to go bang this year.

Captain Arthur Behrend, 90th Brigade, Royal Garrison Artillery

For many weeks past elaborate orders had been issued to us almost daily telling us what our batteries were to do when the Boche attacked. These orders, with their fresh targets and new rates of fire, became so complicated that it was almost impossible to compete with them and with their numerous additions, amendments, additions to amendments, and

amendments to additions. Luckily in the end Corps Heavies took pity on us and, with a wonderful burst of energy, issued on the eve of the battle a fairly lucid five-page document which, as the Brigade Major remarked, was positively the last word and contained all the winners.

Broadly speaking, the artillery defence was divided into two phases: Counter-preparation and SOS.

Counter-preparation was intended to cramp the enemy's style as much as possible while he was massing for the attack; the targets were such things as communication trenches, support trenches or road junctions through which he was likely to go. The moment the Boche came over the top, batteries were to switch to their SOS targets – a barrage along the middle of no-man's-land. As it had been realized that communications would probably have 'gone west' by this time, more elaborate instructions had been issued telling the batteries how to recognize the fateful moment. …

The practical side of the defensive arrangements had not been neglected. Since Christmas, the front-line system had been enormously

A working party taking large calibre shells towards the front line.

strengthened and a fine reserve line, known variously as the Haig Line and the Brown Line, had been dug about 3,000 yards behind the front line. Unfortunately on our front the Brown Line only consisted of a single wide trench. …

The next defensive system was the Army or Red Line and ran just behind our headquarters. It was merely an old Boche trench; consequently the wire was on the wrong side and men were working feverishly on it all day. Behind the Red Line there was nothing but the wastes of the Somme.

The artillery defences were thorough and complete. All the battery positions had been wired in and dozens of reserve positions and OPs had been made, to cover both the Brown and the Red Lines.

Our brigade had been responsible for the construction of at least a dozen reserve positions – one of which, to our disgust, was in the middle of our headquarters. All this had meant weeks of real hard work as six gun-pits had to be dug at each position, wooden gun platforms had to be laid, camouflage had to be erected over each pit, command posts had to be sunk in the ground (and drained), and hundreds of rounds of shells dumped on each position (and counted). Even the Adjutant did his bit for, apart from indenting for all the pit-props and the rabbit wire and the duckboards and the nine-by-three and the camouflage and the fuses and the sandbags and the corrugated iron and the 1-inch nails, apart from organizing their collection, apart from fighting with Siege Park for more lorries and more lorries and more lorries, apart from wringing huge working parties from abusive battery commanders, apart from imploring corps heavies to send up less ammunition, apart from all these things and a hundred more, he was responsible for erecting boards at each position so that inspecting generals should know, for instance, that the neat little notice board 'H.A. 107' beside that nasty wet hole covered with a sheet of corrugated iron really marked the Battery Commander's Post of Heavy Artillery Reserve Position No. 107.

Opposite: On the ranges at Catterick Camp. Seventeen-year-old Reginald Kiernan won extra pay for his 'marksmanship' with a little help from a friend.

Such, in a nut-shell, was the situation at seven o'clock on the morning of the twenty-first of March in the year of grace nineteen hundred and eighteen, when the Colonel and the Adjutant of the finest Heavy Artillery Brigade in the British Army sat in a shack near Beugny, in the Province of Artois, France, staring at a map-board in front of them and wondering what on earth was going to happen next.

The troops that Lloyd George had kept in Britain continued training, oblivious to the tremendous efforts being made in France and Belgium by their comrades. Nineteen was the age at which men could serve overseas, but a few were younger. Private Reginald Kiernan had managed to beat the rules of conscription and had enlisted aged seventeen. He was undertaking his final course of musketry and was, despite his inexperience, not beyond some shenanigans.

30th February: We have fired at the butts by the sea. We were told before we went that the regiment was proud of its firing and that we had to keep up the standard. I got 125 marks out of 200, and so can wear crossed guns on my sleeve. I got this score because the marker on Number 8 Butt (mine) slept next to me in the musketry camp. I gave him fourpence for a drink, and he signalled up ten 'bulls', three 'inners', an 'outer' and a 'washout' in

Private Reginald Kiernan, Training Reserve Battalion

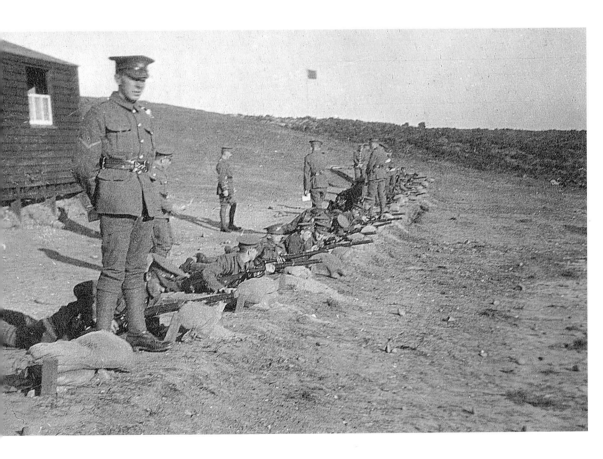

the fifteen rounds rapid. Actually my rifle had jammed at the fourth shot and I could not finish.

The sergeant at my elbow had been cursing me steadily, but now he grinned and chuckled, and said, 'Yo' bastard, yo' little _____ bastard.' The more men of his squad who are 'marksmen' the better for him. …

In our hut there were two old soldiers. They ran a Crown and Anchor board, and did very well. At night, in the darkness, they told filthy stories, and sang horrible greasy songs. The worst were those called *The One-Eyed Reilly* and *I love My Wife*. I struggled not to listen, but sometimes I could not help almost laughing in my mind at the stories, against all my will. And the 'Reilly' song had a catchy air, and ran through my head during the day.

5th March: We are back in another camp in Newcastle. There are the same old parades – 'jerks', musketry, lectures on the parts of a rifle and the Lewis gun. We also have had a mock battle over some model trenches. My job was to sit in a sap and hammer with a trenching tool handle on a bit of corrugated iron. I was a machine gun. After the battle a corporal came to me and said, 'Yo've done some bleedin' execution, yo' 'ave. I telled yo' to

An officer's servant fills a bucket outside a hut in Catterick Camp, 1918.

bang that bleedin' tin when yo' seed anythink, and yo've been a-bangin' it for a bleedin' week. Yo'll 'ave all the bleedin' munition works doin' overtime, yo' will.'

The battle was really for the benefit of officers who are in training here. It was nice to hear their voices. I have hardly seen an officer in all my training. It is the NCOs who have us all the time. I have thrown my first live bombs here. We threw three each from a trench, and an officer stood by all the time to pick up bombs which men might drop in their nervousness, and throw them over the top. He was a big, bony chap and very decent and understanding to talk to. He said, 'Here you are, son. It won't bite you. Out with the pin – away she goes.' It did not seem to go very far, but he said, 'Good man.' When the next man dropped his bomb, he picked it up like lightning and threw it away all in one movement. He said, 'Hell save us,' but he did not curse the man. I hope we have officers like that in France. I'd go bombing anywhere with him.

Juggling with hand grenades, an officer shows off his skills. He would soon be on his way back to France.

10th March: This morning I was talking to an 'Expeditionary' man, that is, one who has been out in France. He has finished his convalescence, and is just ready to go out again. Most of the flesh has been torn from the back of his thighs by a shell, and the skin there is all brown. He is very pale and limp, and his voice is soft and pleasant. He was very earnest. He said, 'Don't you believe this comrades in arms stuff. In France it's every man for himself. Don't volunteer for anything, not whatever it is. They'll call for volunteers and you'll think it's grand. If you get killed nobody'll know – if you do the job, you'll get no thanks for it. There's nothing in it, this comrades in arms stuff. Every man for himself, there. Look after yourself, and don't think of anything but that.'

This Expeditionary man has a look about him which they all have. You can feel it though you can't say what it is – it's something behind the eyes.

In March, Second Lieutenant Wilfred Bion was home on leave. He was also due to receive the Distinguished Service Order from no lesser personage than the King.

Second Lieutenant Wilfred Bion, 5th Battalion, Tank Corps

King George V pins a medal to the chest of an officer. Lieutenant Wilfred Bion found the whole experience of being awarded his DSO awkward and could not wait to get away.

There were about sixty officers and men present in a large room which turned out to be the ante-room to the Hall in which the investiture was to take place. A private, who had been awarded a DCM, and I were the youngest there. I was by far the youngest officer to be up for the DSO so a large, fierce and extremely important colonel addressed me personally.

'Now, mind what you are at. March up to him, and stand to attention facing him. You've got your ribbon on? Well that's something at any rate,' he said with the tone of one who must be thankful for any mercy however small. He continued, 'His Majesty will put the medal on you so keep your hands out of it. For God's sake don't try to help; just stand to attention. Don't move and above all *do not try to engage in chat* with His Majesty. When he's done, step back and march out. Remember – no chat!'

I couldn't possibly have engaged in chat with anyone, let alone 'His Majesty'. The only thing I could have thought of saying was 'For God's sake get me out of this hole.'

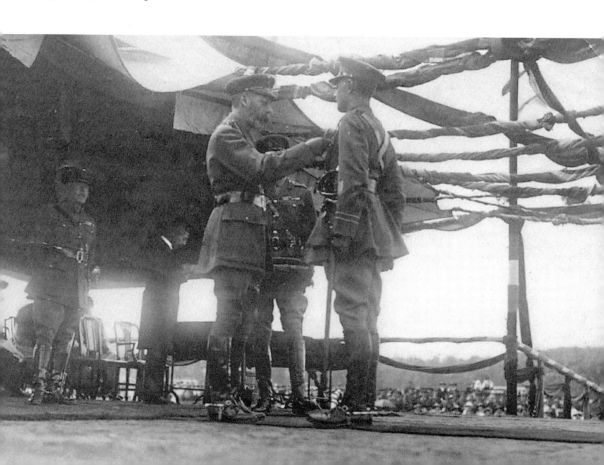

At last the ghastly moment came. There were few DSOs and before I could tell how, I was in front of the King with what looked like a picture hook stuck in my ribbon. On this he hung the DSO. As I was about to back out *he* started to chat.

'You were at Cambrai? That was a very fine action. You lost your tank I believe. Did you get it back?'

'No sir, but the infantry did.'

'Ah! Excellent.'

I could almost feel the Colonel breathing fire down my neck; why had he not told His Majesty 'and above all – don't chat!' Why pick on *me*?

As I was going out, a large hand whipped off my DSO and slapped it into a box. Before I could defend it or myself he was handing me the box. I didn't dare to see if the medal was there or if he had just substituted the box and stuck to the medal.

Wilfred Bion had not been in France for long, but Cambrai had battle-hardened the young subaltern making him surly and uncommunicative with those closest to him. Many men looked forward to leave, but too many were bitterly disappointed with the actuality: Britain had become 'another world'.

Outside the Palace gates was a small knot of press photographers and civilians. Through the lane they formed I escaped to the end of queue where my mother waited for me. It seemed a shame that she had not been allowed in to see and share the glorious moment which was in fact so much hers and so little mine.

I could not have explained to anyone why it weighed so heavily upon me....

I have little memory of that leave other than fierce unhappiness. Seared into my mind was one silly, trivial occasion, and one stupendous and numbing.

My mother, defeated and helpless in the face of my taciturn moroseness, asked if I knew the riddle of the miser's most hated flower. 'It's the anemone,' she said, 'because it reminds him of someone asking "Any money? Any money?" My response was a stony silence which was so hostile that it frightened me. After a moment I felt stealing over me such

Second
Lieutenant
Wilfred Bion,
5th Battalion,
Tank Corps

pity for what I was sure was her utter misery that I looked at her, caught her eye and the fleeting trembling of her lips. The tension was released. 'Damn silly things, medals,' I said, 'but very nice to look at don't you think?' She wiped away her tears, relieved at being able to weep openly.

Driver Percival Glock, Royal Field Artillery, 1st Division

For the benefit of anyone who has not experienced leave, I will try and explain or rather describe it. The first question I was asked was, 'When are you going back?' Just think of it, one comes home with the idea of forgetting the war and the first question reminds one of it and so it happens, every person one meets asks the same question, which is invariably followed with 'Have you seen any Germans?' 'Do you want to go back?' 'Have you seen any fighting?' 'What's it like out there?' 'Have you had many narrow squeaks?' 'When's the war going to finish?' and so on, but of course you can't blame them, it is only natural.

The first three or four days one is home after, say, eighteen months away seems more like a dream than anything else, but one soon wakes up to the fact that you have to go back. What struck me as funny was how ignorant I was as to how the war was going on; all I knew was of one particular part and everybody else had the whole fighting line at their finger tips. I was also struck by the numbers of fellows going about all poshed up in khaki and swanking as to what they had done in France. I was speaking to one of these fellows and happened to mention St Pol, which at that time was quite 20 miles from the firing line. The fellow jumped at the sound of the word (as he probably heard it somewhere) and said 'My word, that's a pretty hot shop now isn't it? I was there the week before last.' I didn't call him a liar as he was about three times my size.

Opposite: *A boat arriving at Folkestone harbour. Many battle-worn soldiers did not enjoy their leave with civilians, who could not begin to comprehend what they had been through.*

I have a few days in Northampton and on to Pontypool: fourteen days' leave soon goes. It all seems strange to me but somehow I am not happy. I feel it is not my place. I feel somehow I belong to another world, not this civilization. Every day seems the same here, although I have been looking forward to my leave and waited so long. Now it seems I am longing to get back. Why, I don't know.

Private Charles Heare, 1/2nd The Monmouthshire Regiment

On leave, soldiers became aware of how many men at home were in uniform or in civilian clothes, men who could be usefully employed abroad. They may have been kept back by Lloyd George, or they might have wangled an easy job, but either way it was hard to see so many 'swanking' when the offensive was palpably close.

While home I met an infantry officer friend who was on leave from the front opposite St Quentin. He declared that the Germans could break through opposite him as easily as anything – there was nobody to stop them, for we had taken over a very extended front from the French. Each division in those regions held an average line of about 4 miles for a stretch of over 40 miles, brigades were reduced as elsewhere to three battalions,

Driver Aubrey Smith, 1/5th The London Regiment (London Rifle Brigade)

reserves were scanty and defences were in a bad state. What was even more worrying was that my friend was confident that this was the portion of the front where the blow would fall. …

There were large numbers of soldiers at home and it puzzled me why more could not be sent out to thicken the front in view of the impending attack. They still kept a good-sized army for coast defence, just because it was thought possible for the Germans to effect a surprise landing. …

But the number of troops on the wrong side of the Channel came as a surprise, the swarms of civilians still sheltering as 'indispensables' amazed me still more. I recognize that many were doing vital work, but it was still riling to see men – to all intents and purposes fitter than many who were in the trenches – leaving banks and offices or shop working or driving buses, taxi and carts. The engineers' trade union was on the verge of a strike because the Government's dilution proposals [increasing the number of women in industry] meant that more of them would have to join the army: why should they have the right to threaten the paralysis of our munitions while the soldier would be shot for the same offence? Yet down by St Quentin 'the enemy could break through as easily as anything: there was nobody to stop them!'

9th March: Left Folkestone, feeling this was perhaps really the last time I'd see old Blighty's shores unless it be from a hospital ship. Crossing was perfect. Everyone fed up as usual, especially at Boulogne, where the Military Police tried to form us into fours and the entire leave party 'struck', calling the police all sorts of nice names and asking them when they had last heard a shell.

Driver Percival
Glock, Royal
Field Artillery,
1st Division

Everybody in the train and boat were right fed up. Anyway, we managed to get back and went straight up the line again. If ever I felt windy, I did then, for about two days. At the least sound I would almost jump out of my skin. It was a very quiet part of the line, too, hardly saw a shell burst, but the cause of the windyness was coming from peaceful surroundings straight into the line. After two days I got settled down again in the same old style, didn't care a button.

There was every reason to be jumpy. The Germans were poised to go and they were putting every chip on the table.

15th March: We get the first secret order for the attack; and again and again you have to gaze in wonder at this careful work which the Staff people are putting in, working things out right to the last detail – after all, that is the secret of our greatness. I don't want to write anything about it here, because it is forbidden to do so, and because there is also the real danger that one might be taken prisoner, and secret notes like these might be useful to the enemy. The whole thing can only be compared with the gigantic general mobilization of 1914 in volume, but concentrated on a comparatively short front; and on top of that, all things which did not exist in 1914 in the way of new weapons, new equipment and unbelievable

Lieutenant Herbert Sulzbach, 63rd Field Artillery Regiment, Imperial German Army

masses of men, and with the difference that in 1914 an advance was completely taken for granted, and all that counted then was to win the battle; whereas here and now, it is a question of our being successful in breaking through the enemy's gigantic fortified line and then winning the battle afterwards: in fact, it's a question of two victories. Shall we be able to achieve this immeasurably great objective with just a few divisions, and with our own troops no longer fresh, having regard to the enormous masses of men which the chaps over there have available? The enemy facing us are supposed to be mainly British. We'll be giving them good service, with a large number of new specialties. The preparations are getting more and more urgent, sleep is getting more and more unthinkable, every battery commander and every battery officer is a miniature General Staff. Even if you were tired, the excitement and enthusiasm wouldn't let you sleep anyway.

Driver Aubrey Smith, 1/5th The London Regiment (London Rifle Brigade)

12th–15th March: Up the jolly old line once or twice more. Germans rather more aggressive, flinging plenty of stuff around the 'red' and 'green' lines. We seemed to be taking up plenty of ammunition and bombs. Great feeling of excitement: pretty certain Germans about to attack. Supposed to be huge enemy dumps everywhere, which our aeroplanes were busy bombing. Weather really delightful and spring-like with dry ground and nice sunny days. Difficult to realize a sword was hanging over our heads.

16th March: Harbord and I started to receive *The Times* each day, as I paid a subscription while on leave. Every evening we were to get the copy of the day before, sometimes as early as mid-day. The paper of 15th – I think – contained the following announcement by Ludendorff: 'We can now think of attack. We are entirely confident that the battle that is bursting forth will be successful for us.' He would not talk like that unless he meant business, but let him try it on, that's all!

Lieutenant Colonel Rowland Feilding, 6th The Connaught Rangers

16th March: I was up this morning at three o'clock and marched forward with the battalion to man trenches again, as yesterday. At 6.25 one of our SOS rockets went up, and was followed by many others along the front. Immediately, the artillery and machine guns opened uproariously all along the line.

Today (as have others which have passed) had been officially mentioned as the likely date for the great German effort, and all naturally thought for a short while that at last the expected had arrived.

However, after half or three-quarters of an hour of deafening din, all became silent, and it was evident that it was a false alarm. Such are the 'jumpy' times through which we are passing.

We then marched away to bury telephone cables, and afterwards home.

17th March: We again marched forward at three o'clock this morning to man Bois switch and the Ronssoy sunken road. It is a wearing life, and all are feeling the strain. We are still the counter-attack battalion.

Our pyrotechnicians are testing some wonderful new parachute lights, which illuminate the whole country for miles around, and to some extent enliven those early morning watches.

17th March: The German attack is expected very shortly; consequently a 'nervy' atmosphere is commencing to make itself felt. To stir up our brutal instincts and passions we have been treated to a morally disgusting harangue by a major of the Physical Jerks Department. The whole brigade was marched out to a field a few kilometres away where we squatted down in a hollow while the blood-red major (straight up from the base) delivered his oration in a strikingly melodramatic manner. He endeavoured to make us 'see red' and it is a matter for sad reflection that civilization should come to such a sorry pass. The authorities apparently think that the civilian-soldier is too soft hearted and gentle so it is necessary to raise the spirit of Cain in him. The whole speech was utterly disgusting and I am sorry to think that England should consider such a thing necessary. It was revolting and I believe I could better have withstood a dose of the abject platitudinous piffle that deals with the 'nobility and righteousness of our cause' 'the honour of dying for England' 'Remember Belgium'.

Sapper Albert Martin, 122nd Signal Company, 41st Division, Royal Engineers

St Quentin: officers of the Worcestershire Regiment enjoying the beautiful weather prior to the German assault.

The waiting game: an unknown officer relaxing in unseasonable good weather.

17th March: Hauteville, where we move into billets, i.e. bivouac beside a hedge, because this little place, which may have had 700 inhabitants in peacetime, is sheltering about 15,000 people. Around the village there is bivouac after bivouac, battery after battery, battalion after battalion. At the moment I am sitting up here on top of the village church at Hauteville and trying to get my impressions together. It occurs to me that I forgot to record a little scene which made quite an impression on me as we were pulling out of Le Hérie: among the detachments moving past was one marching with instruments playing and drums beating; it only consisted of corporals and sergeants, and they too had been on a course and been discharged to get back to their regiments. The music was playing *Muss I denn, muss I denn zum Städtle hinaus ...* (Must I go, must I go, must I leave the little town ...). They marched on, waved to us one after the other, with such a nice look on their faces that you felt warm and enthusiastic: but then suddenly you felt an icy shudder run over you and thought: 'Which of these good men, and which of us for that matter, is going to come home from this battle which lies ahead of us?'

Lieutenant Herbert Sulzbach, 63rd Field Artillery Regiment, Imperial German Army

1V Corps Summary

Information obtained from a deserter of the 28th Reserve Infantry Regiment, surrendered in our lines near Bullecourt on the night 17th–18th March 1918

Prisoner was on a fatigue carrying duckboards to the enemy's front line. The line was thinly held and he seized a favourable opportunity to desert. …

The last few nights prisoner's company has been employed in carrying trench mortar ammunition towards the front line. … Prisoner has never seen any tanks or heard anything about German tanks but he states that on the 15th, when on a daylight patrol, he had seen a notice board on which was written 'Tank Stelle 7'. Prisoner thinks the board is placed on a track which has been prepared for tanks as he noticed that a track had been to a certain extent levelled by shell holes having been partly filled in.

There is a great deal of talk about an impending offensive and a state of tension appears to exist amongst the troops. All sorts of rumours are current. The back areas are said to be full of troops of an assault division. …

Several days have been mentioned for zero day, the original date having been the 12th; then the offensive was said to have been postponed to the 14th, then to the 18th. …

Prisoner is a genuine deserter. He is very talkative and rather excitable but, only having joined his regiment in January, he has little military experience and therefore is not in a position to form a critical opinion of his own.

Sapper Albert Martin, 122nd Signal Company, Royal Engineers

19th March: There is little to think or talk about except the imminence of the German attack. Gradually we have been making the preparations necessary for our part, and as a final touch we were treated to a false alarm this afternoon for the purpose of seeing how quickly we could turn out with wagons packed and everything ready for the march. As it was we were packed up and all in line in a remarkably short time, and the Brigadier was very pleased. But we didn't tell him that we knew what was coming, four or five hours before the alarm was sounded. I am on night duty tonight and judging from the tone of one or two telegrams that have passed it is pretty certain that the attack will commence on the 21st.

<u>Third Army Summary</u>

Special examination of a prisoner of the 121st Bavarian Reserve Regiment, captured near Bullecourt on the night of the 18th–19th March

Prisoner states that a huge offensive was to be carried out on the front from Rheims to Bullecourt, but the main attempts to break through would be made at both extremities.

Orders had been issued that they were to be ready by noon on the 19th, but prisoner understood that the attack had been put off, presumably owing to the weather. He had no idea how long it would be delayed.

Prisoner stated, as the main opposition was expected from our airmen, a considerable concentration of hostile aircraft had been made. …

The initial assault was to be made by specially trained Assault Divisions, but prisoner was under the impression that his division would also take part in the attack.

Lieutenant Herbert Sulzbach, Germany artillery, in confident mood, sitting on the shoulders of a friend.

19th March: Early in the morning I rode over to the survey section and could hardly get along the roads – it's a mass concentration of troops completely impossible to describe. The columns making for the front line are moving up the roads four abreast. Thank goodness the weather is dull and no enemy planes are coming over, so that so far there is no danger that the British will have noticed us moving up.

Our kicking-off point for the offensive is going to be the 'Island Suburb' of St Quentin and that was once a gay, pleasure-loving rear-echelon city, and now it's pretty well a front-line position: but it will soon be in the rear again! Every house in St Quentin that is still standing has received two or three direct hits.

The British are firing into the city every day, with sweeping fire, and now and then one of our ammunition depots goes up.

We have moved into our emplacements in the firing line, and the limbers are already going into their waiting positions, so it can only mean a day or two at most before the huge offensive starts, but the date and time will only be passed through at the last second. We are already imagining what it will be like when the order comes: 'prepare to move!' We are most conscious of the greatness of the moment, and have got into a terrific state of tension, and even when we have any time to rest, we genuinely can't sleep any more, not for a second.

Lieutenant Herbert Sulzbach, 63rd Field Artillery Regiment, Imperial German Army

On the night of March 19th our chief guest was the youthful lieutenant colonel who a very few weeks before had succeeded to the command of the [battery]. Tall, properly handsome, with his crisp curling hair and his chin that was firm but not markedly so; eyes that were reflective rather

Captain George Nicholls, C Battery, 82nd Brigade, Royal Field Artillery

than compelling; earnest to the point of an absorbed seriousness – we did right to note him well. He was destined to win great glory in the vortex of flame and smoke and agony and panic into which we were to be swept within the next thirty-six hours. My chief recollection of him that night was of his careful attentiveness to everything said by our own colonel on the science of present-day war – the understanding deference paid by a splendid young leader to the knowledge and grasp and fine character of a very complete gunner.

By 19 March, GHQ knew where the German attack would fall; it was impossible for the Germans to hide such a huge logistical effort to move men and guns into position. This was no feint, or diversionary attack. This was the real thing and General Gough commanding 5th Army in front of St Quentin knew for certain that his men would be battered. 'We knew we were to be attacked in overwhelming force,' he wrote. 'We knew our line was dangerously thin.'

Lieutenant Rudolph Binding, German Cavalry (Dragoons)

20th March: I hardly know how to write – I have had to keep silence so long – but tomorrow, they say, the field-post will start again. Tomorrow there will be nothing to keep secret, for then hell breaks loose. Before the letters go to the rear, which will be in a few hours, I want just to come to you in these lines. Of course, I know that I cannot entirely escape the day which is so relentlessly approaching. It is a tremendous thing for every one of us. Aeschylus says that a drama ought to excite Hope and Fear, but here is one already showing behind the curtain and awakening both of these sensations before it even rises. It will be a drama like a Greek tragedy, with a fate hanging over it, shaped and created by man alone, and ready to descend on the head of him who is responsible.

Opposite:
Dubious geography: German troops off to the front apparently headed for Paris via London, according to the graffiti on the door.

The preparations are quite inconceivable in detail, and can only be described as the last word. The troops are packed in position so tight that those in front have been there for the last ten days. For weeks past ammunition has been hauled and hauled, night after night, to be piled in mountains round the guns. All that is to be poured out on the enemy in four hours from now. One division lies behind another to an incalculable depth, and three armies, the 18th, the 2nd, and the 17th, are to attack together in unison on an infinitesimal front. So far as possible the troops

will advance over ground which they know from the Somme battles. Our own objective is the area where we lay in January and February of last year. The attack will be delivered over the territory which we laid waste, and where there are neither roads, trees, nor villages.

We belong to the second wave. It is impossible as yet to say whether this will have the easier task or the first. Since March 1st the horses have been getting a ration of 10lb of oats, and all the attacking divisions have been provided with first-class remounts from the Quartermaster General's reserve. God knows how Ludendorff has got them together. I am still 200 short for the division, but they are to be given me when we advance, or during the battle. Naturally the railways have been working day and night

A pause for food at a German field kitchen.

at this business; waiting for thousands of trains with men, horses, guns, wagons, ammunition, tools, rations, bridging material, and a hundred other things, was a trying business for everybody.

We are all going as light as possible. All unnecessary baggage has been ruthlessly prohibited; we all left it willingly behind, buoyed up by a final hope. The organization is really great, but it was, of course, impossible to keep the secret. In Brussels every child knows that the offensive is to begin on March 21st.

20th March: In the evening an order arrives from Sub-Army Group, Central Sector:

Lieutenant Herbert Sulzbach, 63rd Field Artillery Regiment, Imperial German Army

> After years of defence on the Western Front, Germany is moving to the attack; the hour eagerly awaited by every soldier is approaching. I am certain that the regiment, true to its history, will enhance its reputation in the days which lie ahead.
>
> This great objective will call for sacrifices, and we shall bear with them for the Fatherland, and for our loved ones at home.
>
> Then forward, into action! With God for King and Fatherland!

So it was at seven in the evening that we had this order through by telephone. It says quite enough. *21st March* has been fixed for the start of the barrage. There is a terrible lot of work to do, we are in the highest possible spirits, and everybody lends a hand in distributing the huge quantities of ammunition.

At 5.10 pm on March 20th I was in the mess, casting an appraising eye upon the coloured study of a girl in pink – dark-haired, hazel-eyed, *très soignée*, but not too sophisticated, one would say; her beauty of the kind that glows and tells of abundant vitality and a fresh happy mind. The little American doctor had sacrificed the cover of one of his beloved *Saturday Evening Posts* for this portrait, and with extreme neatness had scissored it out and fastened it on the wall – a pleasant change from the cocaine and chocolate-box suggestiveness of the languorous Kirchner type that

Captain George Nicholls, C Battery, 82nd Brigade, Royal Field Artillery

in 1916 and 1917 lent a pinchbeck Montmartre atmosphere to so many English messes in France and Flanders.

The day had been hot and peaceful, the only sound of gun-fire a 6-inch howitzer registering, and, during a morning tour with the second lieutenant who had come from one of the batteries to act as temporary signalling officer, I remembered noting again a weather-beaten civilian boot and a decayed bowler hat that for weeks had lain neglected and undisturbed in one of the rough tracks leading to the front line – typical of the unchanging restfulness of this part of the front.

Suddenly the door opened, to admit Colonel, CO of the infantry battalion who were our near neighbours in the quarry.

'Have you had the "Prepare for Attack"?' he asked abruptly as we held ourselves to attention.

'No, sir,' I replied, and moved to the telephone to ring up Divisional Artillery Headquarters.

'Just come in,' he said; and even as I asked exchange to put me through to 'DA', the brigade clerk came in with the telephoned warning that we had talked about, expected, or refused to believe in ever since the alarm order to move into the line a fortnight before.

The formal intimation was sent by wire to the batteries, and I telephoned to find which battery the Colonel was visiting and gave him the news, which, according to our precise and well-thought-out scheme of defence, was a preliminary warning not intended to interfere with any work in hand.

Then the doctor and myself and the Divisional Artillery gas officer, who had called in while on an inspecting tour, settled down to tea, jam, and water-cress.

That night our dinner guest was the former captain of our 4.5 howitzer battery, now in command of a heavy battery that had come into action within a quarter of a mile of our HQ. The 'Man Battle Positions', the order succeeding 'Prepare for Attack' in the defence programme, was not expected that night, and we gossiped and talked war and new gunnery devices much as usual. No story goes so well at mess as the account of some fatuous muddle brought about by the administrative bewilderments that are apparently inevitable in the monster armies of today.

Midnight: I had sent out the night-firing orders to our four batteries, checked watches over the telephone, and put in a twenty minutes' wrestle with the brain-racking Army Form B. 213. The doctor and signalling officer had slipped away to bed, and the Colonel was writing his nightly letter home. I smoked a final cigarette and turned in at 12.30 am.

3.30 am: The telephone bell above my head was tinkling. It was the Brigade Major's voice that spoke. 'Will you put your batteries on some extra bursts of fire between 3.45 and 4.10 – at places where the enemy, if they are going to attack, are likely to be forming up? Right! – that gives you a quarter of an hour to arrange with the batteries. Good-night!'

My marked map with registered targets for the various batteries was by the bedside, and I was able, without getting up, to carry out the Brigade Major's instructions. One battery was slow in answering, and as time began to press I complained with some force, when the Captain – his battery commander was away on a course – at last got on the telephone. Poor Dawson. He was very apologetic. I never spoke to him again. He was a dead man within nine hours.

I suppose I had been asleep again about twenty minutes when a rolling boom, the scream of approaching shells, and regular cracking bursts to right and left woke me up. Now and again one heard the swish and the 'plop' of gas-shells. A hostile bombardment, without a doubt. I looked at my watch – 4.33 am.

Overleaf: 'Even the ruins are ruined.'

2. 'Even the ruins are ruined'

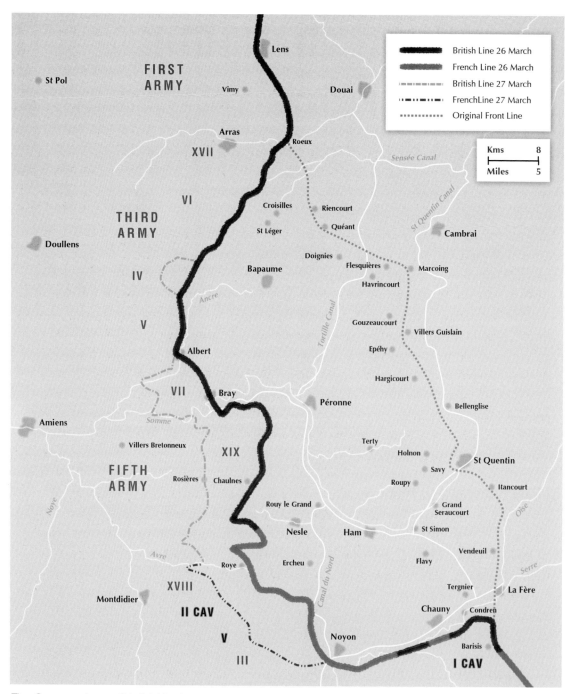

The German advance, 21–26 March.

'We bivouac on the road and enjoy the wonderful British grocery supplies, which even include biscuits, ginger, whisky and English cigarettes.'

Lieutenant Herbert Sulzbach, 63rd Field Artillery Regiment, Imperial German Army

––––––––––

21st March: The starting time had been fixed for 4.40 am. The exact time, down to the last second, was given through three times. Four o'clock. The darkness begins to lift, very, very slowly; we stand at the guns with our gas-masks round our necks, and the time until 4.40 crawls round at a dreadfully slow pace. At last we're there, and with a crash our barrage begins from thousands and thousands of gun-barrels and mortars, a barrage that sounds as if the world were coming to an end. For the first hour we only strafe the enemy artillery with alternate shrapnel, Green Cross and Blue Cross. The booming is getting more and more dreadful, especially as we are in a town between the walls of houses. Meanwhile an order arrives: HM the Kaiser and Field Marshal von Hindenburg have arrived at the Western theatre in order to command the battle of St Quentin in person.

Lieutenant Herbert Sulzbach, 63rd Field Artillery Regiment, Imperial German Army

I awoke with a tremendous start, conscious of noise, incessant and musical, so intense that it seemed as if hundreds of devils were dancing in my brain. Everything seemed to be vibrating, the ground, my dugout, my bed. What on earth was up? By Jove! The great Boche offensive must have begun! It was still dark. What time was it? Just five o'clock.

I lit a candle, seized the telephone receiver beside my bed and buzzed up the exchange.

'Any messages coming through?' I asked.

'No, sir!' …

The door of my dugout opened and in hurried the Colonel, clad in spectacles, pyjamas, and gum boots.

Captain Arthur Behrend, 90th Brigade, Royal Garrison Artillery

In action: a German 10.5 cm field gun surrounded by its distinctive wicker shell baskets.

'Any report from the OP?' he asked.

'Gardiner's speaking to them now.' Suddenly a terrific crash half lifted me out of bed. Out went the candle.

Captain George Nicholls, C Battery, 82nd Brigade, Royal Field Artillery

It was hours afterwards before I realized that this was the opening bombardment of perhaps the mightiest, most overpowering assault in military history. Had not the 'Prepare for Attack' warning come in I should have been in pyjamas, and might possibly have lain in bed for two or three minutes, listening quietly and comfortably while estimating the extent and intensity of the barrage. But this occasion was different, and I was up and about a couple of minutes after waking. Opening my door, I

The destructive power of high explosive shells.

encountered the not unpleasant smell of lachrymatory gas. The infantry battalion headquarters' staff were already moving out of the quarry to their forward station.

I awoke about 4.30 am to discover that a terrific bombardment had opened on us. I lit a candle and a cigarette, not realizing for a few moments what was really happening, then by all the tremendous crashes all around I was convinced that something unusual was happening so tumbled out of bed and started to dress. A head poked in my door and asked me what we were going to do (he was one of my sergeants). I told him to turn out the men and get the horses out.

Company Quarter Master Sergeant Edward Lyons, Army Service Corps, 6th Division

It was pitch black with a heavy mist. The din was terrific, the shells seemed to come in thousands screaming and crashing everywhere.

We were situated on the brow of a hill in a very exposed position, and we got all our horses out without much trouble, though they wanted to bolt once they were untied.

It was a ticklish job while it lasted. Every shell seemed to be coming straight into the stables and the poor beasts were getting desperate. We assembled in a sunken road alongside the hospital and for the time being it gave us some feeling of security. We stuck there until about 8.30 am, and although the shells were striking the banks on either side of the road not one had landed in the road itself. From a camp down the road regimental stretcher-bearers were continually passing with men who'd been hit.

I received an order for three horse ambulances to clear wounded. I then decided to go back and save what we could. So I ordered everybody back to our billets to harness up and hook into all vehicles. While doing this a shell landed right in the middle of the yards, but by all that was lucky it burst in a mud heap and all we got was splashed with mud.

By simple good fortune, the Germans were aided in their assault by thick fog, one of the first that spring. In places, visibility was down to a few metres, throwing British defensive plans into confusion. Strongpoints, which the British had hoped would frustrate initial German aspirations, were rendered useless as the men could see nothing and were either surrounded or overrun. The speed with which the enemy infiltrated the British forward zone was terrifying.

Lieutenant Herbert Sulzbach, 63rd Field Artillery Regiment, Imperial German Army

So we are stationed right at the most decisive place, and the hottest.

In the middle of this booming I often have to make a break in my fire control duties, since I just can't carry on with all the gas and smoke. The gunners stand in their shirt-sleeves with the sweat running down and dripping off them. Shell after shell is rammed into the breach, salvo after salvo is fired, and you don't need to give fire orders any more, they're in such good spirits, and put up such a rate of rapid fire, that not a single word of command is needed. In any case you can now only communicate with the gun-teams by using a whistle. At 9.40 the creeping barrage begins, and under its cover the thousands, and thousands more, and tens of thousands of soldiers climb out of the trenches, and the infantry assault begins: and the infantry assault has now succeeded.

The limbers come up, and we reach our finest hour when 2/Lt Knauer gives the order 'To the front – limber up!' We move through St Quentin at a trot, and the British are hardly firing. And now come the scenes of the advance, the scenes of the ravaged, shell-torn battleground that we still have in our memory from 1914. Everything has gone brilliantly, the

Engl. Gruben Rück nach dem Sturm.

sappers have already thrown bridges across the British trenches, the whole supply column is working successfully. We move forward on the second line of advance, and columns and troops on the move are blocking the advance routes, which of course we ourselves have largely shot to craters. The first prisoners are coming through, well-built chaps, with very good uniforms and equipment, in hard training for field sports. All thorough-going 'Tommies' walking along cheerfully with a fag in their mouths. I had a quick word with a few British gunners, they had been completely surprised and were speechless at our massed infantry assault.

The capture of gunners told its own story of the speed and depth of German penetration into British lines: gunners were not normally seen amongst any haul of prisoners.

Indistinct but evocative snaps showing the Germans urgently pushing on.

Villers-Outréaux, 21st March: An awfully good-looking young English captain is just waiting, with a smiling, interested face, for me to speak to him; so I do. It appears they had been expecting the attack for the past twenty days, but did not expect it today; the preliminary bombardment by our guns seemed to him much too mild for that!!! Although the English reserves were very close up, they could not be used owing to the fog and the quickness of our infantry. This officer wore the most wonderful riding-boots. When I looked him up and down he apologized for not being properly dressed for marching. He said he had just been going for a ride. He appeared to take it rather amiss that our attack had not left him time to dress himself in proper style with boots and puttees to be taken prisoner.

Lieutenant Rudolph Binding, German Cavalry (Dragoons)

We move through Essigny, but there is such a traffic block in the town that we hardly manage a kilometer in three hours. On our right and left flanks it's the same situation, all the troops pushing forward, taking the advance for granted as well, as though static warfare had never existed.

However did we people, who have been enduring a starvation blockade for a good four years, manage to do the *very* thing that the chaps over there couldn't do in some fifty pitched battles? We pass the first British battery emplacements, and we're soon in their second-line positions. …

From our observation post I can see the fighting in progress; our infantry support planes are coming in quite low to attack with machine guns, the fighter planes keeping above them to protect their colleagues. The advance had got moving to such an extent that even the captive balloons at our rear are being brought forward. We are not able to judge where the line is to our right and left, nor how far the divisions next to us have advanced, but the position near Arras is supposed to be favourable.

General Foch is said to be marching against us with the well-known French Reserve Army. Incidentally, since 21st March we've had the most beautiful spring weather – it might have been laid on specially, and our men are in splendid spirits. We are still second-line troops and now only occasionally join in the fighting.

Lieutenant Herbert Sulzbach, 63rd Field Artillery Regiment, Imperial German Army

Overleaf: St Quentin: German troops are entertained by a military band while they await orders.

Towards midday the sun forced its way through the heavy mist, and shortly afterwards a large number of German aeroplanes appeared and must have seen that transport was taking cover in the sunken road for in a short time 11-inch and 12-inch shells commenced to fall on either bank of the road near the hospital entrance. They came through the air with a terrific roar exploding with a crash that shook the whole place. One pair of horses in a limbered wagon leaped through a hedge and went down an almost vertical slope of about 25 feet onto the road without hurting themselves. Soon after, another 'aerial train' crashed on the side of the road causing the same pair of horses and two more pairs in wagons to bolt. One driver got hit and his horses bolted never to be seen again, one pair reached the stables with the limber smashed. The other pair went in the opposite direction and I found them soon after on the roadside with the driver unhurt, but with two wheels off the wagon.

Well, about 4 pm it slackened down for a while, and orders came that if nothing unusual happened we could return to our billets or rather what was left of them, as the General considered things were getting more favourable.

About 4.30 pm the unusual did happen and the storm broke forth afresh, so just after 5 pm we were ordered to clear for Tincourt. I sent everything off after one or two minor accidents and then cleared myself taking a cross-country route, breathing much more freely when I had put a couple of kilometres between myself and Villers-Faucon.

Company Quarter Master Sergeant Edward Lyons, Army Service Corps, 6th Division

On the skyline could be observed little black specks moving over the hills from whence we had come. Like ants they appeared, so many there were and so methodical their movements. Quickly the enemy had followed on our heels. He had tracked us down and as my eyes took in the vision of those hordes of advancing Germans, my heart sank. I knew I could never escape, that my baptism of fire and slaughter was at hand and I must prepare to face it. Nearer and nearer they came and my blood ran cold as I realized they must eventually come up against us – and that dusk was descending. Behind us a wood, a dense mass of trees and undergrowth. To retreat through this in the dark would be madness yet no other escape offered itself. With the little time left to us we attempted to dig some kind of cover.

Private George Fleet, 7th The Queen's (Royal West Surrey Regiment)

How I feared to be left alone that night or sent on a journey but at long last dawn arrived only to display a heavy mist through which nothing could be observed. We went forward – we fired – the enemy replied – we paused for the fog to lift – and then just in front of us I saw a German machine-gun post. I am sure I was trembling all over from fright, or, if you like, from sheer funk. The scrap began and as the moments flew by it became hotter and hotter. We left our cover and took up another position. Bewilderment – anxious glances – lack of any kind of leadership, or was it we realized we were outnumbered – a fellow running – others following. I quickly joined them. Back under cover of the wood we paused. An officer took command of the situation and held us together for a few hours, but later to our distress we discovered the machine-gunners were almost out of ammunition. For a while the semblance of a fight was put up but finally the cry 'Every man for himself' was shouted by the officer in charge. Nothing has ever put fear into me as that cry did. I ran through the wood not knowing in which direction I was heading, urged on by sheer fright.

British troops were in headlong retreat, nearly 10 miles on the first day at the deepest point. Over a 50-mile front, covering both Fifth and Third Armies, there was nowhere where the Germans had been held. Well-equipped German assault battalions plunged on, using tactics of quick infiltration, bypassing strongpoints in the knowledge that these could be mopped up later in the day. British artillery was hastily withdrawn or abandoned.

Lieutenant Rudolph Binding, German Cavalry (Dragoons)

St-Emilie, near Épehy, 23rd March: We are going like hell, on and on, day and night. The sun and moon help. One or two hours' halt, then on again. Our baggage is somewhere in the rear, and nobody expects to see it again. We are glad if ration-carts and field-kitchens can get up to us at night; then men and horses feed for the next twenty-four hours at one sitting. Today this happened at 7 am. Then the ration-carts disappear again until further notice.

We have reached the zone in which all the wells and streams have been wrecked, and the water for the attacking troops has to be brought up in water-carts. That applies to the men. The horses have got to wait until we cross the canal at Moislains-Nurlu; we are supposed to reach it today.

Spent the night on the bare floor of an English dugout, with the GOC Artillery and his officers. Now we go forward, past craters and trenches, captured gun-positions, ration-dumps, and clothing-depots. Another wonderful spring day with an early mist, which helps us. Our cars now run on the best English rubber tyres, we smoke none but English cigarettes, and plaster our boots with lovely English boot-polish – all unheard-of things which belong to a fairyland of long ago.

There are limits to personal cleanliness. Comfort consists in a horse-bucket full of very doubtful water out of a shell hole, but one treats it as if it came straight from the springs of Baden-Baden, so glad is one's skin to be refreshed. We assume that it will be at least eight days before we are under a roof again. The devastation is immeasurable. There is hardly a cellar left of the villages which we destroyed and over which the unexpected attack now rages. Of course, the really hard part will begin when we get on beyond.

Myself and several other fellows had been running for some time when suddenly we came upon open ground. We paused to take our bearings but the bullets commenced to churn up the turf beneath our feet. Again we took to our heels. In the distance we saw a road down which vehicles of all kinds were hurrying helter-skelter. Crossing a fairly narrow and shallow stream we gained this road and joined the motley crowd. Horse-drawn gun carriages seem to have pride of place as the drivers lashed the animals to a frenzy to escape capture. The Germans, hot on our track, were pushing forward quicker than we could retreat.

Sheer chaos reigned – already it was late in the afternoon – men and officers, tired and haggard, many severely wounded, hurrying away in odd groups – a sprinkling of civilians scampering along with a few personal possessions – supply wagons and guns rushing by at breakneck speed – all the paraphernalia of a great army dashing headlong to the rear – eager to escape a persistent and powerful pursuer. Where would it all end? What would happen to me in this awful turmoil? At last under cover of darkness we were collected and sorted out into battalions. Each given a couple of blankets and instructed to snatch a few hours' rest. In an open field adjacent to a small village we settled down. However, with the dawn we

Private George Fleet, 7th The Queen's (Royal West Surrey Regiment)

Directly in the line of the enemy's advance and just 15 miles due west of St Quentin was the 34th Casualty Clearing Station. In this photo the walking wounded crowd around tents. This CCS alone admitted 1,375 patients on the first day of the offensive.

Above left: The caption says, 'March 22nd. Can this ward take any more?' That day a further 1,700 wounded men were accepted. Above right: Men awaiting evacuation from the 34th CCS, which was soon abandoned owing to the German advance. A further 250 men arrived from the battlefield and 2,100 were sent away on afternoon trains. Right: 9.00 am, 24 March: personnel and salvage of the 34th CCS about to leave. All these pictures were taken by Captain Howard Somervell, RAMC. In 1924, Somervell was a key participant in George Mallory's assault on Everest.

awoke to the crackle of machine guns. Once more we retreated, once more the day was spent marching, marching from a victorious and triumphant enemy.

I was hungry. There had been little to eat except 'hard rations'. The agony of thirst nagged me, thirst being harder to bear than hunger. Occasionally I drank water from wayside ditches and although discoloured it afforded me great consolation. My feet were sore, yet pause we could not.

23rd March: Five of us spent the night in an ammunition trench lying on the ground; we were all wrapped up in blankets but were still cold, and dripping with dew in the morning.

Our first-line troops have taken Ham, and we shall soon have made enough progress to reach the old positions we were in before the 1916 retreat; we have only sustained light casualties. There is now less of a jam on the roads and you can advance at a better pace. The 5th Guards Division moves at such a lick that soon we can't keep up with them. We bivouac right in Artemps, which was a British camp, and suddenly we're in another world. English posters, sign-posts and name-boards. We take a lot of prisoners and spend the night in a British officers' dugout.

Lieutenant Herbert Sulzbach, 63rd Field Artillery Regiment, Imperial German Army

23rd March: We moved on or rather back again towards Péronne. The congestion of traffic now was very great and double banking was quite a common thing. Long halts were continuous on arriving at crossroads, as traffic was converging on Péronne from all directions. Things were getting anything but comfortable, as on various parts of the road, low flying enemy aeroplanes were firing on the traffic, but luckily we got none. We got on the move again and entered Péronne, which was absolutely deserted but for one or two police. We had a bit of a fright before we got out of the town. An enemy aeroplane flying very low started shooting at us but nobody was hit. As we crossed the river outside the town, engineers were hard at work preparing to blow up the bridge.

Reaching the heights on the other side we pulled off the road again, watered and fed the weary horses and had some food ourselves. Here, there was no one apparently controlling the traffic, and later when the order to move came, it disgusted me to see the wild scramble to get on to

Company Quarter Master Sergeant Edward Lyons, Army Service Corps, 6th Division

the road. The traffic previously was two deep, which was bad enough for an ordinary road, but in a very short time it became three abreast. Blocks were continuous, transport from the field were forcing their way into the columns on the road, and for a time absolute disorder prevailed simply because there was nobody there to regulate it in any way whatsoever, and I could not help giving a bit of my mind to a few of them. Most of them seemed afraid they would be captured. It would have been no loss to the army if some of them had.

Lieutenant Herbert Sulzbach, 63rd Field Artillery Regiment, Imperial German Army

24th March: Our sappers build a bridge over the canal, and we pass some really very heavy British guns. Then we move on to Dury. We are still second-line troops. In the first three days the offensive in our sector of the front alone has brought in more thousands of prisoners than you can count.

We've been made front-line troops now: the division is following on in order of march. But the pace is pretty slow up to Ham, a little town I passed through in 1916 when it was a rosy little rear-echelon station. Now it's a pile of rubble; we forage, and find some splendid British supplies. There's really everything you could think of. Plenty of oats for the horses and tinned food, bacon, cheese and wine for us. There are huge masses of troops rolling forward again towards Nesle.

Such had been the confusion that vast numbers of British troops were taken prisoner in the first two days, far more than were killed or wounded. Many battalion commanders became casualties too: thirty-eight in the first twenty-four hours, of whom twenty-eight were captured, including five captured and wounded. In addition, hundreds of junior officers were snapped up. Captain George Foley was not in the initial trawl of officer-prisoners, but he did not remain at liberty for long. Overtaken by the enemy, he suddenly found himself looking down the wrong end of a rifle near the Somme village of Ham.

Captain Henry Foley, 6th Prince Albert's (Somerset Light Infantry)

At 20 yards' distance the leading Hun raised his rifle and aimed it with dispassionate care at my head. It seemed to me that to be shot like a pig in a poke was in no way furthering the cause of the Allies. Consequently, and in rather less time than it takes to tell, I indicated that we were willing to capitulate. Somewhat to our surprise, the Hun, evidently a gentleman,

Wounded and prisoners: captured British troops make their way through German lines.

Alive and unscathed: British prisoners momentarily stop for a photograph hours after capture.

A column of British prisoners captured in March moving off.

lowered his weapon, at the same time pointing out that our best course was eastwards. We complied. In a few minutes we had joined the little straggling despondent groups who were trailing back through the German lines. With all those grey figures round us, I had the sensation of being swallowed alive.

As we approached the village we had to pass through a wave of the enemy just emerging. Their bayonets glistened, and they were filled evidently with the lust for blood, and the desire to kill everything in khaki within sight. Never was frightfulness more fiercely displayed, and how we got through them unstuck I cannot imagine. This accomplished, however, we soon found ourselves in the main street of the village, into which our guns were sending an occasional belated shell; and so began our long journey through the enemy country.

Very little notice was taken of us at this point. I joined company with two officers of the Liverpools who were amongst the party. Our first stopping place was a small dressing station, where a little crowd of interested spectators gathered round to have a look at us. They were quite friendly, and gave us cigarettes. The whole country-side seemed to be alive with Germans, and all the way back we met battalion after battalion of grey-clad, steel-helmeted troops marching with a steady, inexorable pace towards the battle line.

Shortly after crossing the canal, we met a battalion that had just suffered some casualties from our bombing aeroplanes. The officer in command rode up to us and shouted something in his native tongue, which we, of course, failed entirely to understand. This rather annoyed him, and I thought we were 'for it', but he merely called up one of the cycle orderlies who were following the battalion, and detailed him as our escort. Then with the words 'Behold, your guide, gentlemen', he saluted and rode away. My party, by the way, now consisted of the two Liverpool officers and two French soldiers, our own men having been stopped some way back.

A German soldier recently wounded by a bomb from an aeroplane was lying on a rough wooden bed. He had to be taken back to a clearing station, and my party was commandeered for the job [of carrying him]. So for three or four weary miles we toiled along, taking it in turn to carry the dead weight of this unfortunate fellow.

The very fact that officer prisoners of war had to be utilized as stretcher-bearers was one of the many signs of the German Red Cross Services' lack of organization and efficiency. Those who were not being lugged along as our hero was were being shaken almost to death in ramshackle transport wagons. It was incomprehensible to us how an army which was in so many ways the perfection of discipline and organization should allow such an important branch as this to be so ill-equipped and primitive.

Foley was eventually led back to St Quentin where he joined large numbers of British prisoners already collected and waiting to be taken away. Foley estimated that there were around 2,000 men in all. 'We must have been a gratifying sight to the Huns,' he wrote, 'and an equally depressing one to the French inhabitants.'

The havoc caused by the German advance caused consternation in England. In response, the age for overseas service was cut by six months to eighteen and a half and the desperate need for reinforcements saw the rapid embarkation of thousands of young men overseas, as well as others who had only just recovered from wounds.

Everything is commotion here. We have been issued with full war ammunition – pack, rifles, trenching tools, 'ammo', iron rations, and spare shirts. We have been trying the equipment on, and laying the whole skeleton of it on the hut floor, adjusting straps and buckles.

Private Reginald Kiernan, Training Reserve Battalion

Hundreds of troops marched out to the station this morning, and they were all Expeditionary men. Many of them had medal ribbons, and all had blue Vs on their sleeves, some of them had three Vs [each denoting a year of overseas service]. They went off very quietly, column after column.

The physical training staff has the wind up. The whole camp is being cleared, and they are afraid they will be put on a draft. There is a PT sergeant who had been the terror of recruits since 1915. Men he trained in that year have been back, wounded in 1916 and 1917, and each time he was the same. He is utterly changed now and is very quiet. We feel triumphant over these NCOs – we know we will soon be the real soldiers, and we do not care a damn about France. We feel twice as strong as they are, and, anyway, we have always known they were 'lead-swingers'.

Night

It is just before 'lights-out'. I have been to confession. It was a lovely bright evening and I did not wait for tea. I walked into the near suburb of Newcastle. I longed to talk to the priest, but he did not seem too pleased to be brought out into the church at six o'clock in the evening to hear confession, though he tried to hide it. The priest never said a word to me, except the words of absolution.

As I walked back the evening had clouded over, and it was raining thinly, coming in from the sea, very cold, as it does here. Perhaps he was tired.

Lance Corporal Frederick Hodges, 53rd (Young Soldier) Battalion, Bedfordshire Regiment

In the streets of Norwich, a rumour began to spread among the young soldiers who thronged the pavements of the city. It was that our troops in France were retreating, and that we youngsters were to be drafted to the front without completing our training.

The rumours proved to be true; at the early morning roll call, as we paraded outside the billets, we were told officially. The situation on the Western Front was so grave that all those who had reached the age of eighteen years and eight months were to be drafted to the front immediately. My age was eighteen years and eight months on 18th March, and so I was eligible.

We signallers reported for the last time at the Sussex Signal School, handed in our flags, and said goodbye to our instructors. We returned to our companies, where all training had also ceased, and we spent every moment of the day in long queues, being kitted out for the front. We put on our best khaki and handed in the tunic and trousers we had been wearing. In great excitement, we queued to have our bayonets dulled and our rifles inspected by the armourer sergeant. We marched through the town to the gas school, and queued up to pass through the various gas chambers and tunnels for a final test of our gas masks.

Everyone was happy and full of youthful high spirits, and that evening, when at last we were free, we all went down into the city centre where many thousands of excited youngsters of eighteen laughed and talked as we milled round the city. We already wore coloured ribbons – red, yellow, green, blue, etc. around our service caps, to distinguish the many young

Two officers practising wireless communication.

soldier battalions in that area. Now we added to these, red, white and blue ribbons which we bought at Woolworths, trimming our uniform caps across the front above and below the cap badge. …

As we roamed the city centre in large groups, the military police who would normally stop us for any infringement in our dress or behaviour, now took no action. Authority was being tolerant and unusually friendly; our own officers were very friendly and informal as they stood chatting to us as we waited again next morning in long queues for boot repairs. They seemed … or was it we, who now suddenly seemed to be a race apart. We were now bound for the front, from which they had returned with wounds, to train us.

The door is suddenly opened, and I look up to find the orderly sergeant, Corporal Duckworth, standing, notebook in hand.

'Come on, you lazy louts, time you were up,' says the corporal cheerily, and continues: 'Any of these men here?' commencing to read out a list of names.

I am wondering what is about to happen now, for I have a presentiment that something much bigger than an ordinary fatigue is about to take place. With much anxiety I wait to hear 'Private Christopher Haworth'

Private Christopher Haworth, Training Reserve Battalion

*Ripon Camp: a
draft of Scotsmen
preparing to
leave for France.*

and at that moment my name is called, followed by more names until the list is exhausted.

'Now all you men who have just answered your names,' the corporal now speaks more seriously, 'report at Company Office at nine-thirty. You're all for draft – France.'

He leaves the room, which is buzzing with the excited chatter of the occupants. I feel a peculiar sensation in my throat, and although I realize it is a dangerous undertaking, I am happy to be included for have I not been looking forward to service in France since I joined up on my eighteenth birthday almost a year ago. At last I am to come face to face with the grim reality of war; I am to be put to the test, and my youthful exuberance overflows with the possibilities of the great adventure before me.

*Private Reginald
Kiernan, Training
Reserve
Battalion*

Dover, March 24th: We arrived here last night. We marched out of the Newcastle camp, light of heart, glad to be going, and we sang *Good-byee* and *Away o'er the Jordan* right to the station. It was a tremendously long train, and we stopped only once on the way to Dover. We were allowed to get out then, but the station gates were locked. Hundreds of people were round the station, cheering us. Going through the fields the men were taking pot shots at the sheep and cows with their new rifles. There was a real 'crackle of musketry' along the train.

It was night when we passed through London and children and women came on to the verandahs of the slum tenements and cheered us.

Their cheers sounded shrill and faint over the noise of the train. Many were in nightclothes, and we could see them dimly, and their little rooms, by the light of their tiny gas jets.

In the yellow light in the carriages the men sprawled in all sorts of queer, curved positions. They lay against each other, asleep. Some were curled up on the floor, their heads on their new packs. They snored and slavered and broke wind. They were exhausted with singing and excitement. The racks were full of packs and brown, shining rifles, all oiled, straight from the armourer's store.

I am writing this in an empty house. It is one of a row of empty houses which stands crescent-shaped on the hill over the town. We are ordered not to go out.

In France, troops were tumbling across the old Somme Battlefield and past the camps of Nissen huts built after the German withdrawal to a new, shorter, and in-depth defensive line in early 1917. On the Somme, on what was defiled ground, Corps Officers, clerks and typists had worked conscientiously and, to the interest of exhausted troops, in noticeable comfort.

These weary soldiers were also aware of the plentifully stocked tents and marquees of the YMCA and the Expeditionary Force Canteen, purveyors of cherished items, from cigarettes to chocolate, from writing paper to razors, and other more luxurious items beyond the fragile finances of ordinary soldiers. These stores were now being abandoned and were open and free to all comers, for if Tommy did not help himself then Jerry surely would.

In the late afternoon we got orders to move our batteries into positions half a mile west of Bapaume.

Corps Heavies were still in their old quarters at Grévillers; the Colonel decided that we should go there too as Corps Headquarters were moving out and there were sure to be plenty of superior billets to let. …

When we reached Grévillers we found that all the best billets had been snaffled by the infantry so we took possession of a miserable hovel beside the ruins of the church; Corps Heavies were living in a suite of luxurious Nissen huts on top of the hill, barely a hundred yards away. The Colonel and the Orderly Officers went off in the car to reconnoitre battery

Captain Arthur Behrend, 90th Brigade, Royal Garrison Artillery

Destroyed
artillery in a gun
pit. It appears
this German
105 cm gun
suffered a fatal
detonation in the
breech.

positions; I went up the hill to Corps Heavies to see the Staff Captain about rations and ammunition supply.

As I climbed up the broad duckboard path, neatly covered with strips of rabbit wire to prevent you from slipping, I felt even more like a tramp than usual. The lawn was as neat as ever; the garden, fringed with its decorous row of huts, had never looked better. In the middle of the lawn stood the trophy, a Boche pipsqueak [light gun], resplendent in its new coat of paint. Above it on a line dangled a row of magpies shot by the Reconnaissance Officer with the Brigade Major's gun. Sleek gentlemanly clerks, carrying papers and what not, hurried in and out of offices. Even the huts, with their tarred and sanded roofs, daintily camouflaged ends, and neat notice boards, eyed me askance.

I entered a hut labelled AMMUNITION OFFICER where friend Smithers told me – um yes – that 6-inch ammunition was very scarce owing to large amounts that had been dumped on the reserve positions, and – er – handed over to the Boche. However there were a few thousand rounds lying at Puisieux; we could draw from these if we liked – um yes – but they weren't likely to be in very good condition as they had been salvaged from the [1916] Somme. Failing that we would have to send our lorries 15 miles back to the railhead at Acheux where ammunition was being sent up as fast as possible; it wasn't considered safe to bring the trains any closer to the line – um yes – under the present circumstances.

Rations were to be drawn from the railhead at Achiet-le-Grand which was being evacuated. Everyone could take as much as was wanted; no indents were required.

Next I went to the Counter-Battery office where one could always rely on hearing the very latest news.

'Anyone in?' I asked a clerk, who was quietly packing up a typewriter. 'Oh no, sir,' in a surprised tone, 'they are all in the mess having dinner.'

I went into their pretty mess.

'Good evening, sir!' said I to the Counter-Battery Colonel.

A British 9.2
howitzer battery
abandoned by its
gunners as the
Germans swept
forward.

'Hullo Ninety! Sit down and have dinner with us!' said the Counter-Battery Orderly Officer affably.

'I haven't got time!'

'Have a drink, then! By the way excuse the candles – the electric light plant's being packed up you know. Beastly nuisance shifting isn't it?'

So I sat down and passed a pleasant ten minutes [and] after a final whisky and soda I crept back to our hovel, wrote a few letters to the batteries and so to bed.

[The next morning Behrend spent time vainly trying to discover how much ammunition the batteries of 90th Brigade had, while around him the evacuation of Corps Heavies headquarters continued. Following their departure, 90th Brigade Headquarters moved in, albeit temporarily.]

'Lorries, lorries, lorries!' The cry was always for more lorries, but we could do nothing. … Corps Heavies had detailed all that they could lay hands on to go off and fetch ammunition from the railheads.

During the morning one could not help noticing that despite the shortage of lorries Corps Heavies were doing themselves pretty proud. Lorry after lorry rolled up to be loaded with such delightful etcetera as the electric lighting set, armchairs, and a fine kitchen range that had certainly not been paid for by its present owners. Even the trophy [the German light gun] went off tied to the back of a lorry; its gaily painted little wheels twinkled round so fast that it looked like a toy.

I opened our office in what had been the Brigade Major's, and prepared to enjoy the usual comfort of our surroundings.

Enter Captain 'Gilly'. Always well groomed and immaculately dressed, even under the very worst conditions, he bears a slight, very slight, resemblance to the Crown Prince and is one of the very best.

'Hullo, B.!' said he, 'Busy? Where's the old man?'

'Not very! Out thank goodness! Oh, by the way, you know the rations dump at Achiet-le-Grand is being evacuated? Well, the Old Man wants you to send a lorry there *tout de suite* to pick up as much rum as poss. and dish it out to the batteries. It's a jolly good idea if no one else has thought of it and the batteries will be damned glad of it during the next two or three nights if I'm not mistaken. And don't forget to leave a jar or two here, Gilly!'

'Right-ho, old dear. It shall be done!'

Exit Gilly.

Late that night my phone rang.

'OC Toc 1, sir!' the exchange told me.

'Adjutant here, sir!' I cried, sleepily.

'Hullo, is that you?' said the Major of Toc 1 coldly. 'You know those rum jars you very kindly sent to us this morning?'

'Yes, sir; you mean the ones the Colonel told you to keep unopened until we get on the move again?' I interposed politely.

'Yes, those are the ones,' replied the Major hastily. 'Well, that isn't the point!'

'No, sir?'

'The point is that they don't contain rum at all; they contain Nut Oil for Chinese labourers.'

And the remarkable part of the affair was that during the next hour Toc 2, Toc 3 and Toc 4 all rang up to make the same complaint.

[At midday the Colonel of the RGA Brigade and another officer named Gardiner came back to the camp from a trip to Bapaume. Gardiner went straight to see Behrend.]

Gardiner burst into the office, his face one big grin.

'What d'you think?' he cried. 'Toc 2 are running the Bapaume Canteen!'

'What?' I exclaimed.

'Toc 2 are in action in the canteen grounds just beside the marquees and the EFC [Expeditionary Force Canteen] people are clearing out! They wanted to set it on fire but old Aglionby wouldn't let them. Toc 2's quartermaster sergeant is in charge and he's giving everything away! Have a cigarette!'

He tossed me an unopened tin of De Reszkas.

'I'd advise you to go down before it's too late,' he added. 'Ask the Colonel for the car; we've brought back with us a case of bubbly, two cases of whisky and umpteen boxes of Coronas!'

The Colonel came in.

'May I have the car to go to Toc 2, sir?' I faltered.

'Yes,' he growled.

The news had spread like wildfire; as Thompson and I were starting, the Sergeant Major came running out of his billet.

'May I come with you, sir?'

'Jump in, Sergeant Major!'

It did one's heart good to see the happy faces we met on the road. Every lorry driver had a pile of cigarette tins on the seat beside him. Every infantry soldier had his pockets bulging with them. Even the walking wounded had their arms full. Everyone was laughing.

Private Edward Williamson, 17th The Royal Scots (Lothian Regiment)

The columns marched up the hill to Maricourt, or what was left of it, and to our surprise suddenly came upon scattered units of the famous 51st Highland Regiment, in groups of ten or twelve with walking wounded among them, very battle-stained, but in high humour for they had evidently helped themselves to abandoned YMCA stores. They carried in their arms a varied assortment of articles: shirts, socks, pants, bottles of wine, tins of beer, cases of whisky, boxes of cigarettes, cigars. The officers were not immune either! Some of the Scots had drunk too much and gave voice to their favourite ditties as they ambled or staggered by. From their unwashed weary faces and bedraggled kilts it was obvious to our curious gaze that continuous fighting and lack of sleep had taken their toll, hence no one could begrudge them this demonstration of elation now that tension was relaxed as they streamed down the hill from the vicinity of Hardecourt. Andy Swanson hailed a tall lean Highlander, who carried a Lewis gun over his left shoulder and a pile of cigarette tins under his right arm, with a fancy shawl under his tin hat that added a comic touch, 'Where's the auction, Mac?' The Scot relieved himself of the gun for a moment and jerked his thumb over his shoulder, 'Yon storeman told us to help ourselves before they fired the canteen, and we couldn't leave this loot to the bastard Germans.'

Captain Arthur Behrend, 90th Brigade, Royal Garrison Artillery

The scene outside the great Canteen was wonderful; it might have been Christmas Eve. A queue of lorries and GS wagons and cars and SAA [Small Arms Ammunition] carts and every other sort of cart stretched for hundreds of yards down the road. In almost every case they were unattended; their drivers were inside seeking something for nothing.

On the grass in front of the canteen were Toc 2's howitzers, drawn up in line 20 yards apart and firing steadily away, one round per battery per minute.

Across the road I saw a party of them with their tin-hats at rakish angles posing for the official photographer of all people. Heavens, look at that Number Two pulling the lanyard with a long Pantello [cigarette] in his mouth and a bottle of Bass in his other hand!

An Expeditionary Force canteen overrun by the Germans at Itres. Most stores were ransacked by passing British troops aware that the Germans would take what was left.

The officers of Toc 2 were dining in an outhouse and had reached the sweet course; before each one of them was set a big open tin of peaches. A confused medley of shouts greeted me.

'Hullo! Here's the Adj.! What does he want? Come in! Go away! Sit down! Have some fruit!'

'What can we offer you?' asked Aglionby to me a few minutes later. 'It's as much as we can do to keep our soldiers on the guns.'

We walked into the marquee. The mob inside was growing unruly; the quartermaster sergeant of Toc 2 and his assistants were unable to cope with the rush. Men were clambering over the counters; others, already across, were pulling down piles of boxes to see what was on top.

'It's getting a bit too popular,' remarked Aglionby gloomily. 'Help yourself while there's time!'

An EFC attendant came up to Aglionby.

'I'm going now, sir,' said he cheerfully. 'No objection – everyone 'elping themselves as 'ts better our lads 'ave it instead of them 'uns but pleash purra guard over – hic – whisky or theshe chaps won't be 'alf blind!'

On the way back we examined our spoils. The Sergeant Major had a case of tins of Café-au-lait, 17 tins of biscuits and 5 pounds of tobacco. I had 1,160 cigarettes, six dozen Gillette blades, one Ingersoll watch, one patent combined tin-opener and corkscrew, one whole roast chicken, two bottles of Grand Marnier and one package which, on investigation, was found to contain 144 boxes of Beecham's Pills. At a guinea a box these would have been worth £152 4s.

A noisy luncheon party was in progress in our hovel.

The menu   Prawns in aspic
                  Cold boiled ham
                  Pineapple and tinned cream

                  _____

                  Pol Roger '06
                  Johnny Walker

'… Yes, I'm a pretty good hand at choosing battery positions!' I heard the Colonel saying with a chuckle.

The orgy of excitement at the rapidly emptying canteens was a moment of light relief for soldiers who had fought themselves almost to a standstill. They would now have to devour what food they had acquired and push on once more.

Second
Lieutenant
Michael Baines,
55th Battery,
Royal Field
Artillery

25th March: Shrapnel bullet from airburst missed me but broke teacup. Very serious. Rumour that Hun just over hill. Slight stampede, two guns and mess cart upset in stream. Gramophone ok. Retreated to Vrely, in action in quarry. Two pip squeaks through roof of mess and dinner spoilt but no one hurt.

26th March: Sent up to find front line and what is happening. … Involved in German attack from Méharicourt and blown into shell holes with OC. Durham Light infantry by shell from own battery. Went forward with infantry but guns shooting short so galloped back with orders from DLI to lengthen range. … Rejoined battery in quarry. Shell burst on gun 11 yards away, had to shoot three horses, poor old 29 and 63, my black wheelers. Fired all night.

Lieutenant
Rudolph Binding,
Staff Officer
German Cavalry
(Dragoons)

Crater-Field, near Le Forest, March 26th: There was the corner of a little wood where the English put up a desperate resistance, apparently with a few machine guns, and finally with only one. When the defence was broken down, out from the lines of our advancing infantry, which I was following, appeared an English general, accompanied by a single officer. He was an extraordinary sight. About thirty-five years old, excellently –

one can almost say wonderfully – dressed and equipped, he looked as if he had just stepped out of a Turkish bath in Jermyn Street. Brushed and shaved, with his short khaki overcoat on his arm, in breeches of the best cut and magnificent high lace-boots, such as only the English bootmakers make to order, he came to meet me easily and without the slightest embarrassment. The sight of all this English cloth and leather made me more conscious than ever of the shortcomings of my own outfit, and I felt an inward temptation to call out to him, 'Kindly undress at once', for a desire for an English General's equipment, with tunic, breeches, and boots, had arisen in me, shameless and patent.

I said, 'Good morning', and he came to a stop with his companion. By way of being polite, I said with intention: 'You have given us a lot of trouble; you stuck it for a long time.' To which he replied: 'Trouble! Why, we have been running for five days and five nights!' It appeared that when he could no longer get his brigade to stand he had taken charge of a machine gun himself, to set an example to his retreating men. All his officers except the one with him had been killed or wounded, and his brigade hopelessly cut up. I asked for his name, to remind me of our meeting, and he gave it. He was General [Frederick] Dawson, an Equerry of the King [and CO South African Brigade].

We have now spent two nights in the crater-field of the old Somme battle. No desert of salt is more desolate. Last night we slept in a hole in the crumbly, chalky soil, and froze properly. It is impossible to sleep for excitement. Really one would like to be after them day and night, and only longs that there shall be no rest until one can feel the first breath of the Atlantic in Amiens. Tomorrow we hope to be on a level with Albert, where there will be villages again. Here the villages are merely names. Even the ruins are ruined. Yesterday I was looking for Bouchavesnes, which used to be quite a large place. There was nothing but a board nailed to a low post with the inscription in English, 'This was Bouchavesnes'.

The whole battalion and probably portions of others were lined up in a huge square in what appeared to be open country. Save for some artillery scampering across the sky-line on our right, presumed to be French, and an occasional shot in the distance, everything was fairly quiet although shrapnel could be seen bursting in the far distance. Yet there we were, lying

Private George Fleet, 7th The Queen's (Royal West Surrey Regiment)

on our stomachs in the open – why? I asked my neighbour the reason. It meant a fight to a finish, he said. My finish, I thought.

Secretly I registered a determination to be rid of that square if it were humanly possible. Eagerly I scanned around for places to which I could run for cover. In the course of a few hours, when shots began to whizz through the air and the atmosphere had become a trifle hot, the square collapsed, the result of a movement by certain men to obtain better cover. The Brigadier, seeing the break-up of his lovely square, tried to stem the tide but failed and again we retreated, towards the village of Bapouf. The other side of the village we were lined up across a field to meet the approaching enemy but again the scheme was abandoned.

Eventually we retired from the fray and moved towards another village some kilometres distant where we were to stay the night. Housed in some kind of hut, or it may have been a school-room or local recreational hall, we were told not to remove any clothing and to be ready to don our equipment and move off at a moment's notice. Tired out, we flung ourselves down hoping to obtain a few hours' sleep. About two o'clock in the morning we were awakened and told to be ready to move off in five minutes. The Germans were expected to take the village within the next couple of hours. Our weary tramp recommenced and in spite of fatigue we were thankful to be marching away from the firing line. At dawn we halted and I recall sleeping in a dugout beside a road until late in the morning. Jerry had not made the progress anticipated and for this we were all thankful. For the rest of the day and the following night we stayed beside this road, then moved on to more comfortable billets in a small village much damaged by shellfire but which afforded a little comfort. With rest, food and drink we became normal human beings again.

Lieutenant
Herbert
Sulzbach, 63rd
Field Artillery
Regiment,
Imperial
German Army

26th March: At Nesle, taken by our infantry assault in the course of the morning, I requisitioned three pigs and several hens for our cookhouse, out of a burning house; at the pace we are going, of course, our supply column can't keep up, and we have to look after ourselves. … Our infantry are bringing large numbers of British prisoners past us on their way to the rear; and a few French among them as well. The British really must have run like rabbits. It appears that the French who were thrown in to support the British were brought up from Paris at top speed in motor-cars. …

I must record a highly expert trick performed by a British pilot. Among other installations, we have occupied a British airfield (in fact we have pushed so far into British positions that we have reached the British Air Corps' living quarters), just a few hours ago. We are riding past it, and what do you think, a plane takes off nice and comfortably from the airfield; we are thinking it was pretty daring of our own Air Corps to occupy the enemy airfield so quickly, and then suddenly, in view of the whole division, the plane reveals itself as it climbs to be not a German one – not in the least, it was a British plane which had been left behind; the pilot had hidden, jumped into the plane, and before our eyes there he was off and away!

At Carrépuis we get our first dose of air bombing from an enemy squadron which has been shooting away at us like mad with machine guns. Among other casualties in this attack, our battalion commander, Captain von Schleicher, has been wounded. In an advance you are quite helpless against being bombed from the air, and it is a much more uncomfortable feeling than being bombed in static warfare when you have decent dugouts. The casualties were correspondingly greater.

The grave of an artillery sergeant in Sulzbach's regiment, killed during operations on the Somme.

Using a hastily built pontoon, a German field kitchen crosses the river Somme at Happencourt, south-west of St Quentin.

Lieutenant
Rudolph Binding,
Staff Officer,
German Cavalry
(Dragoons)

Meaux, to the South of Albert, March 27th: We are through at last, through the awful crater-field of the Somme. After 25 miles of unbroken waste the first house, ruined though it was, was saluted like a vision from the Promised Land. Our troops passed to the south of Albert. Now we are already in the English back areas, or at least rest-areas, a land flowing with milk and honey. Marvellous people these, who will only equip themselves with the very best that the earth produces. Our men are hardly to be distinguished from English soldiers. Everyone wears at least a leather jerkin, a waterproof either short or long, English boots or some other beautiful thing. The horses are feasting on masses of oats and gorgeous food-cake. The inhabitants deliver up chickens and pigeons with the usual tears. Cows, calves, and pigs find their way unobtrusively out of their farmyards into the field-kitchens, and there is no doubt the army is looting with some zest.

Yesterday evening we witnessed the wonderful spectacle of the English blowing up all the munition-dumps in this area, and there were not a few. Millions of shells will have no further chance of being fired at us.

If we had not had this weather we should not be nearly so far as we are. To push the enemy through 25 miles of desert at the most unlikely spot of all, with horse, foot and artillery, rations and ammunition, that was a conception worthy of a leader. Fighting by day, movement without stopping by night of troops and transport, along ten roads simultaneously. Like the wandering of a people, like a sea of tailless serpents moving their heads all level before them, so was this advance.

Today I was mildly hit, so mildly that it only raised a weal. A rifle bullet went through two coats which I was wearing in the early morning on account of the cold and struck my thigh like a blow from a hammer. I was wearing a pair of riding-breeches of English cloth, against which the English bullet stopped respectfully and fell to earth. I picked it up almost like a friendly greeting and stuck it in the pocket of the breeches which it had failed to pierce.

Men of both sides lived in an endless whirl of activity and pressure. Sleep was so fleeting that they wondered at their experiences, unsure whether these things had actually happened. It could feel like one long hallucination.

27th March: Infantry retreating through gun position, had to go back to Caix. Worst day we have had. Went into action behind Le Quesnoy in long valley watched by German sausage balloon, however he stopped shelling infantry pouring back. Rumours of forty French Divisions coming up from south, we shall need them.

Richthofen's Circus put in an appearance, bright red plane flew whole length of brigade without firing, he waved to us and we waved back. Perhaps the Baron himself?

28th March: Troops very nearly beat, all ammunition used up and horses all galled. At 5 pm entire front gives way. French retreat over Somme and we bolt across fields to Rouvrel. Sent to get ammunition from Cub, ride to Jumel 12 miles away, horse lame.

Second Lieutenant Michael Baines, 55th Battery, Royal Field Artillery

Each day was an age and the horrible thought would take shape in my mind that the war was endless. I felt as one must feel on being sent to prison. My mind became a blank. The mud – when it rained – and often when it did not – the lice (how utterly wretched I felt the first time I found one on me) – the dead: unless one had experienced these things it is impossible to describe the conditions. If you are in no way sensitive to body filth and lice, if disgusting sights have no terror for you, if mud and rats do not revolt you, if dead bodies and the smells that frequently emanate from them do not make you retch, then probably you did not suffer unduly unless a German bullet or shell played havoc with your anatomy. But to me all this was vile and revolting. The period I spent in France reduced me to a mere automaton.

Private George Fleet, 7th The Queen's (Royal West Surrey Regiment)

March 28th: Everything is still a tremendous strain for us all. For eight days we have not been able to take off our clothes and boots. Often there is no water even for washing, let alone drinking. All that is available is the icy-cold water of the shell holes, quite clear above the green scum at the bottom. We first take a mouthful each to drink, and then use it successively for cleaning our teeth, then for moistening our shaving-brushes, and finally for washing.

Today the advance of our infantry suddenly stopped near Albert. Nobody could understand why. Our airmen had reported no enemy

Lieutenant Rudolph Binding, Staff Officer, German Cavalry (Dragoons)

between Albert and Amiens. The enemy's guns were only firing now and again on the very edge of affairs. Our way seemed entirely clear. I jumped into a car with orders to find out what was causing the stoppage in front. Our division was right in front of the advance, and could not possibly be tired out. It was quite fresh. When I asked the brigade commander on the far side of Meaux why there was no movement forward he shrugged his shoulders and said he did not know either; for some reason the divisions which had been pushed on through Albert on our right flank were not advancing, and he supposed that this was what had caused the check. I turned round at once and took a sharp turn with the car into Albert.

As soon as I got near the town I began to see curious sights. Strange figures, which looked very little like soldiers, and certainly showed no sign of advancing, were making their way back out of the town. There were men driving cows before them on a line; others who carried a hen under one arm and a box of notepaper under the other. Men carrying a bottle of wine under their arm and another one open in their hand. Men who had torn a silk drawing-room curtain from off its rod and were dragging it to the rear as a useful bit of loot. More men with writing paper and coloured note-books. Evidently they had found it desirable to sack a stationer's shop. Men dressed up in comic disguise. Men with top-hats on their heads. Men staggering. Men who could hardly walk.

And therein lay a huge, unforeseen problem for the German Army. The British troops ransacked their own canteens because they could, it was free, but these men did not habitually lack decent supplies. The Germans ransacked canteens (and homes) because they could, it was free, and they had not seen such copious wonders for far too long. The German economy could not supply delicacies the British Army received. German troops halted, lured into lining their pockets, and this halt had serious consequences for the entire offensive.

They were mostly troops from one of the Marine divisions. When I got into the town the streets were running with wine. Out of a cellar came a lieutenant of the Second Marine Division, helpless and in despair. I asked him, 'What is going to happen?' It was essential for them to get forward immediately. He replied, solemnly and emphatically, 'I cannot get my men

Opposite:
German soldiers,
starved of quality
supplies, could
not help but
gorge themselves
on what they
found. Ultimately
this distraction
slowed the
German advance.

Lieutenant
Rudolph Binding,
Staff Officer,
German Cavalry
(Dragoons)

out of this cellar without bloodshed.' When I insisted, assuming from my white dragoon facings that I belonged to the same division as himself, he invited me to try my hand, but it was no business of mine, and I saw, too, that I could have done no more than he.

I drove back to Divisional HQ with a fearful impression of the situation. The advance was held up, and there was no means of setting it going again for hours. When I considered what was happening up in front it seemed to me to be merely a magnified expression of the passion and craving which we were all experiencing. Had not I seen yesterday an officer younger than myself sitting beside me in the car suddenly call out to the driver to stop at once, without so much as asking my leave. When I asked him in astonishment what he meant by stopping the car when we were on an urgent mission, he answered, 'I must just pick up that English waterproof lying beside the road.' The car stopped. He jumped out, seized an English waterproof which lay on the bank, and then jumped joyfully back again, as if refreshed and waked to new life.

If this lack of restraint seized an officer like that, one can imagine what effect it must have on the private soldier to have craved and hungered and thirsted for months on end. Where in the case of the officer it was the waterproof which tempted him so irresistibly as to make him forget his most important duties, with the private soldiers, according to taste, it was the coloured picture-postcard, the silk curtain, the bottle of wine, the chicken, or the cow, but in most cases the wine.

Private George Fleet, 7th The Queen's (Royal West Surrey Regiment)

Rushed north in lorries to Boves we disembarked about midday immediately moving forward to Cachy, on the right of Villers-Bretonneux. Ahead of us stretched acres of open ploughed fields with a few trees and a church spire on the skyline. Evidence around us indicated the village had been hurriedly evacuated by its inhabitants. Houses were unlocked and in some instances unconsumed meals were on the tables. Fowls and pigs roamed the one or two streets. With the fall of dusk we moved forward over the naked fields to a point about a couple of kilometres, perhaps more, in front of Cachy where instructions were given to dig in.

How frantically I dug that night, and how slow I appeared beside the others. I ached in every limb but thankful in the morning to perceive I had pierced as deep as my fellows. We were under cover from the enemy's fire, if not from the rain, which in some way was as annoying. If you could penetrate beneath the earth's surface you felt safe. Shells failed to terrorize in a trench as they did in the open yet one could explode there as easily as elsewhere. With daybreak I proceeded to dig myself a funk hole at the back of that portion of the trench I occupied but well above its level so that should it rain some measure of protection would be mine. Rain meant mud and filth wherever you looked or trod. Each time I entered a new trench I would commence to make myself a hole where I might crawl for a little protection from the elements.

Looking towards the skyline we beheld figures silhouetted against the brightness that precedes the dawn. Difficult with the light behind them to distinguish their nationality yet they were within hailing distance. Slowly it filtered through to us we were the front line and the figures Jerries. They too, were anxious to obtain cover yet seemed unaware of our presence and careful we were not to display ourselves.

A goods truck purporting to hold French civilians escaping from the German advance, March 1918.

Second
Lieutenant
Michael Baines,
55th Battery,
Royal Field
Artillery

29th March: Lose my way going back in dark, crawl into infantry limber and go to sleep. Wake up 4 am and rise by accident into 'front line' manned by P Battery RHA, told to clear off. Find battery and own section at Domart. Horrible place all shells and gas. Haystacks OP blown up, brigade retreat to behind Hangard Wood. Hangard captured by Hun, retreat to Domart and fire all night, four guns out of action through overheating. Several men sick and shellfire casualties. Only two guns in action.

Lieutenant
Rudolph Binding,
Staff Officer,
German Cavalry
(Dragoons)

March 29th: We are searching for the weakest spot. As yesterday the advance was stopped at Albert while the Eighteenth Army to our left thrust forward as far as Montdidier, our division is being withdrawn today behind the left wing of the Second Army, which is to push on past Amiens, some 6 miles to the south.

We are quartered in the huts of an enormous [British] camp which was partly artillery workshops, partly dump for a thousand different things, and partly prisoners' camp. There are new guns of the latest type, masses of gun-parts, valuable brass fittings, cables, electro-motors, axles, wheels, gun-carriages, and everything you can think of, standing about in such colossal quantities that one runs amazed and staring from one to the other just as if it were an exhibition.

Under normal conditions wealth does not attract such attention, but when even the rottenest hut has brass hinges and latches, when every electric-light switch is entirely composed of brass, when one sees depots of thousands of pairs of rubber trench-boots, piles of rubber tyres, a pyramid of iron nails of every sort (while with us a packet of nails is a rarity, to be indented for in writing in the most elaborate way), when one sees bath-houses with enormous rubber baths and so on, then one realizes the difference between poverty and privations and wealth. I got an impression that the English made everything either out of rubber or brass, because these were the two materials which we had not seen for the longest time.

At every crossroads there are little towers of machine-gun ammunition which anyone can reach. Anybody who needs ammunition can take a box. Why not? Who would steal or carry off machine-gun ammunition, or take it for himself if others needed it? Although lots of material has fallen into our hands, there seems, nevertheless, to have been time to get the most valuable away. Only the enormous plenty which was there makes the residue still seem unnaturally great.

From a point in the neighbourhood one can see Amiens Cathedral. The fighting has been awful. In the church at Raincourt English and Germans are still lying locked in death. The number of dead horses which have still not been cleared away surpassed all imagination, and gives some idea of the loss in human lives. I only hope victory will not drive us to death.

The difficulties of reinforcement are now beginning. Our former camp for details is 50 to 60 miles behind us, and the new camp has not yet been chosen.

30th March, Easter Saturday: It is evening, I'm writing down my impression of the day, which must have been the nastiest of any blessed day in the whole war, full of many dreadful situations, each one following closely on the one just before: at 7.30 our infantry attacked, and by way of a reply to that a hail of machine-gun fire come out of Le Mesnil, worse than I've ever known; our command system breaks down; at 8.30 am my battery commander, 2/Lt Knauer, rides forward, in spite of the heavy fire and the fact that on a horse you make a beautiful target for the French, to look for a new position. I bring the battery up behind, and now we've got so much shrapnel rattling down on us that you can hardly hear or see anything. The machine-gun fire, chattering away at us from only a few hundred metres distance, keeps on as heavy as ever.

All hell has been let loose. The French seem to be transformed; they must have thrown completely fresh, properly rested troops into this sector, and a large number of them too. Amongst others, good old Hermann has been wounded. We pull up a steep track on to a plateau, and there is our No.3 Battery next door to us. And up there it's a witches' cauldron, compared with which the business we had before was child's play: machine-gun fire and small arms fire so strong that it might have been thousands and thousands of enemy gun-barrels being trained on our one battery. The concentration of fire is so heavy that all we can do is lie on the ground beside the guns, with the infantry hardly 300 metres in front of us; and we haven't reached the peak yet, because suddenly we start being

Lieutenant Herbert Sulzbach, 63rd Field Artillery Regiment, Imperial German Army

Below:
Manpower: the need to press on and move the artillery forward was exhausting for these Germans of the 5th Field Artillery Regiment.

fired on from the right and left flanks as well, and it looks as if we are on a pointed wedge of ground offering a marvellous target for the French on all three sides.

Times like this are really unbearable, as you haven't any way of seeing how you're ever going to get out of this witches' cauldron. Our own attack never gets off the ground, and now it begins to rain in torrents, and we are already very tired from the efforts of the last few days and from not getting a second's rest last night; and just in front of us, 2/Lt Mayer of No.8 Battery gets killed in action; that's the tenth officer our regiment has lost since 21st March. Now it gets even 'lovelier'. Our infantry start coming back, in groups or singly, because they can't stand it any more up there at the front, and finally they are lying between the guns.

Captain Eric Bird, Machine Gun Corps

I am still alive, strangely enough. I have had a terrific time during the last week; we have been scrapping almost continually, and until two days ago I had practically no sleep at all. I cannot tell you much, but have had a week more packed with incident than any year of the war. Three times I was nearly finished with the Hun, and once should have certainly been if my horse had not been with me. I have lost all my kit, and have only what

I stand up in, plus my rain coat, three pairs of socks, shaving tackle and towel. I have had on the same clothes for a fortnight, but I wouldn't have missed the battle for anything. I wish you people at home could see how cheerful everybody is out here, and how little 'wind up' there is. None of us want to go into battle, but if we have to, all we ask is a clean fight and a stopping one – I mean a fight without gas and with our flanks holding firm. Too often in this last show we were ordered to retire because our flank had gone, a perfectly horrible business; it is so much more difficult than it appears to withdraw successfully with the Boche in superior numbers on three sides; at least it is easy to retire, but it is difficult to stop and stand again. On one day we made five stands in eighteen hours.

You ask if I received the gramophone records all right. I did, thank you, and so did the Hun. He has them all now, also the gramophone.

30th March: Lamont CRA send Brigade across River Luce thinking the Boche has gone back. He hasn't and we get bad scare. Major Duncan OC Battery wounded. Major Claude Lindsay OC Battery killed. Battery heavily shelled but only eight men hit. Gramophone is still working order. Maynard and I go off to shoot rabbits in nearby wood but get shelled in doing so. Stove going strong. Kill two pigs and a goose in Domart, cows killed in field nearby, very useful.

Second Lieutenant Michael Baines, 55th Battery, Royal Field Artillery

31st March: In action at Hailles, very unpleasant time yesterday. Boche plane almost come down in battery position, we plug stones at him having nothing else, but he gets away. German attack down Avre valley from Rifle Wood, Canadian cavalry counter-attacks and vanish into wood.

Just as am turning in sent up to recce front line near Thennes, walk into German listening post but escape.

Following a day or two spent in peace we moved back to a farm midway between the front line and Cachy. A trench had been dug to the rear into which we were put. Within a few hours the enemy discovered our presence and commenced to bombard us with shells. Casualties were heavy and the place rapidly became untenable. The following afternoon an alarm of a kind was sounded. How or why no one knew, except that officers and men were

Private George Fleet, 7th The Queen's (Royal West Surrey Regiment)

seen running in disorder from the farm and its outbuildings. Foolishly these buildings were being used by the brigade. The whole battalion followed suit immediately all retiring in disorder across a ploughed field. The officers in charge threatened us with their revolvers. For a moment the position looked ugly but we moved on heedlessly. The slaughter would have been too great; besides there were officers with their backs to the enemy. Shooting a private soldier offered no difficulty but an officer cannot be accused of cowardice. In due course the retreat petered out. We paused for a while until everyone had been collected and then commenced our return journey. Dusk came down and in the thickness of the night three or four of us conveniently lost our way. An old shed stacked with hay stood in our path and here we spent the night upon a bed of sweet smelling fodder.

Nearby a transport section was camped and to them we took the precaution of reporting before turning in. Throughout the night rain fell but we slept warm and dry. Early next morning we reported back to headquarters. No questions were asked and that same day the battalion moved back to a well earned rest.

Lieutenant Rudolph Binding, Staff Officer, German Cavalry (Dragoons)

Beaucourt Château, near Moreuil, March 31st: The atmosphere of neglect of this French château can be felt and smelt like an odour even through the terrible filth and mess which has been spread through it owing to the successive use of the building by French, English, and finally German HQ. French and English officers' names still stand under my own on the door of the room where I sleep at night on a bare mattress, and we all share one kitchen. One can hardly move in the hall for dead and wounded, the steps are littered with straw and hay, left by the soldiers who have carried it up to the attics to make beds for themselves there. The French guns are sending their shells whistling flat over the roof, but they still go too high. Most of them land as 'duds' in the mud of the park, where horses and wagons stand in the wet. Endless columns of transport move backwards and forwards. Men, dispatch-riders, cars, guns, and stretchers appear inextricably mixed up together, but in the end most of them find their right place; the cookers reach their companies, the ammunition gets to the batteries, the wounded are brought to the dressing-station, though maybe they are dead by the time they get attended to. The horses are having a good time; there is oats and hay in abundance everywhere. But for that the bivouacs would be fatal on these cold nights.

There is no help for the wounded horses. Hundreds of horse-trains would be needed, and this would burden the lines of communication more than would be justified. The result is that one sees hundreds of dead horses about, dumb reproaches to human folly, whereas dead men, once buried, make no complaints.

Undoubtedly if the statesmen and politicians of all countries, who count for anything and have any word in affairs, could have taken part in this progress through the desert and stopped here for a while in this most recent devastation, if they could bear the privations in the dirt and blood and have to sit tight under constant fire from in front and above, none of them would be against peace. Any peace would be good enough for them. But as it is they sit at their conference tables and regard it almost as a scandal that the armies cannot succeed in advancing on all the fronts together.

We have now got French troops in front of us as well as English. One can tell that from the systematic direction of the artillery and the bombardment of vital points behind the line. The English never do that. Our divisions are much thinned, but the enemy must have had unusually heavy losses. Captured English officers complain bitterly of the complete failure of their Staff work. They say, moreover, that, in spite of their recommendations that the troops should be trained for open warfare, their GHQ refused to do so on the grounds that it was unnecessary. They represent the confusion as something awful, and it is true that we have intercepted wireless messages in which the GHQ asks whether it is to send reinforcements. Meanwhile our own divisions are out of breath for the time being, and the troops are looting into the bargain, as they suddenly become aware of their long privations.

1st April: Do nothing but sleep.

Second Lieutenant Michael Baines, 55th Battery, Royal Field Artillery

General Gough's Fifth Army had been battered but had performed heroically, although it may not have looked like that at times. As the British fell back on their resources and reserves, so the Germans over-stretched their lines of supply. The offensive was faltering, irrespective of looting.

The river Ancre
near Aveluy after
the Germans had
swept over the
old 1916 Somme
battlefield.

Lieutenant
Herbert
Sulzbach, 63rd
Field Artillery
Regiment,
Imperial
German Army

2nd April: My staff of the 2nd Battalion is being relieved, and two of my batteries, No.4 and No.6 as well. The other battalions are staying here and taking part in the artillery preparation for the attack on the 3rd; then the whole regiment will certainly go to rest stations, because they're worn out with fighting and have done a huge amount of work. Our 18th Army has thrust 60 kilometres deep all told, and in this sector alone has taken 1,100 guns and a huge number of prisoners. It is difficult to see how it's going to continue. In any case we are no longer east of Paris, but practically north of the city, and we hope our army will have the good fortune to get the job of breaking through the enemy line to the south; except that it appears, as I foresaw, that we have pushed much further ahead of our neighbours to the right and left; this means that we have pushed out in a big wedge, very tempting to the French for the purposes of a flank attack. …

The supplies – rations and ammunition – are now gradually able to get forward, mainly by lorry and by freshly laid railway spurs. Positions are being surveyed, listening and flash-spotting sections are at work, and the whole business will soon be starting up again.

Lieutenant
Rudolph Binding,
Staff Officer,
German Cavalry
(Dragoons)

2nd April: One cannot go on victoriously for ever without ammunition or any sort of reinforcements. Behind us lies the wilderness. It is true that the railway is running again as far as Péronne, but it has too many demands to meet. …

The thing which annoys and upsets us here again and again are the exaggerations of the newspapers and the telegrams to crowned heads about the decisive victory, and the words – the same old words. The same may be said of the premature decorations. Nobody grudges Hindenburg the Blucher Cross, but the proper occasion on which to confer it would have been after the capture of Amiens. The Crown Prince becomes colonel of a famous regiment, and in this connection the hope is expressed that the regiment will at all times prove itself worthy of its exalted commander. It does not appear to be recognized that the appointment imposes a corresponding obligation on him.

Beaucourt, 4th April: The hardships are very great. One does not think about them, because it is natural that they should exist and that they should be insignificant compared with the greatness of the issue – if, indeed, wars are to be considered great things. The private who lies day and night in the mud in the open, waiting for a shell or an air-bomb to blow him to bits, is worse off than I am, but I can only speak for myself.

Imagine a series of stinking rooms which yesterday or the day before were a château. The wind and rain come in at the windows, in which fragments of glass tinkle at every shell-burst. The walls tremble all day and all night. When the heavy shells are seeking out their mark by degrees and draw nearer, the men run to the cellar. There is no room there for us officers and we go on working. Stretcher-cases get smothered there in the darkness of the night by others who are trying to get shelter. The place stinks of blood, sweat, urine, excrement, iodoform [an antiseptic], and wet clothes. Down below in the passages they peel potatoes, but nobody thinks of throwing away the peel; one puts down the wounded on top of it. The house rings day and night with cries of pain, but with craven and selfish demands as well. The numbers of dead on the lawn of the park steadily increase, while the scum of the army stand round and stare at them with revolting curiosity. In the corner there is a man digging graves without ceasing.

A single shell lays out ten horses at once under the trees. They are not removed; they would be just as much in the way anywhere else. No sooner have thirty wounded been evacuated than there are fifty more in their place. The hospital in the church has had 631 entries in one day and there is one surgeon. Of course, there are other hospitals just as full. All rations and ammunition have to be brought up from Péronne, 20 miles away. All wounded, damaged guns, and transport trains have to be sent back there or even farther. We have had no fresh meat for a week; only one or two chickens serve to supply the illusion that chicken-broth was invented to stay one's hunger on in war-time. The wells have been exhausted or defiled through the carelessness of the men. One or two sheep and cattle which might have been some use had they been properly slaughtered get butchered anyhow as if there were thousands of them. It is impossible to keep a room or any sort of shelter or bed-place clean because there is no water, no brooms, nor even the most primitive utensil available. Chairs and cupboards are broken up to light fires; we have no other fuel, and when this is used up there is nothing left. By the light of a guttering tallow candle two officers are writing reports and orders which will settle the fate of thousands of others, possibly our own. My bed is as hard as a board; when I get up from it I feel more of a wreck than when I lay down, but by changing my position I try to pretend that I am getting rest.

Our division has not struck it lucky. It is ours which has had the heavy fighting on the heights to the north of Moreuil, which are mentioned in the reports. We can make no progress here. Even the fresh divisions do no better. The slippery ground is against us; for every step forward one slides back two, and the ground rises all the way.

I suppose the march and the fighting through the devastated zone were really harder work, but we were fresher then and we had a retreating enemy in front of us. I can still find no word nor image to express the awfulness of that waste. There is nothing like it on earth, nor can be. A desert is always a desert; but a desert which tells you all the time that it used not to be a desert is appalling. That is the tale which is told by the dumb, black stumps of the shattered trees which still stick up where there used to be villages. They were completely flayed by the splinters of the bursting shells, and they stand there like corpses upright. Not a blade of green anywhere round. The layer of soil which once covered the loose chalk is now buried underneath it. Thousands of shells have brought the stones to the surface and smothered the earth with its own entrails. There are miles upon miles of flat, empty, broken, and tumbled stone-quarry, utterly purposeless and useless, in the middle of which stand groups of these blackened stumps of dead trees, poisoned oases, killed for ever.

This area ought to remain as it is. No road, no well, no settlement ought to be made there, and every ruler, leading statesmen, or president of a republic ought to be brought to see it, instead of swearing an oath on the Constitution, henceforth and for ever. Then there would be no more wars.

Three officers crowd into a temporary dugout in a wood near the town of Corbie, close to the Somme River.

5th April – Regimental Orders: 'Days of supreme important action lie behind us. The regiment has done what it promised to do. Every individual has given of his best. The things which the regiment has done belong to History. With sorrowful but proud hearts we mourn our heroic dead. We wish a speedy recovery to our wounded. With eyes fixed on the way ahead, we gaze with rock-hard confidence into the promised land of the future!'

Lieutenant Herbert Sulzbach, 63rd Field Artillery Regiment, Imperial German Army

Happy survivors: B Squadron sergeants serving with the 4th (Royal Irish) Dragoon Guards.

Overleaf: German observation officers peer towards the British lines.

3. 'Mein Gott! New troops!'

'It was dusk and the room was lit by an oil lamp. A soldier sitting opposite, his head in bandages, suddenly fell forward and crashed to the floor. A padre came in and helped him up and then commenced a tour of the room speaking to each man in turn. "He wants to know my religion," I thought, "in case the worst happens!"'

Lance Corporal Victor Cole, 1st The Queen's Own (Royal West Kent Regiment)

———————

The Government's agreement to reduce the age of overseas service reflected the critical position in France. Men would be permitted to go on active service aged eighteen and a half provided they had completed six months' training. Under 'normal' circumstances, Fred Hodges would not have been sent abroad until July at the earliest, but now he was preparing for embarkation with his friends. First, on the eve of departure, there was a parade in Northampton; it would be a stirring and emotional moment.

On 4th April, there was a big ceremonial parade in one of the city parks where the many thousands of youngsters in the young soldiers' battalions were assembled. After a grand ceremonial march past a general, we stood in long ranks, our breath condensing in the cold air and our young pink faces glowing, as we waited expectantly for the General's farewell address before we left for the Western Front. Every eye was directed to the lone figure of the elderly general on the dais as he began to speak.

'You men,' he began, and then paused as he surveyed our eager young faces, 'I know, of course, that you are only boys of eighteen. … I know that you have not completed your training … however, you are now to proceed overseas at a very critical time, and you have to play the part of men. You all know that a great battle is going on at this moment on the Western Front. On 21st March, the Germans launched a tremendous attack; they have broken through our fortifications; they are being continually reinforced; in fact, they are attacking in massed formation. Their objective is Paris

Lance Corporal Frederick Hodges, 53rd (Young Soldier) Battalion, Bedfordshire Regiment

Opposite:
A touching image of a horse tethered to a church altar rail.

and the channel ports, and … THEY HAVE GOT TO BE STOPPED. You young men are NEEDED at the Front … without delay. I know that you have not completed your training, but I trust, indeed I am sure, that the training you have had in this division will stand you in good stead. You have all fired your course with the rifle, and some of you have learned to use the Lewis gun. What we have taught you on the ranges, you have now to put into practice at the front, and from what I hear, there is no lack of targets there! Good luck to you all.'

He then descended from the dais, and proceeded to inspect us at close range, walking along the many long lines of boys drawn up, and occasionally stopping to talk to a few who appeared to him to be exceptionally young or small.

On 5th April, in full overseas kit, we marched through the streets of Norwich for the last time … to the railway station … for London … for Dover … and for the War!

This draft of 18-year-olds was exceptionally large, and attracted a large crowd in the street leading to the railway station. The pavements were crowded, especially near the entrance to the station yard. The majority were women, some no doubt our landladies from the many streets in which we had been billeted. Others were probably housewives who had often enjoyed watching the boys washing up for thousands in the yard of the large Drill Hall. Today they were in a very sombre mood, many of them in tears as they watched the long column of fours march proudly past in full overseas kit. Some shouted 'Poor little beggars, they are only boys. Fancy sending them to the front to die for us.'

My feelings as we marched past the Military Police at the gates of the station yard were a mixture of patriotic pride and embarrassment at this public display of feeling. I could not, or rather did not want, to show emotion or to be affected by other people's feelings. Two days earlier, when saying goodbye to my parents at this same railway station, I had felt the same. My mother had clung to me and begun to weep. I remember it was her 53rd birthday, and she said 'If you don't come back …' I just squeezed and kissed her and broke away, saying 'Don't worry, mum, I shall come back.' Then I hurriedly left the station.

I enjoy myself until departure time arrives when I feel a lump in my throat. People appear calm but a mask is hiding the all too obvious fears. The crowded train and the cheerful banter with relatives. The last farewell kiss.

Good-bye. A shrill whistle and we are off.

The occupants of the compartment become acutely quiet. The train gathers speed and the sound of the revolving wheels dins into my head, *Over the top, over the top*. The clamorous sound will persist in singing, *Over the top*. It changes as the train proceeds. *Will you come back?* on and on. *Will you come back?* and the words are almost choking me, for I have as much certainty of escaping with my life as a condemned man. Will I ever see the old home again? Have I seen all my loved ones for the last time? And the sound of the wheels says, *Don't be so certain*. Oh, the mocking wheels, have they no brighter message?

The other occupants stir out of their lethargy, Woodbines are produced, and conversation comes like an angel from above to drive away our morbid thoughts. The voice of the wheels now proclaims a more confident note, *Don't be a fool – You will come back – All will be well!* One of the fellows returning to France is in a 'Pals' battalion, and amuses us with vivacious anecdotes of life in France.

Private Christopher Haworth, Training Reserve Battalion

It was evening when we arrived at Dover and marched up the steep hill to the castle. After mugs of hot tea and sandwiches, we bedded down on blankets on the floor of the castle, but were awakened about 4.30 am and ordered outside. After tea and porridge we were soon marching down the winding hill to the quay, where we boarded a paddle steamer.

Lifebelts were issued as we went up the gangways, and soon the old boat, a cross-channel steamer, was full of men; decks, stairs, passages, all

Lance Corporal Frederick Hodges, 53rd (Young Soldier) Battalion, Bedfordshire Regiment

Men of the Royal Irish Fusiliers boarding a ship for France. An officer makes his own way up the gangplank.

A ship with dazzle camouflage taking men to France. Dazzle camouflage was intended to confuse enemy U-boats, making a ship's direction harder to discern and so harder to range on.

crowded with soldiers in full equipment. During the crossing we were accompanied by a Royal Navy cruiser and two or three destroyers which circled us; while overhead several aeroplanes flew to and fro to spot any German U-boats. The excitement among the boys was intense.

Private Reginald Kiernan, Training Reserve Battalion

The English Channel: We are just outside a port. They say it is Boulogne. It is night and we have been hanging about outside for a long time. A rumour is going round that a ship has been torpedoed near the harbour. We sit or stand about or lie flat on the decks, wearing life-belts.

As we went aboard at Dover a woman in black said, 'Finish it off this time, boys.'

It is twelve o'clock. We are running alongside a stone quay. We can see houses rising in dark terraces against the sky.

Private Christopher Haworth, Training Reserve Battalion

Disembarking at Boulogne … we are faced with a stiff climb to St Martin's Camp on the hill. Costermongers are persuading us to buy pears at sixpence each, which are being sold in England for twopence.

'*Soldates Angleterre* plenty money – plenty big mug is Tommee *anglais*.'

A boy about ten years of age is following us, crying: 'Come and see my sister …' the rest of the remark being lost in the exclamations of members of the draft: 'So this is France! It's not us they welcome, but our money!' …

We were disappointed with the catering arrangements at a base with every facility, easy supply route and away from danger. Cooks and others were in abundant supply, not so the rations for the 'poor bloody infantryman'. In effect, we had to be made as miserable as possible for when in such a condition a fellow does not worry whether he lives or not. A happy soldier does not want to die and this looked like the start of our conditioning.

'The same old crowd of Base Wallahs,' comments Patterson. Men clinging to a cushy job to keep them from the front while they bully the poor devils going to fight for them. And all those delicate NCOs, the physical jerks instructors and footballers who could not abide the trenches.

But we had seen other things no less intolerable since landing. I was distressed when I passed one of the buildings on the dock and saw a party of German wounded waiting to be conveyed to hospital; I could not help but sympathize with the men I am supposed to hate. What am I to make of it all? I am not at all happy about this business, but the job has to be done, and the only course open is to fight and finish war for ever.

After spending the night at Boulogne we entrain for Étaples. On the journey we experience much fun owing to the prehistoric French railway carriage we occupy. The seat is hardly wide enough to accommodate our persons, having apparently been designed for the frail forms of infants, and the parcel rack is too small and fragile to receive our packs: the only useful purpose I imagine it can serve is that of a handy receptacle for a workman's roll and butter.

After his medal ceremony in London, Second Lieutenant Bion was relieved to be going back to France. His stay at home proved awkward and he was disturbed by his own impatience and aggression. Landing at Boulogne, he returned to his unit as the crisis was deepening once more.

The technique of travel was simple – thumbing lifts. At the end of the first day I found myself at Étaples – where the communion service was said to be right behind the front line under gunfire. Well, perhaps it *was* a bit exaggerated, but the news from the front seemed likely to make the lie

Second Lieutenant Wilfred Bion, 5th Battalion, Tanks Corps

approximate more closely to the truth by bringing the gunfire up to the communion service.

A gunner captain with whom I travelled for about 20 miles said, 'I see the wicked Germans have been bombing one of our hospitals.' He pointed to a newspaper paragraph and winked heavily, 'clearly marked with the Red Cross too. I know the ruddy place – there are ammunition dumps for at least 5 miles along the railway. They've got the hospital right in the middle of it. No wonder they marked it clearly with a Red Cross. I nearly had kittens every hour I was there – wound in my leg; couldn't run,' he explained.

I had been directed to bed down at a small hospital just outside Étaples. It appeared to be a peaceful spot. I found a friendly RAMC doctor who showed me where I could lie up for the night and as it was a lovely afternoon I unpacked my safety razor to mark the spot as mine, and decided to stroll round and move on after a night's rest.

'How is it you are so slack?' I asked him. 'I would have thought you would be chock-a-block with wounded.'

'Efficiency, my lad. The moment this shemozzle started they sent all wounded that the Boche didn't or couldn't capture straight to England. Result – the first decent holiday we've had for years. We've got one poor devil in that hut over there, that's all – he's dying anyway.'

Lance Corporal Frederick Hodges, 10th The Lancashire Fusiliers

We joined a very long queue for a brand-new groundsheet/cape, and it was quite dark when we queued for 120 rounds of small arm ammunition. This made us realize that training days were over. We were going to kill and be killed. Fred Ablethorpe, usually a thoughtful, refined boy, said to me, 'Well, now, they've given us all 120 rounds of ammo, I intend to use it, and shoot as many of the bastards as possible before I'm killed.' I too was thrilled as I realized that we boys were going to face death or wounds for our country. I said to Ablethorpe 'We've GOT to STOP THEM whatever OUR fate.' We accepted the fact that our young lives were no longer our own in this crisis, and that our country expected us to sacrifice them. I felt no fear. The grave situation overwhelmed personal fear.

In the truck was an old soldier returning to his unit, which was the 10th (Service) Battalion of the Lancashire Fusiliers; the battalion which, in a moment of time, had also become mine. This 'old sweat', Brandon, wearing the 1914 Star ribbon on his tunic, had been watching our boyish tricks and our naïve enthusiasm with a great deal of interest. He grinned at us and said 'When "old Jerry" sees your lovely pink young faces in the line, he'll say "*Mein Gott!* New troops! Rat-tat-tat-tat-tat-tat-tat!"' Then, looking us over with a fatherly eye he said 'I expect you kids will DO and I must say, they've done you proud with those brand-new groundsheet-capes. You'd better hang on to them tight out here, or somebody is likely to win them off you.' …

Those who had been transferred to the 10th Battalion marched, in the rain, to Havernas where we met the survivors of the 'old tenth' as they called themselves.

Our young, pink, cheerful and eager faces were a complete contrast to the grey, worn and weary faces of these veterans, who had fought a retreat. We looked with awe at them, men whose clothing was so muddy, so torn and stained; but whose rifles were so clean. They looked at us with a mixture of pity and amusement, knowing that very soon our clean round baby faces would be lined and dirty too.

Four hundred of us marched from Caestre. It was yesterday, yet I still feel exhausted. We were in full marching kit, and we marched on with no band, just slog, slog, slog on, not even keeping step after about 5 kilometres. I have never had such an agonizing bodily strain as the last kilometre. We had not one halt. Some of the men were screaming at the end, though I don't know about what, unless it was the fear that one's head would burst. It seemed to us as though we would march for ever. A great many men fell out and lay by the roadside. We went through Bailleul in single file, as it was under shellfire. Many tall houses had their front torn out, lying in great heaps, showing the rooms inside. No shell came, however, as we passed through. …

The march up has been terrible, but it is over now, and the stragglers are reporting. We are left to ourselves here, and there are no parades. There are only a captain and a lieutenant to the company. The camp, consisting of black, humped, Nissen huts of corrugated iron, is built on mud, and duckboard tracks lead everywhere. We can hear the rumble of the guns and at night there is an occasional deep whining sound and a heavy 'crump'.

Private Reginald Kiernan, 7th The Leicestershire Regiment

Overleaf: 140th Siege Battery pause for a photograph in the Ypres Salient.

29th March: How eerie it is here in front of Ypres. We marched over a broad track made of wooden logs across the flat fields till we came to a shallow trench. It appeared just over a slight rise. We could hear the machine guns. I thought, 'I am at the front', 'I am in the Line'. The machine guns sounded 'Rat-a-tat rat-a-tat'. They sounded from there like someone striking iron with a hollow hammer. Sometimes they are slow and deliberate, sometimes they splutter, as though they cannot fire fast enough.

We move forward in file along narrow duckboards. We have come out of the shallow trench and are 'on the top'. We have divided into platoons. The machine guns are nearer. They sound much louder and more threatening. Sometimes in the midst you could think they were but ten yards away. There is once a swish of bullets overhead and once they hit beneath the duckboards and there is a blue spark.

We go forward as quietly as we can, passing back messages as we learned on night-work in England There are faint whispers: 'Overhead wire', 'Barbed wire', 'Tape', 'Halt', 'Forward', 'Stop that bloody rattling'.

31st March: Our platoon is in a strongpoint in front of Ypres. I feel much happier here than ever I have been in the army. In the daytime, things are very quiet. I am an ammunition carrier in a Lewis gun team. Number One on the gun is Ben Jones. He has been out since 1915. He is very quiet but wonderfully experienced. He was the only gunner in the battalion on the Somme a week or two since who brought his gun out of the fighting. He has the same Number Two as was with him there. Ben is fairly tall but stoops a lot. He is from Cambridgeshire, and says very little, and that slowly and briefly. He has shown us how to fire a Lewis gun at night, tying a wet cloth over the muzzle to dull the flash.

All of us six carriers are 'rookies'. We carry two drums of ammunition on our chests and two on our backs. It is awkward moving quickly with it, as the connecting belt slips from the shoulders. The weight, too, is exhausting. But we are a happy team.

Lance Corporal
Frederick
Hodges, 10th
The Lancashire
Fusiliers

We boys learnt much about the retirement when a batch of letters arrived from England. A lance corporal mounted an old water tank in the farmyard and shouted 'Letters'. A crowd quickly gathered round him.

As he called out the names, very few of them could be claimed; most were addressed to men who had been killed or wounded or were missing.

As the lance corporal called out the name, he was told by the survivors of the 'Old Tenth': 'He's missing', or 'He was killed at so and so', or 'He was wounded, I think …'

I mingled with the crowd and listened to the gossip, and learned quite a lot. The post started them talking, and I heard how they had come out of the retreat with only one Lewis gun still effective, used by a lance corporal who had been recommended for the Military Medal.

I looked with awe at this man who sat at a stable door on a box, calmly splitting wood with his bayonet, for a fire which several other men were trying to start in an old bucket with holes punched into it. The idea was to scrounge some water from somewhere, never an easy task, and make some tea. I heard about the officer who had led some of them through the gardens of a village in the hands of German troops, who had penetrated right behind our front during the retreat.

Others told me of the stand they had made at Havrincourt until the Germans had been almost up to them, and were passing them on the flanks. One man, Morris, said to me, 'I bolted out of one end of that trench while "Jerry" was coming in at the other, they nearly got me!'

The German offensive stalled on the Somme, and Amiens, though tantalizingly close, remained in Allied hands. In seeking the elusive breakthrough, General Ludendorff switched tactics, executing plans for an offensive, near Armentières. If successful, the British would be compelled to withdraw from the symbolically important city of Ypres to the north and they would lose the logistically important town of Hazebrouck. The offensive, originally called Operation George, was scaled down and renamed Georgette. Two German armies, the Sixth and Fourth, would attack: standing in their way would be relatively weak defences. A number of divisions, mauled during the previous month's offensive, had been sent to the sector to recuperate in this hitherto quiet sector. Two divisions of Portuguese troops were also in the area and they were under-strength and lacked morale.

The German preparatory barrage opened on 7 April and continued until the early morning of 9 April, when eight German divisions attacked. Portuguese positions were quickly overrun, survivors falling back in disarray. Once again, favourable weather conditions aided the German assault and British divisions flanking the Portuguese were forced to pull back, while reinforcements were rushed up to plug the breach in the line. The situation was fluid and Allied troops suffered heavy casualties. Lieutenant Bion arrived at his unit just as a bad situation was becoming rapidly worse.

Second
Lieutenant
Wilfred Bion,
5th Battalion,
Tanks Corps

At last we arrived and I reported to HQ. To the voluble inquiries of the Colonel I made the appropriate conversational replies. I had, of course, had a good leave. No, I had not been besieged by bevies of admiring females. I quickly escaped to rejoin my company.

My first impression was that the battalion had not altered. I had met O'Kelly and Fitzwilliam at HQ and here were the old Gang. Both adjutant and colonel had come to us before March, but the Adjutant I had met only when he told me I was to go on leave. Here were all the familiar faces – Homfray, Clifford, Carter, Hauser, Cook. Aitches was a newcomer from A Company where he had been a section commander in the original battalion. He was likeable, but timid. As I know now, and suspected then, A Company would not have transferred him unless they wanted to get rid of him by kicking him upstairs. He was with us to be promoted.

Broome, rosy and youthful as ever, had no horror stories. 'It was pretty thick I can tell you,' was his contribution to the saga of March 21st.

Where were the others?

'What others? Oh yes, you met Cartwright and Robinson didn't you? – I had forgotten. Bridges? We don't really know, but Robinson was killed. In fact all the men in tanks were done in I think. Cartwright may have been captured after escaping from his tank.' That was as far as I went with Broome's story.

As I had missed all the fighting I was first choice to take a party with Lewis guns up to the front at once. It was the Adjutant himself who had come round to our mess to give me the message in person. Written orders were being typed out and would be sent round soon.

British cavalry watering horses in rest billets, April 1918.

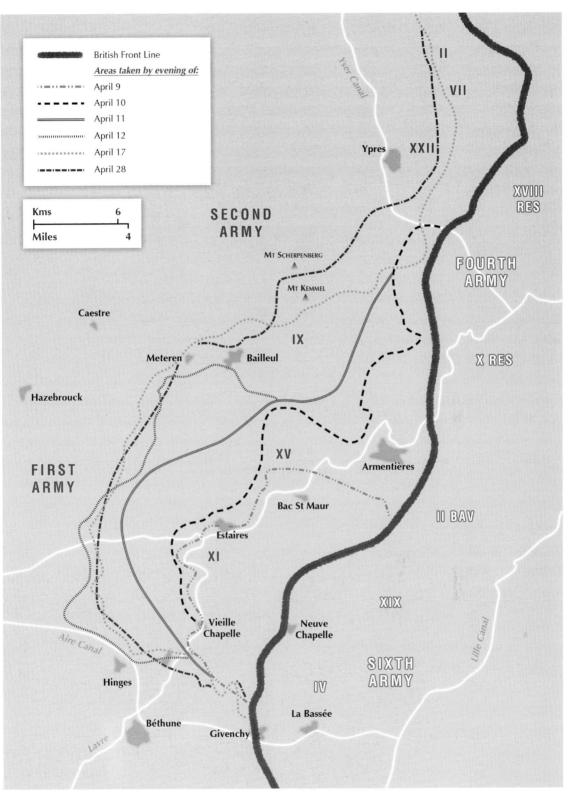

The offensive on the Lys, April.

He drew me into a corner out of hearing of anyone else. 'Things are pretty damn serious I can tell you. We have no tanks and I'm certain the rest of us won't be long after you. I'm sorry it is so soon after your leave. You are really the only officer. …'

I was furious. Why? I cannot have realized that I was supposed to fight. I was dominated by the romantic idea that my business was to be a hero, decorated, and to spend the rest of life basking in the warmth of approval. … I felt it was good of me to have 'won' the DSO – I think I must already have begun to believe this. I hope it didn't show; fortunately the light in our corner was not good. I dredged up some commonsense from somewhere while he talked.

'Of course you realize we are shot to bits – only senior non-tank crew officer left – we useless non-combatants. The Boche have torn another gap in our line; we have to help stop it. I'm expecting orders to come at any time. We are to "stand-to" for immediate movement to the Line – supposing there is one.'

Like Fred Hodges, Corporal Ernie Stevens was eighteen years old and another lad who was rushed out to France. The son of a professional soldier killed during the Boer War, Ernie felt his duty keenly. He joined his regiment, the 20th Middlesex, just a day before the Georgette Offensive began. This would be Ernie's first and last action.

Corporal Ernest Stevens, 20th The Duke of Cambridge's Own (Middlesex Regiment)

Everybody was alive to the fact that the Germans were strafing just behind the lines where the reserves would be congregated.

At daybreak, we learned that a ration party had come up with some bread and cheese and this was dished out. I had just got my share when suddenly the platoon sergeant shouted out, 'Stand-To!' It was a very misty morning and we were in low-lying ground, but it was also quiet at this time and I don't recall any shelling. Two figures were seen coming through the mist and the platoon sergeant ordered us to fire five shots, rapid, thinking they were Germans. As soon as we started firing, up went their hands and as they approached we could see they had no helmets and that they had discarded their arms and equipment. They were our lads and luckily we had managed to miss them, perhaps through our own nervousness, but it was a very bad morning and it was difficult to see. One of them had a

Under attack: the picture caption claims these men are taking cover from enemy fire.

bullet wound in the back of his neck. The Germans had reached our front line and these two had managed to get away.

We stood behind an earthen wall when we heard a chatter of a machine gun behind us. We knew we were in for some trouble but never imagined we would be machine-gunned from the rear. I heard the bullets whizzing past me as I made for a small slit trench and I jumped into it to find myself up to my waist in water next to my platoon commander. He was new out to France and looked very worried. 'Corporal, I'm afraid we're absolutely hemmed in. It's impossible to make a fight of it. The only thing I can suggest is if you have a handkerchief bring it out, tie it to the end of your bayonet and indicate to the Germans that we are prepared to surrender.' I felt like a coward. I was letting my country down, I was letting my unit down and I was letting my family down. I was nearly sick thinking about it. Being taken prisoner, oh what a disgrace!

On April 9th, 1918, I have got [written in his diary] 'The most terrible day I have ever spent.' Up to this time for many nights we had had only three or four hours' rest, and each night we discussed the question as to whether it would be safe to take our clothes off. This particular night

Lance Corporal Archibald Davis, 419th Field Company, Royal Engineers we unfortunately decided to do so, and at twelve midnight we got down to rest. The code word 'Bustle' did not reach us, probably because the [telephone] wire was cut by shellfire, as it often was. We bustled all the same. During the night there was a terrific bombardment, the building we were in was hit, and we woke up and bustled when the wall behind our heads crashed down.

We did not stop to dress but picked up trousers, books, putties, etc., and dashed to the cellar for protection. This was at four o'clock in the morning. Three women and a man were sleeping in the cellar, but it was soon crowded out with soldiers and civilians. Here we managed to scramble into our clothes. The shelling was terrific, the building we were in being hit four times over our heads. At least one of the shells was a 15-inch. Alas, gas was out all the time. To make matters still worse, I had a diarrhoea trouble, and had to face the music outside.

During all this turmoil, and when things were at the worst, the OC found he must send a message at once, and asked for a volunteer to take it. An infantryman (a Cockney), without any hesitation, said: 'I'll go, sir.' He no sooner stepped out of the door when a shell burst and caught him at the bottom of his back. I helped to get him in and bandaged his wound. It was a fearful one at the bottom of the spine, and took an awful lot of bandaging. He was laid out for ten hours on the hard, cold floor, before it was safe for us to move him. During this time he asked for a dog that came and sat by his side and wouldn't leave him. He also asked us to send some cards to his mother and his sweetheart. He had been wounded four times before, and was the pluckiest chap I have ever met. … During a lull in the shelling I and another fellow placed him on a form face down and carefully took him round to the nearest dressing-station.

Throughout the Somme Offensive, Private Frederick Voigt was billeted behind the lines, near a prominent hill named the Mont des Cats, a few miles north-west of Armentières. Voigt had thoroughly enjoyed the spring weather and the surge in flowers and wildlife. Then he had heard about the fighting near Amiens, and soon after, he began to witness a marked increase in enemy activity in his sector, more air raids, greater shelling in the 'back areas'. When the Germans attacked, it did not take long for the evidence of fighting to begin trailing past his camp.

Numbers of soldiers were straggling past. They looked wretched and exhausted. Their boots and puttees were caked with mud. They had neither rifles nor packs. Three men were lying up against a garden wall. We asked them for news. They could not tell us much, except that the Germans were still advancing.

'We was at Dickebusch when 'e started slingin' stuff over – gorblimy, 'e don't 'alf wallop yer – umpteen of our mates got bleed'n' well biffed. We cleared out afore it got too 'ot.' Several famished 'battle-stragglers' had entered our camp in order to beg for food. They sat round the cookhouse and ate in gloomy silence.

In the adjoining field a number of tents had sprung up. Blue figures were moving in and out amongst them. The French had arrived.

The next morning, about breakfast time, the first shell burst near the camp – a short rapid squeal followed by a sharp report. The second shell burst a few minutes after, throwing up earth and smoke. A steel fragment came sailing over in a wide parabola and struck the foot of a man standing in the breakfast queue. He limped to the first-aid hut, looking very pale. When he got there, he had some difficulty in finding his wound, it was so slight. We paraded and marched off. Several shells burst in the neighbouring fields. We reached the ration dump and began to load the train. A civilian arrived with the newspapers. Our NCOs were powerless to stop the general stampede that surged towards the paper-vendor.

Private Frederick Voigt, Labour Corps

There was no earthly chance of us getting away, the Germans were in such numbers, so I waved my dirty handkerchief and in due course a German appeared on the level ground above us, looking down on us and ordering us out one by one. The first thing we had to do was to throw off our equipment which lay strewn all over the place, and then I noticed Sam Simpkins, a mate of mine, lying on the ground moaning. I asked a German permission to go and have a look at him and he nodded. I ran over and saw that Sam had been hit in the left arm. His elbow had been shot away, and his forearm was only hanging on to his upper arm by a piece of flesh no thicker than a finger. I knew nothing about first aid but blood was pouring out and I knew he would be dead within ten minutes. I asked permission to pick up a knife and the German nodded vigorously,

Corporal Ernest Stevens, 20th The Duke of Cambridge's Own (Middlesex Regiment)

Scotsmen of the 51st Highland Division, including two officers, captured during the opening stages of the Lys Offensive.

German artillery near Armientières. The picture is dated 9 April, the opening day of the Lys Offensive.

like 'hurry up and do it'. He seemed to give a little smile as much as to say, 'Good I'm glad someone's going to do something'. Very slowly I cut Sam's sleeve off almost to the shoulder. Sam was in a semi-conscious state as I made two strips out of his sleeve, which I used as tourniquets above his elbow. I stopped the bleeding but I couldn't do anything about his forearm, so it was just a case of gently getting his arm and laying it across his breast.

Owing to the region's reputation for inactivity, the battlefield more closely resembled that of 1914 than the fields of the Somme, Arras or Ypres. Villages and towns were largely intact and inhabited by civilians who lived under the threat of enemy shellfire but accepted the risk. They were suddenly forced to evacuate their homes, taking whatever they could carry and pouring onto the congested roads.

10th April: My poor old rheumatic landlady, sitting in her armchair, was hoisted onto a motor lorry, en route for safer quarters further back. A motley lorry-load it was, embracing as it did an ancient dame of ninety-eight lying on a mattress laid on a long, low barrow – on which movable bed she had spent the last three years of her life – and her daughter of seventy-five. With the latter, I grieve to say, I had 'words'; as she, when her mother had been safely loaded, barrow and all, desired to place most of their household goods after her. …

Lieutenant Colonel David Rorie, OC 1/2nd (Highland) Field Ambulance

Refugees taking flight from the German offensive.

At one farm nearer the line – and all this flat fertile country was studded with little farms – the rest of the people had cleared out, leaving only a young woman of twenty-five and her grandfather over seventy. As the fight progressed it became an Advanced Dressing Station, and the vicinity was heavily shelled. At the urgent request of our troops the girl at last went back, but the old man blankly refused. He spent the day sitting at the side of his stove, occasionally going out to feed his pigs and hens. Why not? His alternative was to bundle and go, along shelled roads whither he knew not; the great majority of refugees had no fixed objective: they were simply trying to get away – anywhere – from it all.

Lance Corporal Archibald Davis, 419th Field Company, Royal Engineers

At three o'clock in the afternoon Sergeant Rainford and I were ordered to go to what was left of the Orderly Room, burn all the papers and make a dash for it. We carried out instructions and made a glorious bonfire; but before going I managed to rake about in the ruins and recover the picture post-card of Gladys Cooper, which had been pinned up on the wall of all our Orderly Rooms; it duly appeared in the next. In order to get away, as there was so much gas about, we had to wear our respirators and crawl a

German prisoners help carry the wounded down a road during the fighting in April.

long way on our hands and knees. Whilst doing this, Sergeant Rainford had the tube of his respirator cut clean through with a piece of shrapnel, which fortunately did not touch him. We set off at five-thirty with the Orderly Room stuff, and arrived at a place called Quatre Vents at 8.30 pm. Here we managed to get some eggs and coffee for supper, having been nineteen hours without anything to eat or drink.

It was said that Fritz had advanced, and that we had afterwards driven him back again. At any rate, I saw about fifty German prisoners. Our lot had fourteen horses killed and wounded and twelve stampeded. The sights in the village of Gorre were terrible, and the civilians suffered fearfully. Near the church there were at least nine men blown to atoms. The church was wrecked, but I was informed that the tower was being used as an Observation Post. The shells, chiefly gas, played havoc with the fish in the canal, and you could stand on the edge and watch the dead ones float by in hundreds.

There were eight of us altogether in that trench. There was a duckboard, very mucky, very wet and very heavy. Our officer was taken away, I didn't see him again, so being an NCO I ordered these chaps to bring the duckboard over, three on one side, three on the other and lifted Sam onto it. We waited around for some time before moving off, taking it in turns to carry the duckboard on our shoulders. We went from our second line up to the first line, over no-man's-land, over the Germans' first and second lines, and eventually onto a road and towards a German first aid tent where we put Sam down.

A medical officer came out. He looked, returned to the tent and immediately came back with a scalpel and he just cut Sam's forearm off and threw it on a heap of other arms and legs, some in German uniform, some in khaki. The heap was about knee high and wide, perhaps fifty all in, and, to be frank, I wanted to be sick.

Corporal Ernest Stevens, 20th The Duke of Cambridge's Own (Middlesex Regiment)

On April 10th, I have a note in my diary: 'On this day I am commencing my third year of service in the army. I have escaped with the transport and am writing up my diary while awaiting further orders.'

When the Germans advanced, official orders came through that under no circumstances was the 55th Division to be given the order 'to retire'; but the division, after suffering awful casualties, had to give way a little this time.

Lance Corporal Archibald Davis, 419th Field Company, Royal Engineers

I shall never forget that retreat. The roads were blocked with miles of transport, also with civilians running away with mail-carts, handcarts and every conceivable mode of transport, loaded sky-high with furniture and their personal belongings, and with men, women and children hanging on alongside. Many of their houses had been blown up, and the streets of Gorre were strewn with dead. One could not but admire the marvellous spirit and pluck of the French women, who waved their hands to us as they passed. One man had buried his wife and two children.

Second Lieutenant John MacDermott, 51st Machine Gun Battalion, 51st Highland Division

It had been a long day of new experiences and I slept the sleep of the just that night in a little cottage, but with enough sense to rest booted and fully clothed. It was as well I did so as I wakened to the sound of shooting and the news that the enemy was across the Lawe and attacking. It was just daybreak outside and there was a heavy morning mist everywhere which limited visibility considerably and had obviously been exploited by the enemy to cover his advance. I saw some of our infantry lying in a shallow depression in the open which slanted at an angle to the river and I joined them with my batman. But if we could not see the Germans they could see us and soon we had the chilly experience of being enfiladed by an enemy machine-gunner who remained invisible but was able to spray the depression we were lying in right along its length. Quite a number, including my batman lying next to me, were wounded and I had a bullet through my trench coat which nearly cut my electric torch in half without even scratching me. About then I saw a lad called Cromerty, from the Orkneys, and another member of my section. They had a machine gun with them, but not the tripod, and also a number of belt boxes. …

With Cromerty and the other member of the section we went in search of a defensive position. I recall going into one farm building to explore the possibilities when I was met by a Highlander coming out whose face was as white as a sheet though he had not been hit. The only reason for this that I could see confronted me when I entered what must have been the best bedroom. There, laid out in a great bed, was the body of an old lady awaiting her funeral. The shock of this scene lay in its utter incongruity with the death and violence that had been taking place outside.

Owing to the continued German offensive and with great concern for the integrity of the entire British effort in France and Flanders, Field Marshal Douglas Haig issued a statement of intent and had it disseminated to all ranks. This, he judged, was *the* critical moment of the war.

Three weeks ago to-day the enemy began his terrific attacks against us on a 50-mile front. His objects are to separate us from the French, to take the Channel Ports and destroy the British Army.

In spite of throwing already 106 divisions into the battle and enduring the most reckless sacrifice of human life, he has as yet made little progress towards his goals.

We owe this to the determined fighting and self-sacrifice of our troops. Words fail me to express the admiration which I feel for the splendid resistance offered by all ranks of our army under the most trying circumstances.

Many amongst us now are tired. To those I would say that Victory will belong to the side which holds out the longest. The French Army is moving rapidly and in great force to our support.

There is no other course open to us but to fight it out. Every position must be held to the last man: there must be no retirement. With our backs to the wall and believing in the justice of our cause each one of us must fight on to the end. The safety of our homes and the Freedom of mankind alike depend upon the conduct of each one of us at this critical moment.

(Signed) D. Haig F.M. Commander-in-Chief British Armies in France
General Headquarters Tuesday, April 11th, 1918

Field Marshal Sir Douglas Haig, Commander-in-Chief, BEF

12th April, near dawn: The gunfire is much nearer; all night, since dark set in, the sky, about 4 miles to the south, has been red and there has been a deep rumbling and heavy crackling with a sound of a great wind. About every ten minutes there is a big thud somewhere far off to the south, that shakes the walls of the trench here. A runner has told the sergeant that Jerry has attacked the 'Pork and Beans' (Portuguese) who are in the line a long way to the south and has gone through them 'like a dose of salts'. The sergeant says that if it spreads, it will be 21st of March all over again.

Private Reginald Kiernan, 7th The Leicestershire Regiment

British divisions sent to Italy at the back end of 1917 to prop up a faltering Italian front line were now rushed back to the Western Front. Battalions, such as the 1st Royal West Kent Regiment, had had a comfortable time in Northern Italy but were now thrown back in the fray with little ceremony.

Lance Corporal Victor Cole, 1st The Queen's Own (Royal West Kent Regiment)

Above:
Portuguese troops marching near Béthune. These troops took much of the brunt of the opening attacks and were forced into chaotic retreat.

We got out of the train, apparently miles from the fighting, and learned that the unfortunate Portuguese had been surrounded and captured. As we advanced, line after line, in extended order, across the green fields and into the sprawling Nieppe Forest, there was no sign of war, the sun shone, birds sang in the trees and startled deer ran leaping off into the brush.

We eventually came out on the other side of the forest and still no sign of the enemy but word came down that we were now the front line.

Beyond the forest there was a field with a chalk road running across and we started along this road. Ahead of me the column veered right, and I thought, 'What's up?' In our path there was a complete section of blokes lying in fours, dead. You couldn't help but look, but a voice said, 'Come on, come on', and hurried us past. About 10 yards away was a little bit of ground with the earth scooped out. It had been a shrapnel shell that had burst, and wiped the lot out.

Ralph Newman and I were attached to B Company for signal duties and this company now took up position behind a hedge running parallel to the edge of the woodland about 50 yards from it. We extended to 6-foot intervals between each man and dug slit trenches for cover. Ralph and I lay in our little shallow trenches and trained our rifles through the bottom of the hedge in the direction from which we expected the Germans to attack. Between us was our portable telephone connected by wire with C Company directly to our rear.

Some yards to the north of our position was an old farmhouse – some of our chaps were scouting around there so I nipped across to investigate. In the cellar was wine, hundreds of bottles of it, and thinking that it would be a pity if it fell into the hands of the Germans I stowed half a dozen bottles in a sandbag and made my way back to where Newman lay with the phone. We opened a bottle and had a good drink, the others we hid in a hole.

A little later an official rum issue came down the line so what with the sun shining, the birds singing, and the mellowing effect of the wine and rum, we were feeling at peace with all mankind. Then, with a shattering crash, the fun commenced and in a moment the air was full of bursting shells, flying shrapnel and the smoke and noise of battle.

Pulling myself together, I noticed that most of the stuff was going over our heads and dropping into C Company lines. The world seemed full of the whine and crash of shell splinters. Behind, in the forest, I saw the trees falling right and left as high explosives burst among them – ricochets spun visibly through the air without bursting.

To our front across a ploughed field, the ground rose a little so that we had hardly any real field of fire, then suddenly, quite close, I saw the Germans – at least I saw the tops of their helmets bobbing up and down as they ducked and dodged in our fire. Aiming at these moving blobs, I fired again and again until there was no longer anything to shoot at and the 'cease-fire' whistle brought respite. A battery of our field guns now joined in the game. Concealed in the forest behind us, they fired over our heads. As poor Fritz came on, our guns shortened their range until their shells were falling just in front of our own position. One fell right among our men, then another, and several were wounded.

I tried my best to get through to the battery on our phone but the line had been cut. The company commander, Captain Scott, was furious with the artillery and ordered me to take a message back to the guns myself, so I shook hands with my friend Ralph Newman and set off. All kinds and calibres of missiles were crashing all about, shrapnel, whiz-bangs, high explosive, all in a frenzied mix-up and at the back of it the steady tap-tap-tap of machine guns.

I reached a little stream, crossed on the plank bridge and turned into the wood where C Company was dug in. Here I found a signaller complete with telephone in a hole behind a tree, and in a minute or so my message had been passed to the guns and the range had been lifted nicely.

As I turned to leave, something hit the tree behind which we were crouching, there was a blinding flash, a whirling sound of splinters, and there I was lying flat on my back looking up at a startled signaller. I had been hit in the lumber region and was already feeling numb from the waist down. Stretcher-bearers arrived and dragged me over to a hole for temporary cover and turned me on my face. One of them let rip a stream of swear-words as he cut away my leather jacket and saw the wound.

My wound bandaged, I lay until the attack slackened off. They lifted me into an empty ration limber drawn by a couple of mules and we rattled off back through the forest. I hardly recognized the place as the same one we had come through such a short time before. Then it had been a lovely peaceful bird sanctuary and now it was a shambles, fallen trees and great holes everywhere.

[Victor Cole had been fortunate to have been wounded in a location from which he could be removed expeditiously for treatment.]

When I came out of the wood, I looked right and left. There were red caps [Military Police] about 50 yards apart and I said to the driver, 'What are they doing here?' and he said, 'They're to stop anybody going back.'

A brief stop at the dressing station to be labelled and off we went again. By and by we came to a roadside farmhouse with a Red Cross flag before the door. My stretcher was laid on the floor and the bearers went away. The place was crowded with wounded men swathed in bandages. At one end of the room a couple of RAMC doctors were bending over a stretcher raised on boxes and it looked to me as though they were trying to amputate a leg.

It was dusk and the room was lit by an oil lamp. A soldier sitting opposite, his head in bandages, suddenly fell forward and crashed to the floor. A padre came in and helped him up and then commenced a tour of the room speaking to each man in turn. 'He wants to know my religion,' I thought, 'in case the worst happens!' What he did say when he came to me was 'Which would you like, my boy, a bottle of beer or a tot of rum?' – a pleasant surprise in that place. I declared a preference for the beer.

Dozing off for a time I awoke to find myself crying like a baby. Nerves I suppose. The doctors made their rounds, put fresh dressing on us and marked most of us for the Casualty Clearing Station. Then came an ambulance driver – a woman! This was the closest I had ever seen a woman to the firing line and although big shells were still whistling overhead the girl took no notice of them. 'I can take four,' she said. So four of us were carried out and lifted into the little Ford Ambulance. The girl gave us cigarettes. To me she said, 'Don't worry, chum, I'll take it easy over the shell-holes.'

A FANY (First Aid Nursing Yeomanry) ambulance driver: Vic Cole was astonished to see women working so close to the firing line. Note the attempt to dry quickly damp blankets on the vehicle's radiator.

Lieutenant
Colonel
David Rorie,
OC 1/2nd
(Highland) Field
Ambulance

13th April: When the Advanced Dressing Stations fell back they had previously cleared all wounded and medical stores, and in several cases this was done with the enemy in sight and the stations under machine-gun fire. In spite of this, RAMC casualties were low – two MOs and one other rank missing (prisoners), and seven other ranks wounded.

In the course of this battle an officer, dodging his way across country amidst heavy enemy fire, thought he noticed some movement in a shell hole. Going up to it he found an old civilian and his wife dressed – as these people often were when fleeing from their homes – in their Sunday best, and crouching at the foot of the hole. The old lady, a ruddy faced agriculturalist, had a bonnet fringed with beads and cherries which dangled and bobbed as she ducked at each explosion. Recognizing her visitor as a British officer and wishing to express herself in a way he could understand, the poor old dame tersely but comprehensively remarked, 'No bon! Ah! No bon!'

One party of King Edward's Horse gallantly held the enemy in check for several hours in the vicinity of a farmhouse and under very heavy shell and machine-gun fire. The men were exhausted and there were many casualties. All the civilians had cleared back except one old woman. During the action she milked her cows, herself taking the milk under fire to the men, and also making hot coffee for them; while, throughout, she tended the wounded as best she could.

Private
Frederick Voigt,
Labour Corps

The eastern sky flickered with vivid gun-flashes and scintillated with brilliant shell-bursts. The night was full of rustling noises and sullen thunder-claps, while a more distant roaring and rumbling seemed to break against some invisible shore like the breakers of a stormy sea.

We retired to our huts and tents. Soon after lights-out the Police Corporal came round and shouted:

'Parade at 4.45 to-morrow morning in marching order.'

The tumult increased as though the surge were coming nearer and nearer. Shells of small calibre passed overhead with a prolonged whistle and burst with a hardly audible report. The thunder of bigger explosions shook the huts and caused the ground to tremble.

As I woke the next morning the din of the cannonade broke in upon my senses with a sudden impact. Rumbling, thundering, bellowing,

German troops relax with drink and cards during the fighting near Armentières.

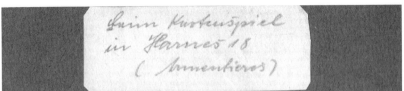

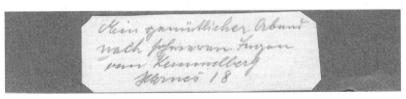

rushing, whistling, and whining, the tumult seemed all around and above us. Sudden flashes lit up the whole camp so that for fractions of seconds every hut and tent was brilliantly illuminated. Multitudes of dazzling stars appeared and disappeared.

We drew our breakfast and packed up our belongings. All was confusion in the hut. We paraded, the roll was called, and as the day began to dawn we marched off.

Second
Lieutenant
Wilfred Bion,
5th Battalion,
Tanks Corps

We passed down the main road in long, swaying columns of fours. We left the wood yard behind us and hoped it would be destroyed – how we hated the place for the dreary months we had spent there! The westward stream of refugees had ceased, but an eastward stream of French infantry and field artillery thronged the roads. The artillerymen were mostly tall and powerfully built. The infantry were nearly all elderly men of poor physique.

They looked desperately miserable. We exchanged greetings.

We were travelling parallel with, about 5 miles from, the front line. What the devil were we up to now? I felt ignorant in detail of my task, of my place in any larger design. We had no rifles; Hauser, O'Toole, Smith and I had revolvers; six Lewis guns were manned by four men each. I did not like Lewis guns; I thought them unreliable and unsuitable for any job we had to do inside or outside tanks. They sounded 'tinny' when they were firing. Our job? – to reinforce infantry.

Cook turned up the next time we left our lorries. 'These trenches here are where Carter and I will be. … One mile in front is the Infantry Brigade; they are down to the strength of one company, spread over a mile. There are no supports so no support trenches – unless of course time lies heavy on your hands and you like to dig some.' He gave a cold, acid smile. 'I don't think time will lie heavy on your hands – we have been told the enemy has to break through at no matter what cost. There's only you lot and this bunch of infantry between him and the sea 30 or 40 miles behind. There are no orders for retreat because there is no retreat arranged. You hold on – unless of course you are dead. Any questions? Of course not – there aren't any.' …

I divided the party into six and we advanced in open order of sections; three infantry guides were there to show us the way. I said I would be with the third section from the right if wanted.

Dawn broke about half an hour after we reached our position. I could see then that our trench lay at the corner of a hutted camp. It stank because it was full of dead horses. An infantry officer told me the enemy trenches were 50 yards in front and that they liked infiltrating through the huts to throw a grenade or two into our line and then disappear. His report cost us many an anxious hour; perhaps it was well for our vigilance. …

I was no longer obsessed with ambition to be brave; that I knew was beyond me, but I did not want to be disgraced. There was usually no danger of disgrace because there was nothing disgraceful to do – you cannot run away in company or, at least, it is relatively difficult. As a section commander I was to learn of problems associated with loneliness and isolation. As I peered into no-man's-land I was to experience one of them almost at once.

A sheet of corrugated iron slithered from a roof and crashed to the ground. I was watching that spot at the time so I knew what caused the grinding metallic sound that preluded the crash. Then the silence which was absolute flowed back and enveloped first the camp and then our party in a hideous fear. I watched. I waited for the grenade thrower. Nothing. At last, to break this evil spell, I looked at my watch. It was twelve minutes past ten. I returned to stare at the camp. The sun was shining, the sky blue. The Lewis gun, flanked by the two intense gunners, glistened. … I kept my stare on the huts for any sign of movement.

At last, feeling it must be now past noon, I looked at my watch again. It was not quite quarter past ten. I looked at my watch incredulously; the second hand was moving and the sun confirmed the hour. Again I felt fear. Could I possibly last till evening? In desperation I stopped thinking about the past or future; I began taking compass bearings on every object within my limited view. To my relief my fear began to ebb away. It was an experience familiar to me in my childhood nightmares but not in waking life.

The Battle of the Lys broke down into a series of small struggles as the Germans probed and pushed to find a breakthrough. Increasingly, tenacious defence eventually overcame determined advance. In Britain, the public was aware of the seriousness of the situation, and in a series of extraordinary notes and letters, diverse groups and organizations wrote to the Commander-in-Chief to offer their moral support. Whether they ever expected a reply is not known but given the circumstances, Haig would have been forgiven for a lack of indulgence. Nevertheless, he replied.

To Field Marshal Sir Douglas Haig from The Chairman, The Union of English Congregational Churches, Oswestry.

16–4–18
The Union of English Congregational Churches in North Wales, in annual assembly at Oswestry, desire to assure the Commander-in-Chief and the Army in France and Flanders of their fervent goodwill, admiration and prayers during the present critical period.

From Field Marshal Sir Douglas Haig to The Chairman, The Union of English Congregational Churches, Oswestry.

19–4–18
All ranks join with me in sending grateful thanks for your kind message. The knowledge that we are in your prayers is a source of comfort and encouragement to all of us.

To Field Marshal Sir Douglas Haig from 'Wells', STABBS.

16–4–18
Stabbs is with you. Raised £3,166 for a seaplane.

From Field Marshal Sir Douglas Haig to 'Wells', STABBS.

19–4–18
Hearty congratulations to you all on the splendid result of your subscription, and grateful thanks for your kind message.

To Field Marshal Sir Douglas Haig from The Secretary, Royal Antediluvian Order of Buffaloes, 29 Uverdale Road, Chelsea, London.

19–4–18
Members of Royal Antediluvian Order of Buffaloes, assure you of their pride in the gallant troops under your command, and are confident with them the cause of right will prove victorious.
From Field Marshal Sir Douglas Haig to The Secretary, Royal Antediluvian Order of Buffaloes, 29 Uverdale Road, Chelsea, London.

19–4–18
I send you the cordial thanks of all ranks under my command for your inspiring message, which has greatly encouraged us all.

Special Orders of the Day: one never knew whether they were intended as jokes, and why Sir Douglas Haig should have to acknowledge every little English club's views in the matter, when everyone in the BEF was so busy stemming the flood of Boches.

Captain Douglas Strickland, Army Ordnance Corps, 34th Division

Throughout April vast numbers of reinforcements continued to pour into France to replace the losses sustained. Second Lieutenant George Atkinson arrived at Rouen and began to sharpen his knowledge of bridge demolition, still a much sought-after skill.

23rd April: Arrived at the RE Base Depot, Rouen, and was delighted to find a pile of letters waiting for me. Damn fools that we are, we are all fretting to get back into it [the war] again – the lines must be very thin nowadays. …

Second Lieutenant George Atkinson, 2nd Army, Royal Engineers

24th April: Wasting time all day at the Demolitions School. God! What fools we are. Up in the line men are dying like flies for lack of reinforcements – here are thousands of troops and we cannot go because the RTO's [Railway Transport Officer] staff is too small to cope with the railway embarkation forms!

25th April: Several fellows posted to companies today, so that it looks as if we shall soon be over the wall that Haig spoke about and with our backs to it again.

26th April: More demolitions – news still very bad – if they don't let us go to the Huns methinks they will come to us.

27th April: Demolitions again. We destroyed a steel rail and heard a fragment of it go humming away over our heads just like a shell. About ten minutes afterwards the Colonel came down with great wind up and chewed us all to pieces for being careless. Our piece of rail had evidently gone right over the camp and landed somewhere near the Revolver Range.

Unfortunately, the Colonel had heard it humming over his hut and it had nearly frightened him to death!

The German casualties were high and, if objectives proved unobtainable, unaffordable. It was clear by late April that the key hub of Hazebrouck would not be taken, indeed not even reached, and so at the end of the month the German High Command called off the offensive, although British troops remained high on the alert.

Private Reginald Kiernan, 7th The Leicestershire Regiment

27th April: There are no trenches here, because there is water just below the surface. There are earthworks back and front, riveted and wire-netted. One of our own shells has carried away the back of our bay only this morning. The Jerries have been dropping their shrapnel about 12 feet above the post, but a few feet behind. There is a constant concussion on all sides and in the air. This afternoon I was sitting in the corner of the bay. There was a sudden roar, like a train coming out of a tunnel, only with a terribly steely screech. Everything went yellow and black. The walls of my chest fell in and I could not breathe. There was a great shower of black mud and water. The whole corner of the bay where I was sitting had disappeared. We were all soaked through and plastered with black mud.

Evening: It is dusk. The shelling has stopped. The corporal says they are coming over, and we are to keep our eyes skinned. I am having a turn under the only cover, a piece of corrugated iron over the remaining corner of the bay.

We have had a lot of casualties, though not in our bay. Mostly shrapnel. They have limped through our post, covered with blood. The West Yorkshires came up to our post over the open fields, on the way to a strongpoint on our left. They were caught by the shelling all the way up. When they dropped into our post they were shaking so pitiably and trying to hide it till they got control of themselves again. They could only talk in gasps.

28th April: They have begun to bump our little trench. There is an aeroplane flying low over it. Shall I live out today? The bumping has stopped. It has started again. A shell drops close in front. A full minute passes; there is a screech. That one is a few yards behind. The stones and black mud fall on us.

Looking towards Kemmel Hill during the later stages of fighting near Armentières, 25 April 1918.

The remains of a concrete blockhouse near Kemmel.

They have stopped again. It is dark. We can stand up in the trench and stretch our limbs, with great burning and pain. An officer has just come from the canal. We are to 'stand-to' all night.

It must be the 29th of April now. I have lived through my birthday. I am eighteen.

Second Lieutenant George Atkinson, 2nd Army, Royal Engineers

11th May: At Last!!! Left Rouen in a crowded troop train and made myself thoroughly miserable by wondering if I should ever come back and what everybody was doing at home, etc., etc. Silly ass!

12th May, Sunday: Passed through Boulogne and Wimereux early in the morning and then through Calais and Cassel and on to Heidelbeck, where we slept in the train. Hun planes came over in the night and tried to bomb the train, but they didn't get anywhere near us.

13th May: Set off at 9 am to find the company, and after walking 11 miles with my pack found them at one of the old camps in the Ypres Salient – quite like home again. The camp is surrounded by guns, and a battery of 9.2 howitzers just behind us make life unbearable. In the evening the Divisional Concert Party gave us a very good show in spite of the fact that the 'theatre' was continually shaken by shell explosions.

16th May: Working in the line all day and saw several air fights but no casualties on either side. At night went up again and had 200 PBI [Poor Bloody Infantry] constructing a barricade on the main Ypres–Poperinge road. Enemy strafed the 9.2 howitzer on the Plank Road, and as we passed, his shells were falling about 20 yards away from us. We didn't stay to observe his shooting, which was a little too good to be comfortable! Arrived on the job and found that half the working party had gone astray owing to Brigade HQ giving wrong orders. Damned asses in their well-cut breeches – if they had to flounder about in trenches all night they would be more careful.

The Ypres Salient on an ordinary lively night is a sight to be remembered. The rise and fall of Very lights makes a circle of fire all round us, and except just where the Poperinghe road connects us with the rest of France we appear to be completely surrounded. It is more than a marvel to me how they have failed to cut us off in that little bottle-neck. On this particular night Fritz was raining shrapnel into Dickebusch and our people were giving him a warm time in reply. The 4.5 howitzers were firing hammer and tongs, and as I watched the angry shell-bursts on the ridge in front I began to feel quite sorry for the Boche infantry. However, his field guns sent some high explosive over just to the left of my barricade, and my sympathy rapidly vanished.

19th May: Rode round with the Skipper, taking over all the demolitions from him as he goes to the Gunners tomorrow as Liaison Officer. I am now responsible for the explosive charges under all the bridges behind Ypres, and in case of evacuation of the salient I've got to be the last man to leave, blowing up everything before I go. It's a regular suicide club, as I know that fully half the charges won't go off unless I fire my revolver into them.

Overleaf:
A woman and
her young child
escape with
whatever they
can carry.

4. Wrong Place, Wrong Time

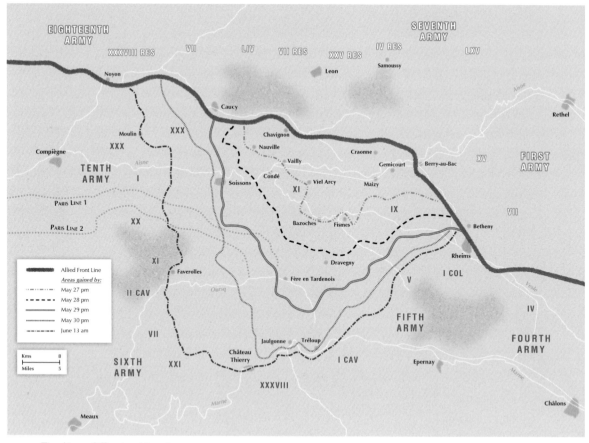

The Aisne Offensive, May–June.

View from British front line just before the German offensive of 27 May 1918. Picture taken by an unknown British officer, 149 Infantry Brigade.

'One retreat is much the same as another ...'

Sapper John Gowland, 50th (Northumbrian)
Signal Company, Royal Engineers

———————

In May, five exhausted British divisions were sent to regroup in the relatively tranquil Champagne region north-east of Paris. All had been engaged on the Somme and the Lys and all had suffered severely. A period of recuperation was urgently required while reinforcements were bedded in. These British troops would release fresher French divisions to head north where, intelligence suggested, the next German effort would fall.

As British troops took the trains south in late April and early May, they gazed at the sights: the 'great pencil in the sky', as one described the Eiffel Tower, while others were afforded glimpses of the Palace of Versailles, both reminders of normality and of a half-forgotten civil life.

The men entered a province largely untouched since the fighting of autumn 1914. The countryside, heavily forested in parts, had become a backwater. Fighting had erupted in the spring and autumn of 1917 when the French seized the imposing ridge, the Chemin des Dames, but since then a policy of 'live and let live' had been adopted by opposing troops. British soldiers discovered a rural idyll, warm, bursting with early summer life; the 'sanatorium of the West', the Germans called it, with good reason. The British troops could put their feet up after weeks of intense fighting.

We have been having a great time since we arrived here. We took the train just beyond Cassel, and travelled by it for two days and nights. It was very slow, and the fellows got off at the back and ran up to the engine for shaving water, and then jumped on as their own truck passed them. Towards night we passed what I think was the Eiffel Tower, sticking up over the fields many miles away; and we passed a place called St Denis, which I think is very near Paris. The next day we reached a country where names were strange to me, like Ville-en-Tardenois, La Ferté-Milon.

Private Reginald Kiernan, 7th The Leicestershire Regiment, 21st Division

We are on the French front. We have taken over French huts, big commodious huts, with wire beds. At Ypres we slept, when 'out', in an inch of dust on the floors, and wrapped our puttees round our feet for warmth. Here we lie with nothing on at night, because of the heat and fleas.

All round, the country is heavily forested, and there is long, lush, rich grass, and a very cold river to bathe in, near a place called Châlons-le-Vergeur, a lovely name. There is an empty town near Hermonville, and it is fine to walk through the deserted streets. All the houses are standing, roofs on, shutters up. There is Trigny, too, where business is as usual. It is all a scream to us – you can't find a shell hole anywhere, and it is only about 10 kilometres from the front. …

Fellows back from the line say it is a doddle. In parts the trenches are 12 feet deep, and so narrow and stretch so far that they have to walk sideways for kilos [kilometres] when they are carrying the dixies. The district is called the Champagne.

Taking a slow train to the Aisne region proved restorative for men of the exhausted 50th Division.

There is never a sound from the line; no machine guns, no artillery. The trenches are a thousand yards apart. The Jerries used to come out of their trenches, but they don't since one of our fellows fired at them. The man who fired was cursed by the others, because they don't want to start any unnecessary trouble. The corporal says they have only a few men to cover every 300 yards of the line, and that there is so much cover that it would be hard to stop Jerry if he came over.

The whole area was eloquent with memories of the war from the first great battle of the Aisne in 1914, to the stupendous storming of the Chemin des Dames in the spring of 1917. The Aisne canal became a favourite bathing-place, and in the generous warmth of the excellent weather helped us to forget the dark days of the previous months. Reims, with its cathedral glorious even in ruins, was not far to the east of us; Soissons, almost equally beautiful, away to our left. Even the villages, such at any rate as had escaped the devastation of war, were things of beauty. I shall not soon forget one midnight ride down the hillside through Longueval. The clustering houses, with the quaint old church set in the midst, were bathed in the full light of a gorgeous moon, and the silver and shadows created a magic scene. Scarcely had we passed the village than from the thickets and hedgerows came the thrilling notes of a score of nightingales, singing away in the silence and the moonlight a sad song whose ecstasy touched us almost to tears.

Reverend Wilfrid Callin, Chaplain, 1/4th The Northumberland Fusiliers, 50th Division

22nd May: The weather for the last week has been glorious, the Boche have been good, we are in a very pretty part of the line and still have our charming HQ – so what more can the heart of man desire? I sent you the other day some 'lilies-of-the-valley' – I don't know whether they will ever arrive home, or if they do, whether they will be quite dead. But anyway I thought it would be worth trying. You might let me know in what sort of condition they arrive. Lilies-of-the-valley simply abound here – only alas! they are nearly over. We also have an asparagus bed of our own, with far more asparagus in it than we can eat. We have asparagus for breakfast, dinner, lunch and tea, and still there is plenty to give to battalions (which we do).

Captain Lancelot Spicer, 9th King's Own (Yorkshire Light Infantry), 21st Division

All of which does not sound very much like war, or the tales of our 'brave fighting men', does it? Well, no, but then just at present this is a quiet bit of line, but one always lives on the edge of a volcano, and you never quite know when the eruption is going to start. One minute all is quiet and the next minute a perfect tornado of shells are raining down upon the earth.

Private Reginald Kiernan, 7th The Leicestershire Regiment, 21st Division

From the road nearby I can see the towers of Reims Cathedral, as though it were only a hundred yards away, yet it is some kilometres. The 'feel' of the place is different from Ypres. Up there, on those flat, grey fields, where it is winking red and yellow stabs and flashes all night, with the unending rumble of guns, it seemed that it always had been like that and would be so for ever. It was what we expected: the British front, frightfulness, dullness, rain, mud, dead bodies, stench, the whistle of stray bullets far behind the line, the Very lights, the hollow sound of the machine guns, never wholly quiet ever, anywhere, as though both armies could never sleep. Ypres was just what I expected of the war. It was exactly like what the papers said, that I read at school.

But here it is all green and blue and bright. Everybody is interested in us. The French soldiers grin, are friendly, and ask us questions about the underground railways in England. They give us *pinard*, their red wine, which they carry instead of water. There are lovely bottle green woods with little dark streams in them.

What we noticed most was the silence. Two out of three of the Germans' shells were duds and these were very infrequent. It seemed that both sides hated to disturb the peace. Sometimes a whole day would pass without a gun being fired and for a few weeks we had the most pleasant time we had ever spent in France. George and I had a dugout in the centre of a dense wood. The wires we had to look after rarely gave any trouble, and there was one armoured cable containing sixteen wires buried 6 feet beneath the ground. Most of the time we walked about the countryside. The front-line trench was a splendid affair. The French had certainly done themselves well. The officers' dugouts contained armchairs and beds and were fitted with electric lights.

There was a little village tucked away in a hollow behind our wood. Here, life went on as usual. Fields of grape vines were everywhere and fruit trees grew by the wayside. The wood we were in was carpeted with lilies of the valley and thousands of birds were singing. It was spring and to us was very much like I supposed heaven must be; compared with the flat, uninteresting, war-torn miles of mud we had been used to, this was indeed paradise. The Tommies in the line could sit on the parapet and read magazines or study their shirts without fear of sudden death, the German trench being on an opposite hill more than a mile away. The whole country was composed of hills and valleys. A few well-made graves with elaborate crosses reminded us that someone was killed here at times, but casualties were very rare. I once saw an officer of an entomological turn of mind catching butterflies in no-man's-land. Evidently the line was only a sort of guarded frontier.

A couple of miles to our rear flowed the river Aisne and a canal side by side. Here we bathed daily. Mr Winthrop told us to make the most of it and do as we liked but to return to our lines immediately should anything in the way of a bombardment commence. …

Sapper John Gowland, 50th (Northumbrian) Signals Company, Royal Engineers

Opposite: *Still standing, and to soldiers in the line, almost touchable in the distance: the twin towers of Reims Cathedral.*

One day a man on guard outside Divisional Headquarters was killed by a nose cap that went through his tin hat as if it were made of paper. It came from an archie [anti-aircraft] shell that had been fired at a plane. The poor fellow was buried with full honours. Half the headquarters staff attended the funeral and two French officers representing the adjacent French headquarters were present. No doubt had the Germans known the man had been killed they would have sent someone too.

This could never last. Something would happen or we would be moved back to Flanders. Once, while we were at the front line end of one of our wires that was faulty we saw a Tommy come out of a dugout and solemnly drop a piece of paper into a box fixed to the side of the trench and marked waste paper. We both stared in amazement. And we were no less surprised when we saw a colonel in a dressing gown taking his breakfast in a deckchair. The distant thunder of guns at other parts of the line almost ceased to disturb us.

Then came the end of it all.

May 1918: 50th Division Royal Engineers enjoy the relative peace and tranquillity of the Aisne.

There were reasons for the Germans' passivity. They were planning the next tranche of their Spring Offensive, this time on the Aisne, near Paris. Having failed to split the Allies, this time they would push towards the capital, 40 miles from the front lines. Smashing through battle-weakened Allied divisions, many, in the fighting, stripped of experienced officers and NCOs, the German troops would pour across the Aisne River and canal before the bridges were demolished. Then they would head south-west in the direction of the river Marne and Paris. Surprise would be the key to success, backed by overwhelming fire-power: the enemy lines would be drenched in gas to cause panic and confusion, followed by a short but intense artillery barrage.

26th May: We have just been ordered to fall in. It is nearly 10 pm, so something must be happening. It is a beautiful evening. Some Boche planes have been over, a bit lower than usual.

Private Reginald Kiernan, 7th The Leicestershire Regiment, 21st Division

Over 5,200 guns were ranged against the Allies' far fewer 1,400 guns, and proved to be the greatest German tactical advantage in fire-power achieved during the war. The barrage began at 1.00 am on 27 May. The intense use of high explosives quickly wrecked trenches and strongpoints, ensuring telephone communication between units was cut in the first hour. Just as dawn broke, German troops attacked. Eighteen-year-old Percy Williams was serving in the Northumberland Fusiliers with many similar aged boys. It was their first experience of real war.

I was in a dugout in the third-line trenches when an officer came round and said that there might be action tonight. I'd not been under bad shellfire before and I was shaking and almost sick with fright as we waited, just waited until all hell broke loose. When the guns opened up, the noise was deafening, the shells were falling, causing tremendous explosions and destroying not only the trenches above our heads but the stairs leading down to us. We were told to leave the dugout and we scrambled up into a trench that had been practically destroyed. Gas shells had been falling all night and saturated everything, covering our masks with a sulphur film. You couldn't see. I had stomach ache. I felt faint and sick and had to spew up, forcing me to take the gas mask off and vomit as best I could, trying not to breathe in. A man next to me, I don't know who he was, he

Private Percy Williams, 1/5th Northumberland Fusiliers, 50th Division said, 'You must put on your gas mask, you must!' There was no chance, there were no officers that I saw and no communication at all because the bombardment was so terrific that the telephone lines were all smashed to pieces. I was absolutely terrified for hours, and the crying of the wounded – I'd never experienced anything so terrible in my life, and after only a month in France!

There was good reason why Williams felt there was an absence of leadership for, according to one of the senior officers on the division, over and above the normal stress and strains:

Brigadier General Hubert Rees, Headquarters, 150th Brigade, 50th Division

The commanders of the 50th Division were burdened with the further anxiety that they were fully aware that the division was not in a condition to take part in a great battle and required time to recuperate. The company officers were completely untrained, almost without exception. The simplest orders were misunderstood, while the frontage allotted to the division, some 11,000 yards, reduced the forces available for defence to a minimum.

It would have taken time to acclimatize new officers, just as it would have taken time for the thousands of 18 and 19-year-old lads to get used to trench life. Directly in the eye of the German storm was 19-year-old Frank Deane.

Private Frank Deane, 1/6th The Durham Light Infantry, 50th Division

We just sat in the trench while all this stuff just crashed all around us. Everything you can think of was coming over, shrapnel and heavy shells and gas shells. We had been told that our artillery would bombard their trenches at 9 pm, the night before. Well, there was a bit of artillery fire from our side but they started at midnight and there wasn't a whisper from ours after that. All we could do was to sit quietly on the fire-step in the dark and listen, just hoping nothing dreadful would hit us.

As it was dark, you got the flashes of light from the shells and the Very lights. It wasn't just the bangs and shrieks of shells but, you see, whenever a shell fell, earth would come down and it would rattle on your tin hat because it would spread for quite a long way from the point of impact. You

Homes and livelihoods on the Aisne destroyed in moments.

just shrug your shoulders and get as much of yourself under your tin hat as you possibly can and hope for the best. After all, if you walk from one place to another, you wouldn't be any better off so there was nothing to do except sit down, be terrified, and wait until it was all over.

We filed for the dugout, up the steep road to the top of the hill. The road at the top was camouflaged all along the side, and over the top, with long strips of stuff like dried seaweed. But Jerry caught us right away with his shells. They screamed upwards from an immense plain up on to the ridge top. We took to a ditch, and then wound down the hillside, and Jerry tried to hit us all the way. We could hear the gun bang as the shell shrieked towards us. Ben said they were firing point-blank. Our necks shorten and we want to stoop but the officer shouts, 'Keep moving, there.' There are fountains of earth and stones rising and dropping on us.

Private Reginald Kiernan, 7th The Leicestershire Regiment, 21st Division

All the plain below was drifting smoke, just as if it were mist, but it was shells. We could see the yellow flame. We went down to some trenches they said were called the Labyrinth, shallow trenches, with thick, low shrubbery, back and front. Shells were whistling and yelling from all angles. It was no use ducking or dropping. Every second the nose caps hit the earth – drdrdrdrdrdr – thud. A small shell hit the ground near my foot, and slithered along. I did not hear it coming in the row. It was a dud.

The officer and the corporal with two men went through the shrubbery. Looking through it I could see a big *route nationale*. There were hundreds of our fellows running along it, like a football crowd running for the trams. Jerry's machine guns were going and they were dropping, a score at a time and lying in heaps, khaki heaps.

The officer came back and the two men were carrying a corporal. His face and body and legs were all covered in blood, and he was all grey and yellow. They were carrying him back. We said, 'Good luck, Corporal.' He whispered, 'It's you as wants the good luck. I'm out of it.' I liked the corporal. He liked me, and he always smiled as he passed. …

There was shelling from all points. We could see Jerries now, coming over the fields, through the wire and camouflage. We fired at them for a short time, and then fell back.

The Germans were using their well-honed tactics of quick infiltration, just as they had on the Somme and the Lys. Not tackling strongpoints head-on saved time and lives. As before, these men could be isolated and, when it was clear that all hope of escape was possible, could be persuaded to surrender rather than fight to the death.

Lieutenant Alfred Halkyard, 8th The Leicestershire Regiment, 21st Division

The use by the enemy of his infiltration method in the attack was most noticeable on the front under my own observation. Small parties under a junior NCO or senior soldier were most persistent in working forward in dead ground or down communication trenches (of which all could not be blocked and held) and any part of the front where the enemy met with serious opposition was subsequently left alone.

The forward companies were quickly overrun and the enemy was crossing and passing round the flanks of the marsh soon after 6 am. The strongpoints, however, east of Reims – Berry-au-Bac Road and supporting platoons along the road itself – held out for some time and it was not until 10 am that the enemy's infiltration and outflanking methods and use of dead ground and unoccupied communication trenches caused these posts to become untenable.

One by one our telephone wires went dead. We could hear orders flashing about as we tapped in to see what wires were working. Within an hour there was not a wire intact with the exception of the buried cable, and half an hour later that went silent. To reach the front line seemed impossible but we had to try to get a line through. Plunging into the shell-swept wood we followed a wire. It was broken three times in the first hundred yards. Trees fell and huge branches were flung about like twigs. Faintly above the awful din we heard the clatter of gas gongs. …

We were surrounded by gas now. The high ground we were on was like an island in the midst of a greenish sea. We could see the horrible stuff creeping among the trees of the wood, eddying and swirling where the bursting shells disturbed it. Putting on our masks we started back. The wire was broken again in a dozen places. We saw a lamp flashing Morse code from the front line but it was very difficult to read the message, the flash of the shells kept interrupting. I could only catch a few words. Our wire was broken faster than we could mend it.

We reached our dugout again alive. It was not only useless but suicide to attempt to repair the line again. We crept into our dugout which was full of gas. A shell burst near and some of the roof fell in. Dashing out again we saw two tree trunks lying parallel to each other. Squeezing between these we pressed ourselves to the ground. Our gas masks were becoming unbearable and the shellfire seemed to get even worse. Pieces of wood and whole trees were flung about like straws in a whirlwind. Every second I expected a jagged piece of hot steel to rip open my stomach or carry away a limb. The awful sights I had seen passed through my mind. Perhaps a shell would hit me direct. I wondered if I would feel it. There would be a moment of a dreadful agony, I thought, as my body was torn to quivering lumps of flesh which would be unrecognizable as the remains of a human being. A horrible sight, men would turn away from it. Soon the pieces

Sapper John Gowland, 50th (Northumbrian) Signals Company, Royal Engineers would be covered with loathsome blow-flies. I felt George move, so he was still alive too. If it had not been for the trees we lay between we should not have lasted five minutes.

As the shellfire moved away, John's companion, George, went to find some water.

Sapper John
Gowland, 50th
(Northumbrian)
Signals
Company, Royal
Engineers

George came back without any water looking as if he had seen a ghost. 'Get your rifle and bandolier, quick,' he said. 'Never mind anything else. There's a crowd of Jerries coming this way. They did not see me but they will soon find us.'

We were surrounded. I could not understand it. Rifle fire continued up the line. Now we understood why the bombardment had stopped so abruptly. The Germans had broken through somewhere and were behind us.

Artillery was the great killer of the war. Legs and torsos stick out of shell-swept ground.

In the din we could hear casualties shouting for stretcher-bearers, stretcher-bearers, stretcher-bearers. I thought, 'Oh my God, I'm going to die, I'm going to die!' We did not know what was happening, not 50 yards on either side of us. Then Corporal Collins came along. He was panicking, he'd seen tanks, he said that the Germans had broken through, and we were surrounded. 'Every man for himself, everything has collapsed,' he said, 'there's no chance, we must get out of it, otherwise we shall get captured.' As I stumbled from the trench I dropped my rifle, it was panic, the noise was terrible. I was weighed down by my pack, by fifty rounds of ammunition strapped around me, by my entrenching tool, the earth was blown up all around and I couldn't see. Then a shell burst close by, shrapnel wounding me in the leg. It wasn't bad, we had puttees on, but I saw my leg was bleeding and I remember having a towel to staunch it. I couldn't walk, so another chap said we'd better crawl for it, to try and get away.

By this time the gas had lifted and I could see the Germans running across, scores of them, I was so confused, you see, and the noise had left me all of a muddle, I didn't know where I was. Then I turned and saw this German with his fixed bayonet standing over me. He shouted 'Halt, halt, halt!' and then he motioned, 'or else', and grabbed me. I was petrified, I put

Private Percy Williams, 1/5th The Northumberland Fusiliers, 50th Division

Captured British troops in a holding camp behind the German lines. Frank Deane was the last surviving British prisoner taken during the offensive.

my hands up. We were told in the newspapers a few months before that the Germans weren't taking any more prisoners, so you can imagine what I thought. He got hold of me, and ripped my spare ammunition off.

There was absolute panic. We could see the Germans in their grey uniforms, with their rifles and fixed bayonets; I had never seen a German before. I never saw a British officer, there was no command of any sort, we had to act on our own. A lot of the boys ran away to get out of it. You must remember that we were nearly all boys of eighteen and we were up against seasoned veterans, and when you see a lot of Germans coming with rifles and bayonets, well, I think you'd be a very brave man to wait until you were bayoneted, and they were big chaps, they looked so formidable in those big grey helmets.

Private Frank
Deane, 1/6th
The Durham
Light Infantry,
50th Division

Somebody shouted 'Gas!' I put my mask on and was all right. However, I later looked at my silver watch and the gas had blackened the edges of the metal. At about 7 am there was a thick mist and the Germans came across. When it got a bit lighter we looked up over the top and we saw a mass of Germans, I suppose about 100 in a square. They were well to the right and to the rear of us, marching quite quickly. When we saw these men, there was nothing for us to do but to scuttle further back into our trenches to see if we could get ahead of them, because if we just sat where we were we'd have been surrounded there and then. We seemed to be on our own, but presently a few others joined us and we made our way back. There was only a lance corporal who was in charge of our little group but somehow or other we managed to keep together all the way. He was an old soldier, a nice old chap and his name was Lindsey, a coal miner in civilian life. I can't remember a lot, everything was confused, but I recall seeing my platoon officer and he was just sat on the fire-step with two men doing absolutely nothing, he just watched us go by and didn't say a word. He seemed to me to be just waiting there until the Germans caught up with him. I don't know if he actually knew what was going on or whether he was just dumbfounded. That was the only other party of our battalion that I saw that day, so you can imagine that we must have been terribly scattered in little tiny groups. We left the trenches and passed through a wood, crossing a road, the Chemin des Dames they called it, then up a

sloping hill on the other side. A couple of officers on horseback were on that hill, where they'd come from I don't know, possibly headquarters, and it was they who lined us up on the hill facing these woods waiting for the enemy.

British dead on the trench parapet.

The Germans came through, firing their machine guns like billy-ho. We'd been lying low for protection when to the right of us a trench was spotted and we were told to get up and go to this trench. I was next to the last man, a lance corporal, but we never got anywhere near the trench before they were all around us and I was captured. I can't remember a lot, it was all very confused. I do know that just before I was captured, I was wounded. A machine-gun bullet crashed through the first joint of my thumb before going up my hand.

Sapper John
Gowland, 50th
(Northumbrian)
Signals
Company, Royal
Engineers

We skirted the edge of the wood ready to dodge out of sight at a moment's notice. Making for the bridges over the river [Aisne] and canal were some howitzers drawn by caterpillars. A mile farther along some infantry were retiring in open order. If we could get to the bridge before we were cut off we had a chance to regain our lines. There was another bridge where the infantry could be seen retiring but that was too far. It might be destroyed before we reached it and George could not swim. … Our only way was to run across country and catch up the howitzers and chance being seen and fired at. This we did. We were not noticed until we had nearly reached the slow-moving guns. Then a large party of Germans appeared at the edge of a belt of trees and opened fire on the guns. We reached the big howitzers without being hit and these gave us good cover, and in a few minutes we were safely across.

There was an old trench, possibly a relic of 1914, running parallel to the river and in this was an officer and perhaps a hundred men. From this officer we inquired for our company. He said there were no companies any more that he knew of and that we were to jump into the trench along with the others. There were artillerymen who had lost their guns, lorry drivers, officers' servants from headquarters, a few infantrymen and even a French civilian who had got hold of a rifle and a Tommy's coat and refused to budge.

We could see the other bridges in the distance crowded with traffic and German shells bursting close. Men were lining the bank of the river on our side and digging themselves in. A machine gun was brought from somewhere and set up so that it commanded the bridges in front of us. Beyond the river and canal all was open ground and Germans were coming from the direction of the village in force. Four field guns were coming along the opposite side of the river. Evidently it was no longer possible to cross the other bridge and they were making a dash for the one in front of us. The Jerries in the trees who had fired at us and those coming from the village opened fire on them. One horse in the lead of the rear gun fell and the others piled on top of him. They were quickly unhitched and the gun abandoned. The machine gun in our trench opened fire on the belt of trees and this quietened the Boches a bit, but before the other guns crossed the bridges another horse fell. It was one of the wheelers and was dragged along dead in the traces until the bridge was crossed. …

A burst of rifle fire told us the Germans were getting near. Soon after, shelling commenced. Our own guns that had been captured were turned against us. They were 60-pounders. I hated them worse than any crump or whizz-bang. Like the latter they came without warning and burst with a deafening crash that made a whiz-bang seem like a Chinese cracker. Bigger shells fell near the crowded road. One of these made a huge crater in the road itself. A 6-inch howitzer toppled into the hole and the road was blocked. Some of the civilians, crazed with fear, tried to cross the ditches with their carts, and came to grief. Men worked frenziedly to fill in the shell crater and make a passage. The howitzer was left in the hole. It helped to fill in. Then the Hun concentrated his fire on the choked road. The devil himself could have conceived no worse hell. Horses screamed and stampeded. A man beside us clawed aimlessly at his entrails, mechanically trying to put them back in place. We went to him. A dozen field dressings would not cover his wound. With a scarf we bound his stomach in place. He looked at us in a pitiful, dazed manner and mercifully became unconscious. Another shell burst beside a galloping officer. He was blown to shreds. The horse halted beside the remains of its master, its jaw torn away. Slowly it sank down to die. A woman lay beside the wreckage of her belongings cut almost in halves, a dead baby beside her. There were men who spouted blood threshing the ground with their limbs. A shriek of agony would sound above the shells as someone died horribly. A man with a red mass where his face had been ran blindly into the fields. It was the last straw as far as I was concerned. This horror on top of the years that had gone seemed to take the last urge for life out of me. What was the use of living in such a world. … From then on I cared not whether I lived or died and yet somehow I survived. …

We mended our wire, where it was broken, like machines. Coming upon the man with the dreadful stomach wound who we had bound up, we managed to get him on a wagon. A tiny child sat amidst the ruins of a farm cart playing. Its parents were not to be seen. Perhaps its mother lay beneath the wreck. Of course the father was fighting somewhere. I picked the child up and handed it to a lorry driver. It was a road of death and indescribable horror. It reeked with human blood, and of course – brains. They were always present. Old men driving their carts seemed dazed.

Some of the women were hysterical, others just dumb with horror, and children looked on the awful scene with expressions on their faces which I hope never to see again on the faces of children. At last the road cleared of the living and was left to the dead.

Private Reginald Kiernan, 7th The Leicestershire Regiment, 21st Division

28th May: The French were in front in a little thin wood, about 50 yards long. We could hear the Germans rat-tatting, and the French guns spitting back at them. They had very light machine guns, with a crescent-shaped magazine. Many of these French were oldish men. Some were stout, and had long black beards, but they ran like children; from one end of the wood to the other, carrying their machine guns, putting them down in the trees, firing away, and then moving behind the wood to the other end, and going through the performance again.

We fell back 6 kilos that night. In the dark we lined a trench very near a long, black wood. There was no moon. … Suddenly in the wood in front there began a shouting and screaming, high screams of warning and fear and hate, and the crack of bombs, and the clashing of steel, the most horrible sound there is to hear. The officer drew us out of the trench and we lay nearer the wood with our rifles towards it. The clashing of steel and the screaming continued. From the dark of the trees came French stretcher-bearers carrying men all wringing wet with blood. It dropped through the stretchers on the bearers, oldish men who were trembling but grinned when they saw we were English. One man was groaning and crying and muttering words in a deep voice of agony. He was like a large piece of raw meat, so covered with blood.

It grew quiet in the wood, and the German lights began to surge up. We went back to the trench. …

At dawn we left the trench in file. Five Germans came out of a copse 20 yards away. We turned quickly towards them and threw ourselves into the long grass. A sergeant only a foot in front of me gurgled and turned on his back. His eyes turned up and there was a look in them as if he were trying to understand something. He was dead. A lance corporal, one pace behind me in the file, was on his back and rattling in his throat. He was dead. …

I cannot remember all that happened in this day. The Germans were close to us, behind, in front, at the sides, always with machine guns, and were hard to see. But we got some of their transport with our Lewis gun, at 1,500 yards, two lorries which ran wild on a steep road right in front of us, and then turned over and over on their sides. And we got a big target of Jerries on a road, 600 yards. In the afternoon we saw plenty of them singly, but we could not fire at them – only in groups – as we'd hardly a shot left. …

We were taken away from the ridge in the thick black of night. We had formed in fours on the road, waiting for the different battalions to come in, and French troops were passing us in fours on our left. They cursed us and said things of which I could only catch a drift, all about the English – 'Sacres's' and 'Merde's', and deep spitting, bitter things. I hoped they'd find Jerry in the same mood as we'd left him.

Opposite: Dead horses litter the ground, killed during the later stages of the fighting.

A building at the moment a high explosive shell hits the roof.

The destroyed village of Berry-au-Bac with the river Aisne behind.

There were eighty of us left. We waited and there came a few Durhams, then nineteen Northumberlands and some oddments of other lots. There were 119 all told. …

We marched, then slept on the roadside just at dawn. I cannot march as my heels are cracked and caked with blood. My nose and mouth are bleeding and I swallow the blood. We halt by a grove of trees, where the rooks cawing sound like the Germans shouting afar in the woods. I tell the ranker officer. He says, 'If you don't march, you stay bloody here and we go on.'

Four of us who cannot march follow behind the short column. The Medical Officer rides behind us on a horse. After a time he tells the others to march on. Me he puts on a lorry. The lorry soon puts me down, and when the column comes up I fall in and struggle along. I could scream or tear my head with pain. We march many kilos. We come to a great broad river. They say it is the Marne. …

At night we come to a village and we halt. My head is burning. I lie in a barn, and I can hear myself muttering things I do not understand.

The German advance had been spectacular, just as it had been on the Somme and the Lys. Yet once again there was no decisive breakthrough and the German casualties were unavoidably high when moving about in the open. Percy Williams and Frank Deane were two of many thousands of prisoners but as they passed through German lines they could not help but notice the ramshackle nature of the enemy's transport including 'an old harvest cart pulled by a donkey, a mule and a horse', recalled Deane. 'I didn't see any motor transport.' Any depression he may have felt at being captured was eased by what he saw. 'I thought, well, if that's the sort of equipment they've got, they won't last long.'

7th June: I have not written in my diary for two days – but just slept, and my body feels that it could sleep for ever.

We came to a village, and I 'went sick'. The MO took my temperature, and as it was 104 he gave me light duty. When he took it the next afternoon it was still 104. At night he found it 104, and looked down my throat with a torch and gasped. I was sent here in a lorry. It is a French CCS, but there are British doctors as well. They thought it was diphtheria, but it is gas, in the nose and throat.

Private Reginald Kiernan, 7th The Leicestershire Regiment, 21st Division

Sapper John
Gowland, 50th
(Northumbrian)
Signals
Company, Royal
Engineers

We were relieved, but our division was a division no longer. The papers reported it as being wiped out, and indeed it nearly was. The papers were kept from my mother for some days, but some fool brought her attention to the news, and the shock was too much for her after nearly four years of worry. An attack of influenza followed and my mother died. But it was the war that killed her.

For a few weeks the remains of our company worked behind the French lines. The remainder of the division went far back to a base. We saw no more actual fighting. The division was reinforced with troops from the east. Most of them were suffering from malaria or dysentery, and for the remaining few months of the war we were used as reserves. I had escaped whole as far as shells and bullets were concerned.

The Germans were held up on the Marne River and got no further: Paris remained out of reach and although there was a further spasm of fighting in July, the German offensive was spent; they had nothing more to give. The army would return to the defensive and wait and see what the Allies intended to do: the advantage had irrevocably passed from one side to the other. In a few weeks, the Allies would embark on their own series of offensives against a greatly weakened enemy whose morale fractured. The war was lost and the Germans would soon face that reality. Meanwhile, after the extraordinary exertions of the last few months, all sides needed time to take stock. Private Reginald Kiernan had suffered as much as anyone: 'something has changed inside me', he wrote in his diary.

Private Reginald
Kiernan, 7th The
Leicestershire
Regiment, 21st
Division

Fear has come to me. I did not know it at Ypres. There were moments when I threw myself into the mud, and the shrapnel cracked just above me, and the hot pieces sizzled in the pools near me. No one could have been more alert to dodge death – but I know I was not afraid.

It began when the sergeant and the lance corporal died almost on top of me, without the sound of a shell, and as quickly and quietly. At Ypres I hated going in the line because of the body agony of getting along the canal bank. I thought of the canal bank every minute we were away from it – but I know I was not afraid of Death. I do not think I am afraid of Death now – it is the Fear of *being* killed.

From Sézanne here, we can hear all day and all night a loud roaring cannonade, though they say it is 30 kilometres off. Sometimes it rises to a great roaring, sometimes it is just rumbling. But it has gone on for days.

I find I am thinking of the soldiers between all those guns – crouching, running, lying still, as the shriek of the shell passes, and their breath stopping. I feel my neck shortening and my back crouching as I listen to those guns.

I do not want to go back to the battalion.

They have brought in a French soldier next door. The doctor is doing something, and the man keeps screaming 'Assez, assez, monsieur le major'.

I do not want to go back to the line. When I think of it my stomach turns sick. At Ypres one night, before we went back to the post near the canal bank, I got a letter from mother. She wrote, 'I know you will be a

The Chemin des Dames showing the effects of the fighting there in late 1917 and again in May 1918.

man and face it.' For many nights I did not care how much agony and toil I had. I tried to make myself put on one side the cold and the greyness and the weight of the ammunition. I tried to keep upright when we were marching, instead of leaning forward and slipping the fingers through the shoulder straps of the equipment to relieve the weight.

But I cannot feel the strength of that letter now. I am afraid of going up to the front again. I am afraid. Last night I saw in the dark all the khaki and the yellow earth. I turned on my face and shut it out in the stars and lights that you see when you press your face in the pillow.

On the Somme, the German failure to take Amiens had led to a resumption of trench stalemate. A salient had been pushed in the Allied lines, the sort of salient that the Germans had been reluctant to defend a year before, prior to their withdrawal to the Hindenburg Line. Bulges in trench lines required more troops to defend than a linear front, and Germany no longer had excess troops available. Minor raids by both sides became the order of the day, probing, testing respective strength. Men waited and reflected while diligently watching across pleasant fields bathed in glorious summer weather.

Captain George Nicholls, C Battery, 82nd Brigade, Royal Field Artillery

Away to the east muffled boomings as if giants were shaking blankets. My mind turned to July 1916, when first I arrived in France and came along this very road at three-thirty one morning as the sun's rim began to peep above the long dark wood. How easy to recall that morning! I had brought fifty-three men from the Base, reinforcements for the Divisional Artillery, and half-believed that the war could not proceed unless I delivered them to their destination in the shortest possible time; and my indignant keenness when I reached the village behind the long dark wood and learned that no one there knew anything about the two lorries that were to transport my party the remainder of the journey to the front! Did I not rouse a frowning town mayor and two amazed sergeant majors before 5 am and demand that they should do something in the matter? And did not my fifty-three men eventually complete a triumphant pilgrimage in no fewer than thirteen ammunition lorries – to find that they and myself had arrived a day earlier than we were expected? And here was I again in the same stretch of country, and the British line not so far forward as it had been two years before.

The front lay west of the old Somme battlefields, in more or less intact country, and a period of relative quiet supervened. There was a front-line trench on the slopes above Albert, in standing corn over the chalk, which was memorable in a number of ways. A typical sequence of events on quiet days was as follows: at 'stand-to' an hour before dawn, the darkness of no-man's-land would become musical with the songs of skylarks, which continued until sunrise. When the sun was well up, a bevy of beautiful butterflies would appear, fluttering over the trench and perching on the wild carrot that was flowering on the chalky rubble of the parapet. We had ample opportunities for observing these lovely insects: we could almost rub noses with them! Curiously, I do not remember seeing any other butterflies here, though White Admirals and Marbled Whites were common elsewhere. Despite bursts of shelling and small-arms fire, and a nasty smell of phosgene among the corn, they all appeared in mint condition. They ignored us, and we them for the most part, though one or two went home to younger brothers, folded up in green envelopes.

Private Wilfrid Edwards, 1/15th London Regiment (Prince of Wales's Own Civil Service Rifles)

Reserve line, Somme, 8 June 1918. An officer sits outside his dugout. Note the camouflage netting on the ground and the bedding 'borrowed' from houses abandoned by civilians in the spring.

Corporal
Frederick
Hodges, 10th
The Lancashire
Fusiliers

One day I picked a bunch of red field poppies from the old grassy trench and put them in the metal cup attached to my rifle. They quickly wilted in the hot sun, but in any case I don't think the idea would have appealed to my officer if he had seen them. Most of the boys and men I was with apparently found no pleasure in flowers, but I was acutely conscious of them growing there in the midst of all that man-made destruction. Only field poppies and a few other wild flowers, but the persistent charm of nature in such conditions during that period of May, June and July 1918, was more poignant than it had ever been before in my life, or since.

That spring and early summer, I was often conscious of the great contrast between the man-made ugliness and horrors of the war-torn countryside, and the fresh unchanging harmony and beauty of nature. Certainly I have never lived so close to nature since, nor been so acutely aware of life. Between wrecked villages, the crops lay ungathered, and nature, uncontrolled by man, was a riot of scent and colour; oats and barley mingled with blue cornflowers and red poppies, with the song of a lark in a blue sky. This contrast was almost too much to be borne.

In our daily lives in towns and cities, we live with our senses half asleep, but in those fields near Albert, where for nearly four years death reigned, I was never more alive. Even at night, when on sentry duty under the stars, which I seldom noticed when living in a town, I was intensely aware of the orderly arrangement of the stars compared with the disorderly scene all around.

Captain George
Nicholls,
C Battery, 82nd
Brigade, Royal
Field Artillery

About three-quarters of a mile from our headquarters was a tiny cemetery, set in a grove of trees on a bare hillside, sequestered, beautiful in its peacefulness and quiet. One morning, very early, I walked out to view it more closely. It had escaped severe shelling, although chipped tombstones and broken railings and scattered pieces of painted wire wreaths showed that the hell-blast of destruction had not altogether passed it by. I went softly into the little chapel. On the floor, muddy, noisy sleeping soldiers lay sprawled in ungainly attitudes. Rifles were piled against the wall; mess-tins and water-bottles lay even upon the altar. And somehow there seemed nothing incongruous about the spectacle, nothing that would hurt a profoundly religious mind. It was all part of the war.

And one night when I was restless, and even the heavy drugging warmth of the dugout did not dull me to sleep, I climbed up into the open air. It was a lovely night. The long dark wood stood out black and distinct in the clear moonlight; the stars twinkled on their calm abode. Suddenly a near-by battery of long-range guns cracked out an ear-splitting salvo. And before the desolating rush of the shells had faded from the ear a nightingale hidden among the trees burst into song. That also was part of the war.

On our way from the bivouacs to the RE workings we walked along the road, where we were hidden from enemy observation by the brown-green camouflage netting. Then we dropped into a trench for 150 yards, and then crossed several fields which were not under enemy observation, being in 'dead' ground.

Lance Corporal Frederick Hodges, 10th The Lancashire Fusiliers

Several times as I crossed these fields to commence an afternoon shift, I was deceived by the apparent innocence of the summer scene. One afternoon I was on my way, alone, to start work; I was thoroughly enjoying this break from the trenches; having regular food, and sleep in the bivouacs near to Englebelmer. The day was hot, the grass knee-high along the track across the fields to the RE workings. The sun was shining and the bees were humming as they dawdled among the red poppies and other wild flowers along this grassy path. Like the larks singing high in the blue sky, I thought they are not affected by the war. So the hum and dawdle among the wild flowers.

This vivid experience of nature in its simple summer beauty was like a sudden glimpse of my childhood in my parents' garden; it was a swift moment of vision, of normality seen retrospectively through the ugliness of war all around me. I was lulled into a false sense of security, and tempted to loiter along this pleasant grassy path, until I came to four huge howitzer craters, freshly made, and got a whiff of luddite on the summer air.

One of our planes came down in a cornfield near us. It landed all right, but as it ran along the ground after alighting, the growing corn became entangled in the landing wheels bringing the plane to such a sudden stop that it turned a somersault. We ran across to it, expecting to find the pilot

Private Sydney Fuller, 8th The Suffolk Regiment

*The smoking
remains of
a British
observation
balloon destroyed
over the Somme.*

The smoking remains of a British observation balloon destroyed over the Somme.

killed, but he was only badly bruised. Asked if he was all right, he said he had hurt his back, but that he 'guessed it was more "wind up" than anything'. It had been hit by enemy anti-aircraft shells. One splinter had gone through the engine.

26th June: Fine day. Enemy planes rather more active than usual chasing some of our slow planes. Enemy guns very quiet. Our guns were very active, day and night. We watched a bombardment of an area near Ovillers by our heavy guns, and they certainly did raise some dust. Our own planes were out in scores, and I saw as many as twenty-four of them returning from far over German lines, at one time. Saw several scraps, one plane coming down near Thiepval, too far away to be identified as 'ours' or 'theirs'. One of ours was brought down by enemy AA shells, and landed somewhere near Albert. Saw great numbers of our propaganda balloons drifting over the enemy's lines, and dropping papers. I believe it was during the afternoon of this day that I watched an unusual bit of enemy anti-aircraft shelling. I first noticed just above the horizon behind the enemy's line, what appeared to be a cloud of black smoke. This drew nearer, and was soon seen to be composed of hundreds of enemy anti-

July 1918: an officer of the Royal Flying Corps shot down over German lines is given a respectful military funeral as children look on.

aircraft bursts, all to be concentrating on this one plane, for some reason, and they continued to do so until it was well over our lines and out of range. Although shells burst all round it, it did not appear to be hit. There was little wind, and when the plane had got over our lines safely, its trail was marked by a miles-long stream of black smoke, stretching away out of sight behind enemy lines. I often wondered, afterwards, what this plane had done to make the enemy so very anxious to prevent it returning to our lines.

Once the lines were static, 'normal' life resumed and, as had so often been the case, low-level fraternization took place. Where trenches were close, this might be as simple as a shouted 'Good morning, Fritz'. Sometimes, where close observation was restricted, fraternization went further.

30th June: A prisoner was brought down to Brigade Headquarters during the afternoon. He was a tall, fair, young man, a Saxon, said to belong to an enemy 'naval' division. He wore on his shoulder-straps a device consisting of crossed anchors, with a crown above them, all in yellow. He had been

Private Sydney Fuller, 8th The Suffolk Regiment

captured in Aveluy Wood, by means of what, in one sense, was a dirty trick. To explain the manner in which he was captured, it must also be explained that rather strange conditions had been developing in Aveluy Wood for some time. The 'front line' on both sides there consisted of isolated 'posts' among the brushwood that had grown up since 1916. The enemy's posts and our own were very near each other, but practically hidden from each other by the brushwood, which also hid them from behind on both sides. There soon began a policy of 'live and let live', in that particular spot. Soon they began to call across to each other, and before long the enemy and our own men were crawling out to meet one another in the brushwood, exchanging bread, tinned meat, and even photographs. This, according to my informant (one of the Norfolks who brought the prisoner down) took place between the visits of the officers on both sides, information as to visiting times being mutually exchanged.

I was told that two of our young 'new' men were climbing a tree in the wood one day, when the Germans made vigorous signs to them to 'come down'. The young men, not understanding, did not do so, and did not see the reason for the signs (an unexpected 'visit' by an enemy officer), until too late, and both were shot dead by the said enemy officer with an automatic pistol. At another time, enemy whiz-bangs began to drop among our 'posts' and our men shouted to 'Jerry' asking him 'what he was up to'. 'Jerry' understood, and sent up Very light signals indicating to his artillery that they were dropping their shells 'short', with the result that the shells were 'lifted' well beyond the 'posts'. This sort of thing had gone on until the 'Staff' had got to hear of it. They, of course, ordered that all fraternizing with the enemy was to cease, a prisoner being kept the next time they came across to our trenches. In accordance with these orders, the prisoner had been enticed over to our posts by an offer of half a loaf of white bread, and was then kept prisoner. When he understood that he was 'caught' he went into quite a rage, and he refused to give any information of the enemy's troops, dumps, etc., to our Intelligence Staff, when he reached Brigade Headquarters. How much of the story about the two young men climbing the tree, and about the shelling incident, was true, is uncertain, but it is certain there had been a good deal of fraternizing in the wood, for my informant showed me many German photographs, buttons, etc., he had obtained from Fritz. Also, the prisoner certainly was in quite a 'paddy' over his capture, refusing to speak to anyone. It is also certain that after the capture of the prisoner, the enemy became very nasty in the vicinity, using many trench-mortars, and causing many casualties where, before, it was very quiet indeed.

Throughout the Somme summer months, soldiers were billeted in or in the grounds of abandoned homes. On other occasions they lived cheek by jowl with French civilians who had clung onto their homes and farms just behind the line.

A damaged but repairable château being used by British officers as headquarters.

Gunner Raymond Gartrell, 10th Australian Field Artillery, sits amongst the debris of a partially ruined château near Villers-Bretonneux.

Lance Corporal Frederick Hodges, 10th The Lancashire Fusiliers

I used to wonder what the seigneur would say if he could see what had happened to his beautiful château, extensive grounds and gardens and the protecting high brick wall. On one of our working parties, when enemy shells were bursting with loud crashes in the street flanked by the high wall, our officer led us through the village by the back ways and gardens, and I had a good view in the moonlight of the smashed and broken château gardens, greenhouses, statues and summerhouses as we hurried through the tree stumps.

Lieutenant Ivan Simpson, 1st The Monmouthshire Regiment

I was at Company Headquarters seeing my skipper, when the Boche began a concentrated shoot on our unfortunate house. Never choose you HQ at a house by crossroads. After two and a half hours' bombardment, during which time we were unable to evacuate it, we were naturally not particularly cheery. By this time all the house was down on top of the cellar. Then a shell must have come clean through the roof and burst inside. I recovered consciousness to find that out of eleven in the cellar, my servant and my OC were alone unhurt. The rest were all killed except two, and they died within a few hours. We still could not move until dark, and then we got them down. My skipper went temporarily off his 'rocker', so, taking it all in all, I had a pretty close call. In consequence of this catastrophe, I have been running the company

The destruction of medieval churches on the Western Front appalled soldiers on both sides.

since then. Previous to this I was billeted at _____ with my battalion, and there I witnessed the interesting spectacle of the whole town ablaze. No words can describe the scene. After the war is over, I think I will resign my commission in the army, and take one in the Fire Brigade. To see a church, which dates back to 1388, simply wrapped in a sheet of flame, with 5.9 shells bursting round the tower, is enough to turn one positively sick.

Brigade Headquarters retired from the trench dugout and settled in the end house of the village, a white-walled, vine-clad building, with a courtyard and stables and a neat garden that only one Boche shell had smitten. On the door of the large room that we chose for the mess there still remained a request in French, written in a clear painstaking hand, that billeted officers should keep to the linoleum strips laid across the carpet when proceeding to the two inner rooms. But there was no linoleum now, and no carpet. On the otherwise bare wall was hung a massively framed portrait of the proprietor – a clean-shaven, middle-aged Frenchman of obviously high intelligence. A family press-cutting album contained an underlined report from a local newspaper of a concert given in the village on June 6th, 1914.

    One of our servants used to be a professional gardener, and in a couple of days he had weeded the paths and brought skill and knowledge to bear on the neglected vegetable beds. We had excellent salad from that garden and fresh strawberries, while there were roses to spare for the tall vases

Captain George Nicholls, C Battery, 82nd Brigade, Royal Field Artillery

All the creature comforts: an officer's billet occupied by 122 Siege Battery in the village of Gorre.

on the mantelpiece in the mess; and before we came away our gardener had looked to the future and planted lettuce and turnips and leeks, and even English pansies. The Boche gunners never got a line onto that house, and though aeroplanes cruised above us every night not a single bomb dropped near.

Sapper Albert Martin, 122nd Signal Company, Royal Engineers

Much ado over the Countess's Silver Spoons! A few days ago the Staff Officers had a tea party in the château grounds, a large number of officers being invited from the battalions. The Countess provided the necessary silver and crockery so that the business could be carried through in good style. After it was all over and the crockery was being returned to the Countess it was discovered that several solid silver teaspoons were missing. The old lady went up in the air about it – the Brigade Major circularized all the officers who had been present, the whole of the gardens and grounds were thoroughly searched but all was of no avail. Then the BM had us all on parade and, approaching the matter as tactfully as he could without openly accusing some person or persons unknown with wickedly stealing the things, suggested that if any of us could find these things would we, as honourable men, remember the great prestige of the British Army etc. etc., put them into a box which had been fixed in a certain place where absolute privacy was assured so that no other individual could see who the conscience stricken person was. This appeal was the very last forlorn hope for none of the Signals was anywhere near the tea party. It seems to be the general opinion that some of the officer guests 'swiped them up' as souvenirs and now are ashamed to own up to it. I am afraid the Countess can say a final farewell to them.

Captain George Nicholls, C Battery, 82nd Brigade, Royal Field Artillery

For several days Wilde, the signalling officer, and the [American] doctor conducted an acrid argument that arose from the doctor's astounding assertion that he had seen a Philadelphia baseball player smite a baseball so clean and hard that it travelled 400 yards before it pitched. Wilde, with supreme scorn, pointed out that no such claim had been made even for a golf ball. The doctor made play with the names of Speaker, Cobb, and the other transatlantic celebrities. Then one day Wilde rushed into the mess flourishing a London Sunday paper that referred in glowing terms to a mighty baseball hit of 136 yards, made on the Royal Arsenal football ground; after which the doctor retired to cope with the plaque of boils that had descended upon the brigade. This and a severe outbreak of Spanish flu provided him with a regular hundred patients a day.

Captain Nicholls had noted the growing presence of American soldiers in France, elevating a general feeling of optimism amongst British troops. 'Everyone,' he wrote, 'appeared possessed of a sane and calm belief that things would work out in the long run.' Unfortunately, it is believed that American soldiers also brought with them the strain of Spanish flu that was to cause the global pandemic that autumn, killing millions of people.

The battalion came down to a camp in Bernaville, where the majority of men promptly got laid up with influenza. We had heard that there was a great deal of this about and that it was seriously inconveniencing the Germans themselves in their offensives, but so far, as a unit, we had been remarkably free from the germs. Then they assailed us all at once. On the section, first one man and then another developed a high temperature,

Driver Aubrey Smith, 1/5th The London Regiment (London Rifle Brigade)

An officer of a mobile anti-aircraft gun relaxes next to covered boxes of ammunition. These guns proved to be more effective as a deterrent to enemy aircraft than in destroying them.

while in the camp where the companies were stationed whole hut-fulls succumbed to the illness so rapidly that within about two days the bulk of the regiment was temporarily *hors de combat*. The camp was like a field hospital, for, owing to the Casualty Clearing Station and Field Ambulance being overflowing with similar cases from all quarters, it was decided to treat most of them on the spot. Nevertheless quite a number of serious cases were carried off in motor ambulances, and we heard many of them proved fatal. So this was what warfare was bringing in its train!

There was something quite uncanny about the rapidity with which the flu seized its victims. But those who did not get it really badly were able to carry on after a few days.

The hiatus in fighting, while welcome, only seemed to make men wonder 'so, what now?' Had the Germans ended their campaigning? Were the Allies going to attack? After all, summer was campaigning season and not much was happening.

Driver Aubrey Smith, 1/5th The London Regiment (London Rifle Brigade)

The great question was: 'What would the enemy do next?' Time was slipping through his fingers. Our own losses in material and, to a large extent, in men had been made good, while Americans were arriving in incredible numbers. On the other hand, the cream of Ludendorff's officers and storm troops were already wiped out. … Miles behind the firing-line we passed a little village with American troops, who hurried to the roadside to watch us pass. Men fresh from the States, who had never been nearer to the war zone than they were at present, were drilling in these back areas, and it was inspiring to our men to see them. … It was comforting to feel that there was someone between our troops in the trenches and the deep blue sea.

Sapper Albert Martin, 122nd Signal Company, Royal Engineers

The [telephone] line was broken again this morning and of course I suspected the Yanks, and with good cause for I found that they had cut out about 20 yards of it to use as string. They seemed quite surprised to learn that they had caused any trouble.

A Frenchman's pack that was left behind here when we took possession [of the trenches] has not been claimed. We fetched it inside after the first night in case it should rain, but now that all the French troops have gone from the neighbourhood there is no chance of the owner turning up so today we opened it up and shared out its contents, the most acceptable items being five shirts. Fisher had three and I had two. Fisher went down to B Echelon this afternoon and brought back my spare valise. He has also been on the scrounge again and the result is that now we have a table, two chairs, a form and sundry boxes on which visitors are invited to rest their weary bones – also a table cloth – white with red markings – certainly it is in two pieces but neither piece is quite large enough to cover the whole table so we have to lap one over the other. In the centre of the table we have a vase of small marguerites and flaming poppies with a sprig or two of honeysuckle. The vase is an old 18-pounder shell case that we have polished up and made to look very smart.

Yesterday when searching the cupboards in the adjoining cottage we found some stuff that looked like cornflour. It was in a paper packet and from the reading matter thereon I concluded it was good to eat. My little French was not quite sufficient to make out whether it was to be used as a food or applied as a plaster, until I came to a phrase commencing '*Employé au lieu d'Arrowroot*'. Very good – but what about the milk? Some of the neighbouring farms are still occupied by the natives so Fisher set forth with a large can and in less than an hour he was back with it full of milk – about half a gallon.

The cottage supplied us with a cast-iron cooking pot – like a small witches' cauldron, and so I proceeded with the cooking. It was a great success and when it got cool it was real blancmange. We tasted it and found it very good so we issued only a very limited number of invitations to supper.

Milk can be obtained from the one cow on the farm, but no free issue. Having purchased *du lait*, my section scouts around the farm in the hope of locating chicken or other treasures which might be put to good use when darkness falls. We are like primitive man now, and if we are unable to purchase necessities, we 'scrounge' them, which to the mind of the serving soldier is quite legitimate as it often happens that money is worthless. On this farm, however, there is nothing to scrounge: troops have been here before, and Madame understands the psychology of the British soldier, and locks the cow up at night in case she strays. This is a wise precaution, for if Madame left it in the field at night it would be cooked meat by the

Private Christopher Haworth, 14th Princess Louise's (Argyll and Sutherland Highlanders)

'Milk can be
obtained from
the one cow on
the farm.'

morning. When a fellow has not tasted
meat since he left England, and is hungry
– and we are always hungry – it becomes
a natural instinct to kill the cow. …

We enter a house for a meal of
pommes de terre frites and *oeuf frites* – a
plate of chips and one egg – one franc.
The dining room is dirty – we are repelled
by the sight of big black gluttonous flies,
a solid mass covering the plates which
had been used by others.

'Hell!' exclaims Fraser. 'We can't eat
here.'

'It's the best you will get in this godforsaken place, Jock,' says a man
who is finishing a meal. 'All the other places are the same – covered with

*Any contraption
will suffice for a
cup of tea. Sadly,
this officer was
killed shortly
before the end of
the war.*

flies – they breed quicker here than lice on a soldier's shirt – and that's saying something!'

We do not like the idea but must feed, and having dined we get out quickly.

12th July: Had tea with the Brigadier and then dinner with the CO front-line battalion. It is really very amusing the way in which some of these old-time regulars endeavour to preserve their mess formalities. The dugout couldn't have been more than 10 feet square, and yet they managed to produce quite a respectable four-course dinner for seven officers. It was handed onto the table by a perspiring orderly, who crouched in the entrance to a tunnel which could not have exceeded 3ft by 4 ft. How the food was cooked I could never imagine, but the smells of cooking leaked out from behind the orderly, and somewhere in the depths of the blackness behind him there was a voice that swore, mightily and frequently. I judged that the Voice had produced the meal and also that it had been a hot job. Most of the soup got spilt before it left the end of the cavern, but the smell was excellent and gave us quite an appetite for the tinned salmon which followed. This had been brought up with ammunition and a bottle of execrable French vinegar from Division that very afternoon. The next course was excellent. Roast mutton, procured as the result of dark dealings with the ASC, fresh peas from heavens knows where, and lastly some sauce roulade from mint which they said had been growing last night in no-man's-land. The sweet was a treacle pudding. We drank thin whiskies and sodas which were distinctly lukewarm in spite of all the doctor's efforts to keep the stuff cool. All things considered, a very enjoyable meal and a great credit to the Voice.

Second Lieutenant George Atkinson, 91st Field Company, 2nd Army, Royal Engineers

The morrow turned out a fine, dry day and my guest duly arrived. He established his bona fides without difficulty. I cannot remember his name but he was a nice looking person, dark-haired, with a heavy moustache, and I explained the situation as fully and as frankly as I could. Then we adjourned for lunch to the hut and the soup was served. Suddenly I heard the sobbing noise of an arriving shell followed by the distinctive 'phut' at the end of its journey. I said nothing but slipped out and asked the sentry where that one had gone. But he avowed he had heard nothing and

Second Lieutenant John MacDermott, 51st Machine Gun Battalion, 51st Highland Division

I went back to my soup. Soon exactly the same thing occurred again and I slipped out only to get the same answer from the same sentry who was a trustworthy fellow. Perplexed, I returned to my soup only to hear another one on the way. I looked straight across at my companion determined to get his confirmation of the sound and, instead, had the whole phenomenon explained without a word said! My visitor was supping his soup with gusto through his moustache and as the spoon emptied there came that sad, warning 'phut'. I was just able to avoid comment. The 'shelling' finished with the soup and so far as I am aware my visitor never knew of the apprehension he had caused.

Allied forces had engaged in a series of small-scale raids – passive penetration, the Australians called it – that had begun to bully the enemy, nibbling away at German ground and spirits. One significant assault on 4 July by the Anzacs at the village of Le Hamel and a neighbouring hill had been a resounding success, encouraging the development of bigger plans. A new large-scale assault was coming and British infantry officers and NCOs were tasked with battle training.

Corporal Fred Hodges, 10th The Lancashire Fusiliers

How beautiful were those early hours before the heat of the day; how full of life we were. Reveille at 5 am, breakfast at 5.30 am; and it was a good breakfast, berghu [porridge] and then bacon; with the bacon fat as a dip for our bread. Fall-in at 6 am, and then we marched to the woods, where wild strawberries grew thickly in large brambly clumps between the rides which dissected the wood. Our senior officers, the Colonel, Major and Adjutant, mounted on their well-groomed chargers, rode up and down the grassy rides directing operations. We advanced this way and that in short rushes as per the Infantry Field Manual, led by our platoon officers and NCOs.

It was quite good fun. It certainly did little to prepare us for the capture of the blasted, leafless area which had once been Aveluy Wood, which, as we had seen on our night patrols from the trenches, was a foul ruin of shattered tree stumps and stinking shell holes. Here, in Toutencourt Wood, the trees were alive and leafy; and as we lay in the rides and among the tangled undergrowth waiting for the next order, we could eat the wild strawberries. …

Having had good food and regular sleep during this period of so-called battle training in perfect summer weather, we felt strong and very fit. As I looked at my sunburned companions I could not help thinking how sad it was that such strong happy healthy youngsters were training for battle, for wounds and death. Of course, I kept these thoughts to myself, and joined in the laughter and jokes as we stood in line in the hot sunshine waiting for our turn to use the new Egg bombs. There was to me a deep poignancy about this happy scene – a group of lively youngsters, having a break from war, yet training for war.

Overleaf:
Summer sun: British officers of an anti-aircraft battery enjoying an afternoon tipple. The man on the right wears slippers and pyjamas. Slippers and two pairs of pyjamas were a requirement for officers' overseas kit. Note the upturned telephone cable drum used as a table.

5. Turning the Tide

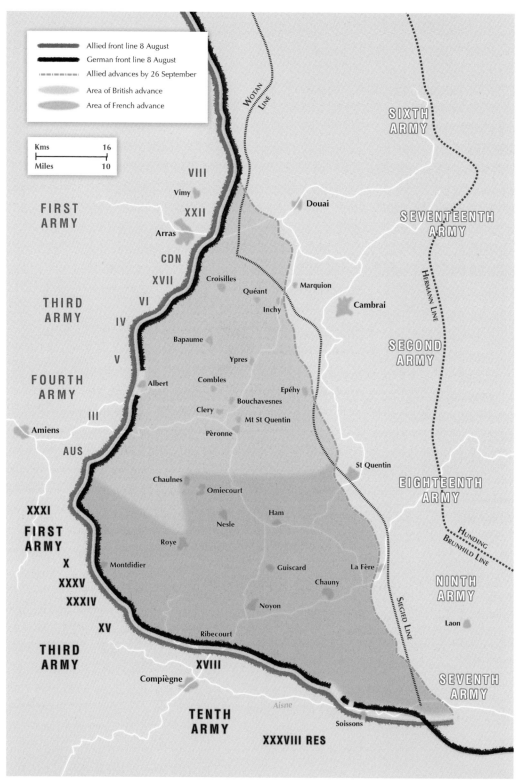

The British Push, August–September.

'During May and June we accepted it that our role would be to stick it out until the Americans came along en masse in 1919. The swift and glorious reversal of things from August onwards surprised no one more than the actual fighting units of the British armies.'

Captain George Nicholls, C Battery, 82nd Brigade, Royal Field Artillery

———

We have left the back area, and come nearer the line. I went to a battalion concert. There was a screamingly funny man, and said,

'No, I ain't none of yer Mons 'eroes.

No I ain't none of your Kitchener's Harmy torts,

And I ain't a Derby Scheme.

I didn't put me name down and I 'ope I wouldn't be called up.

No – I waited till they came and fetched me, they 'ad *to drag* me up.'

After the concert a lieutenant back from leave addressed us. He was very good-looking, dark and smiling, and full of life. He said that the back areas were swarming with Yanks, and they were full of beans and wanting to get stuck into old Jerry. He said they'd soon be in it with us, and what was more important, Jerry knew of these millions of Yanks, and was hopelessly discouraged. He said that Jerry knew it was all up. We felt terrifically glad. But an old sweat said, 'Talkie-talkie; that means we're for it.'

Private Reginald Kiernan, 7th The Leicestershire Regiment

By this stage of the war, the Line had acquired its own history, and the small minority of men in the battalion who had fought in some of the great battles of 1915, 1916 and 1917 spoke of those days as history. 'When we were in the old front line', they would say, meaning before our big Somme Offensive in 1916. Or, they would say, 'Oh that was before Jerry pulled back to the Hindenburg Line in March 1917' or, 'When we came back the first time from Ypres to the Somme.'

Lance Corporal Frederick Hodges, 10th The Lancashire Fusiliers

This was not a war of endless blood, mud and misery. The officers are enjoying bottles of Haig & Haig whisky. Note the soda siphon on the right.

To us, the young soldiers of 1918, whose task it was to finish the war, those old days were indeed simply history. I had read the newspaper accounts of these old battles; I was familiar with all the famous place names, and now here I was on the very spot where some of those old battles had taken place.

Now, they told us, WE were going to finish it. The thinly held Line of General Gough's 5th Army of 21st March was now heavily reinforced. We had held and contained that great work, despite our heavy losses, and NOW, the tide was about to turn.

On 4 August, the fourth anniversary of the outbreak of war, the weather markedly improved after a damp end to July. It was now warm and dry. Unbeknown to all, the last phase of the war was about to begin. As a prelude, the army exhorted all the men to keep their counsel in coming operations.

Slips or leaflets were pasted in our paybooks. On the slips was printed an exhortation:

KEEP YOUR MOUTH SHUT!
The success of any operation we carry out depends chiefly on surprise.

DO NOT TALK.
When you know that your Unit is making preparations for an attack, don't talk about them to men in other Units or to strangers, and keep your mouth shut, especially in public places.

Do not be inquisitive about what other Units are doing; if you hear or see anything, keep it to yourself.

If you hear anyone else talking about operations, stop him at once.

The success of the operations and the lives of your comrades depends upon your SILENCE.

If you ever should have the misfortune to be taken prisoner, don't give the enemy any information beyond your rank and name. In answer to all other questions you need only say, 'I cannot answer.'

He cannot compel you to give any other information. He may use threats. He will respect you if your courage, patriotism, and self-control do not fail. Every word you say may cause the death of one of your comrades.'

Private Sydney Fuller, 8th The Suffolk Regiment

Anything out of the ordinary always attracted attention, and rumours quickly grew and spread if there was an inkling of what was on. Our sense grew that something big was about to happen because there was evidence of strict security. The Mounted Military Police were much in evidence on the 6th and 7th [August]. When we came to Heilly there was an Expeditionary Force Canteen with a crowd of men around it. When we tried to approach we were stopped by the Mounted Military Police and prevented from even speaking to the New Zealanders crowding round it. The Anzacs had been secretly moved south for their attack on August 8th, and we were being moved south to mop up.

Lance Corporal Frederick Hodges, 10th The Lancashire Fusiliers

The attack on the Somme would use British, Anzac, Canadian and French troops: Allies co-operating together in an 'All Arms Operation': infantry, aircraft, artillery, cavalry and tanks working in unison supported and orchestrated by the full use of modern battlefield technologies. The assault, for example, would be greatly enhanced by the destruction or suppression of enemy artillery. This would be made possible by sound-ranging and flash-spotting, improved methods of identifying and accurately locating enemy batteries. The lessons in suppressing enemy strongpoints and accurate counter-battery artillery fire at Le Hamel on 4 July were to be integrated into the scheme, while experts from each of the arms were consulted in the planning process: on the advice of the Tanks Corps, far more tanks would be deployed in the operations than hitherto proposed. There would be no preliminary bombardment to alert the enemy to an attack; rather, a creeping barrage would be employed. Accurate and intensive artillery fire, mixing high explosive and gas shells, would be crucial to success. Above, aircraft of the RAF would strafe the enemy while conducting vitally important reconnaissance. Allied forces on the ground would be aided by significant air superiority. Nothing was left to chance; everything was meticulously evaluated and considered.

Lance Corporal Frederick Hodges, 10th The Lancashire Fusiliers

By our British conventions, they (Australians) were totally uninhibited, having grown up in a society unhampered by a class system. Army regulations, and especially saluting officers, were irksome to them, and they often expressed contempt for the British Tommy's rigid respect for

Australian infantrymen stand next to a British Mark IV tender (supply tank) lying idle near Villers-Bretonneux.

officers. 'None of your Tommy officers for us,' they boasted, 'we pick our own – the best soldiers from the ranks.'

I sat near a noisy group of Aussies one day listening to their backchat with one another; they were always cracking jokes and laughing; they were very witty. I was surprised to see that their colonel was one of them, in all but rank; they chatted and laughed with him quite informally, calling him Dick. As the group broke up, still cracking jokes, their colonel, a lean tanned tough looking man over 6 feet tall, strolled away laughing with no salutes exchanged, just a friendly wave of the hand.

The Aussies couldn't be regimented; they were individualists and their independent spirit was very effective in attack because they acted without waiting for orders during the ever-changing circumstances of battle.

This apparent lack of discipline did not sit well with all men due to fight alongside Australian troops. Prior to the attack, Lieutenant Bion accompanied fellow officer Lieutenant Hauser of the Tank Corps to a meeting at Brigade Headquarters.

It was a large tent, full of officers; they were all Tank Corps. Whatever kind of show required the whole Tank Corps in support?

'They must be arranging to end the war,' said Hauser sarcastically.

Silence fell on us. The General was speaking. 'On your left, extending as far as Villers-Bretonneux, will be the Australian Corps.'

Christ! Those bastards! We did not love the Australians. There had been a local attack, which was a failure, in which tanks had taken an even worse beating than usual because the Australians had gone too far and too fast without mopping up. Uncleared-up anti-tank guns had therefore arisen behind them and destroyed the tanks.

'Those bloody tanks,' said the Australians, 'too slow, too damned

Lieutenant Wilfred Bion, 5th Battalion, Tank Corps

A officer of the Royal Field Artillery sits in an office surrounded by maps, orders and messages.

Tank 9352, Neptune, 14th Battalion, Tank Corps, broke down between the first and second objectives on 8 August and was finally knocked out crossing the Hindenburg Line on 27 September. The officer may be its commander, Charles Gordon Macdonald.

cowardly to keep up. We had broken right through! Where were the tanks? Nowhere – as usual!'

As I say, we did not love each other. For us, their magnificent indiscipline was just indiscipline, paid for in blood – Tank Corps blood. …

The 'lecture' went on; it was not interesting, not novel. The tent was hot, but we listened. The river Luce ran across and parallel to the 5th Battalion front; there was not much water in it. In fact it was not an obstacle; 5th Battalion would find out if it was swampy. In any case there was a brick bridge across it and the 5th would cross by that. The bridge of course was not standing – it had been blown to bits when our line was stabilized at the end of the March 31st show. Still, the rubble might stiffen it up a bit. It would be much safer than anywhere else. Though of course the enemy would shell it … and so forth. He droned on.

'The 1st Battalion will …' I could relax, go to sleep even? Better not.

Private Sydney Fuller, 8th The Suffolk Regiment

8th August: Finished laying the lines shortly before dawn (3.10 am). Our aeroplanes were about, over the trenches, long before this, their engines drowning the noise made by our tanks as they crawled up to their positions for the 'kick-off'. The barrage opened at 4.20 am, rather raggedly. I got a little sleep in a dugout, but about 6.30 am my eyes began to be troublesome – just soreness at first, then a sensation as if I had got grit or sand in them. This gradually got worse. I saw several prisoners go past –

some of them very young men, 16–18 years old. Nearly all were wounded. Many of their steel helmets were 'camouflage' painted. A few (first aid men or stretcher-bearers) had a Red Cross painted on the front of the helmet. My eyes were now too bad to see what their shoulder-strap numbers were.

If Fuller was having problems seeing because of gas, the tank commanders poised to advance could see almost nothing because of fog.

No one had mentioned fog. There could not be a fog; the river, the banks, the low ground, all were as dry as a bone. I myself had seen it. Why, oh why, had I not reported back from the reconnaissance that there was a danger of fog? I could see the report: 'An experienced Tank Corps officer had been sent forward to examine and report on the suitability of the terrain for tanks. Unfortunately he thought of absolutely everything and even noticed that there was no water in the river bed, but still failed to see the obvious point that since the water had abandoned the river, it must have taken to the air.' There it was – thick, solid, impenetrable.

'Now what?' said Carter. I heard my own voice talking. 'Let's go and have a look.' We walked down and came to a wall. The next step and we were trying to see our hands. At arm's length they were out of sight.

The first tank had stopped with engine throbbing. There was the whine of a shell and the burst – a five-nine.

Lieutenant Wilfred Bion, 5th Battalion, Tank Corps

We walked on through the gun lines conversing by gestures, and as the dawn began to break could see occasional tanks through the mist in front of us. After walking for about fifteen minutes, during which period I had my prismatic compass glued to my nose, we struck the main road and walked on down it. The mist was very thick and any number of people were lost. We were amazed to see a tank coming towards us, closed down and looking very ugly. With some trepidation I approached and halted it, and learnt that Lieutenant Cornish, the commander, thought that he was approaching the German lines, and he gave me a few hot words about foolish bravado in exposing myself. I managed to convince him that half an hour spent in swinging his compass and correcting it would have saved him from an anti-climax, and turning him round on the road, I waved him on in front of me.

Major Norman Dillon, 2nd Battalion, Tank Corps

An evocative image of the Royal Berkshire Regiment advancing over open ground, 8 August. The image has been doubly exposed, giving this slightly haunted effect.

The fog may have caused confusion and temporarily halted progress, but it was about the only thing to hinder the Allied advance that day. Clearly Bion had been too hard on himself, and once the fog lifted, the tanks came into their own.

Lieutenant Wilfred Bion, 5th Battalion, Tank Corps

All our objectives had been taken and the infantry, gunners, engineers and signals were in pursuit. For the first time our surviving tank commanders could meet as a victorious unit with less than one out of three killed. Unlike Cambrai there was no point on our front where we had been checked. The army was far beyond its day's objectives.

Private Sydney Fuller, 8th The Suffolk Regiment

Cook, Carter, Robertson, Aitches and I stood beneath a tree. 'Look there!' said Carter pointing back down the road to Amiens. 'Reserves!'

We had not seen reserves before. The road was a mass of troops stretching mile after mile down to the valley of the Luce. Here and there transport and guns had left the road to press on faster than the infantry. It was a clear, sunny afternoon. On the hard ground the gunners, the horse limbers, had nothing to prevent them from travelling fast on the wide open spaces. I had not seen troops marching in column since Le Havre. It was a marvellous sight. …

The Battle of Amiens, August 1918: German prisoners help a wounded comrade through the streets of Bellicourt.

That night the sky in front was lit up by fires, not ours but the enemy's, as the retreating troops set fire to their dumps; for once it did not signify disaster. It might earlier have been a sign for rejoicing, but now it was only a sign for 'what next?'

Casualties were relatively light for such an operation and fortunately Private Sydney Fuller's sight, while temporarily affected, was not permanently damaged. Nevertheless, he had been rendered almost useless on the day.

The dressing-station was in the quarry, and I had my eyes treated several times. The treatment consisted of swabbing the eyeball with a small piece of cotton-wool that had been dipped in a solution of carbonate of soda. This completely stopped the pain for a short time, but each time, it got worse, until ordinary daylight could not be borne, and I could only keep my eyes closed. The burning 'gritty' feelings made one want to rub the eyes hard, yet they were too sore to be touched. Many of our casualties were caused by this gas. Eventually my eyes became so bad that I was quite useless, and was sent back to our old headquarters with another signaller who was in a similar state. It took us a long time to get back, as we could only see a short distance

Private Sydney Fuller, 8th The Suffolk Regiment

from our feet, and were in consequence continually getting in front of guns, missing our way etc. Heard that all objectives had been gained.

Lance Corporal
Fred Hodges,
10th The
Lancashire
Fusiliers

On August 9th we followed the Aussies, mopping up over the ground they had just captured. We were amazed and thrilled at the depth of penetration, 5 miles deep in the German line. This had previously been unheard of. When eventually we came to some German field guns, we swarmed round them, laughing and talking excitedly to one another. Scrawled on them in white chalk were the words 'Captured by the 1st AIF.' We were delighted and said, 'Good old Aussies!'

The Battle of Amiens was an astonishing success and the beginning of the end for Germany, as privately acknowledged by General Ludendorff. He would write that 'August 8th was the black day of the German Army in the history of this war', a telling statement after four years of thrust and counter-thrust and vacillating fortunes. The Germans could only hope to delay defeat and pray terms might be offered that forestalled a complete capitulation. Allied forces had advanced up to 8 miles, and 27,000 German casualties had resulted, just over half taken prisoner of war. Allied casualties were around a third of those of the enemy, a dramatic turn-around from the days when those who went forward suffered disproportionate losses compared to those who stayed put. Recovered ground on the Somme, as further north at Arras, was quickly revisited by refugees keen to return home.

German POWs captured in the summer of 1918 safe behind barbed wire near the French coast.

The corn in the surrounding fields is now almost ripe 'unto harvest'. The whole countryside was under cultivation right up to Fritz's advance in April, consequently the front-line trenches run amid the waving corn. This makes operations more difficult, as it affords shelter to creeping and crawling troops. There have been a few raids by both sides and on several occasions Germans have been found hiding in the corn well behind our front line. The farmer who owns this land came over today with his wife, presumably to have a look at the crops. I could not make out where they are living now but it seems that they cleared out from here very hurriedly last April, but the ripening corn induces them to come back to gather the harvest. Of course the Government is doing all it can to persuade the farmers to reap all the corn possible and the British Army is supplying men to help.

Sapper Albert Martin, 122nd Signal Company, Royal Engineers

One morning, shortly after our arrival, I heard a strange noise outside and saw an old Frenchman with a horse and plough going along the pavé in the general direction of Arras. This was an unusual sight, but on enquiry there was nothing really strange about it. French civilians often seemed to get recent news quickly and this Frenchman explained his presence by

Second Lieutenant John MacDermott, 51st Machine Gun Battalion

As the Germans withdrew, civilians reoccupied their land. French women working near the Somme village of Ribemont.

saying that he had heard that the front had been pushed forward in the neighbourhood of the Scarpe, that his farm was in that part and that he thought the sooner he started his ploughing the better! In fact there had been such an advance of a limited kind, but things were very far from permitting agricultural activities and the old farmer had to go back.

I think his optimism after four years of war reflected a growing feeling of confidence which many of us shared. It depended not so much on hard, detailed news as on the fact that we had seen the enemy depart, albeit reluctantly and with much pushing.

Sapper Albert Martin, 122nd Signal Company, Royal Engineers

17th August: The civilians are cutting the corn – two women and a man are engaged in the business all day long. Where they go at night is a mystery. All day long they are in full view of Fritz but he has left them alone – yet they are in the midst of Fritz's legitimate objectives – and shells are no respecters of persons. One of their carts, loaded high with wheat, broke my [telephone] line where it was carried on high poles across a roadway. It was useless to try and erect the poles again so I came back for a pick-axe and then buried the cable under the roadway. This comic air-line requires some attention. On an average I have had to go out and mend a break about four times a week; only about half of them are due to shellfire.

Second Lieutenant John MacDermott, 51st Machine Gun Battalion

The trenches north of the Scarpe, both old and new, constituted a Labyrinth and one could not wander far without the appropriate trench map. I recollect going out one day with a sergeant to inspect part of the trench system which had recently changed hands after being in German occupation for the most of a year. Little attempt had been made to adapt the position to what might be regarded as the enemy's requirements. The British trench names, painted on metal strips, had been removed but could generally be found stuck behind the riveting a few feet away. And the British fire-steps had been left facing east. On the fire-step we were passing was a German stick grenade with its wooden handle pointing invitingly towards the trench, and round the explosive canister at the end of the handle perhaps half a dozen other canisters had been wired on. I thought how heavy it must be to throw and stretched out my hand. Immediately, and without any ceremony, the sergeant struck down my arm and told me quite clearly that that was a well-known type of booby trap.

Not far from there I had occasion to look over the parapet towards the wire in front which had been our wire when erected. The flutter of a piece of cloth caught my attention and I found lying close together the skeletal remains of several Highlanders with kilts and tunics still recognisable. The booby trap had pointed to no new enemy characteristic, but the rest of what I saw held a glimmer of hope. It was not just that the Germans had been holding the line very lightly: there must have been something eating into their morale as well. Perhaps our troops were not as highly trained, but I'm pretty certain that if the roles had been reversed with the 51st manning that trench for months, they would have put it to rights and given decent burial to the dead.

The advances made by British and Empire troops in August had been exhilarating but the men were still fighting under extraordinary levels of severe and nervous strain. In such an atmosphere, some men thought about their lives: who they now were, what they had become, and the civilian life that might yet be on offer. Second Lieutenant MacDermott lay in a dugout and looked towards a brighter future by briefly contemplating his peaceful past.

I had awakened early in an upper berth in a dugout cut out of the chalk and began to wonder how much my brief military career had put my earlier education out of mind. A wooden beam supporting the roof ran across just in front of my face. I picked a piece of chalk out of the wall and determined to see if I could write along the beam the formula of the binomial theorem which I used to know off by heart. I started only to stick in the middle and all efforts to get further failed. This was quite a shock. At the time I vowed that, if I got through, I would send for my algebra and refresh my mind on things already learnt and forgotten.

Second Lieutenant John MacDermott, 51st Machine Gun Battalion

An officer from the 1/4th Yorkshire Regiment sits inside an elephant iron shelter.

Some managed to do quite a lot of reading on active service, but I was never able to do much of it, partly because there were so many distractions and interruptions and partly because it was virtually impossible to take along with one anything of bulk or sufficient to give a reasonable choice. I only took two books abroad: the first an 'Active Service' New Testament with a printed message from Lord Roberts and an inscription from my father; and the second a small anthology of English poetry. They did not take up much space and I did not profit from them as I should, but they were a lifeline to better things, to all that was worth striving for, and to our hopes for the future when we had time and inclination to think about it.

Sapper Albert Martin, 122nd Signal Company, Royal Engineers

We are not what we were. We are not individuals that walked and talked and went about our lawful occasions in peacetime. Those persons have faded out of existence – we have reverted almost to a semi-savage state. The thin veneer of civilization has been washed away leaving revealed primitive human instincts that at one time we would scarcely have acknowledged. I am quite certain that Man is much nearer the savage than is generally admitted. Brought up in the ease, comfort and conventions of a civilized State we accepted the veneer for the substance. But now we are up against the stark realities of existence. We have experienced real hunger, real fatigue and real horror, and we begin to appreciate the full meaning of 'the struggle for existence' and 'the survival of the fittest'. Animal instincts rise up within us in a manner almost terrifying. We feel but little removed from the wild beasts that prey and are preyed upon. A mixed multitude of primeval passions surge in our hearts. Yet they are kept in check. The social training of generations has proved effective in the main issues but how much our self-control is influenced by the knowledge of the support of civilization behind us it is impossible to say. We regard ourselves rather as detached personalities. Sapper Martin is not the respectable law-abiding Mr Martin of pre-war days. They are quite distinct personalities and are apt to eye each other rather contumeliously at times. Hunger, thirst and fear are fundamental realities and the natural passions that arise from them must be experienced before they can be appreciated.

Slowly and surely I am breaking up, and now I am so far gone that it is too much trouble to go sick. I am just carrying on like an automaton, mechanically putting up wire and digging ditches while I wait, wait, wait for something to happen – relief, death, wounds, anything, anything in earth or hell to put an end to this, but preferably death. I am becoming hypnotized with the idea of Nirvana – sweet, eternal nothingness. My body crawls with lice, my rags are saturated with blood, and we all 'stink like the essence of putrefaction rotting for the third time'.

And there are ladies at home who still call us heroes and talk of the Glory of War – Christ!

Last night something went wrong in my head. A machine gun was turned on us, and instead of ducking I remember standing up and being quite interested in watching the bullets kick sparks off the wire – Day pulled me down into a hole and has been watching me ever since.

Second Lieutenant George Atkinson, 91st Field Company, 2nd Army, Royal Engineers

A gun belonging to 218 Siege Battery is manhandled into position.

If ever again I hear anyone say anything against a man for incapacitating himself in any way to get out of this I will kill that man. Not even Almighty God can understand the effort required to force oneself back into the trenches at night – I would shoot myself if it were not for the thought of my father.

With every infantry forward leap, it would take time for the artillery, especially the heavy artillery, to catch up. Lines of supply would have to be extended over captured ground, bringing forward quantities of food, water and fuel, and ammunition. Lines of communication would need to be run forward: it was always a huge logistical challenge, particularly as Allied troops re-entered the old Somme battlefield of 1916, that old cratered world, cross-cut with old trenches and workings.

While 8 August had been highly successful, the number of tanks knocked out or disabled owing to mechanical failure had been high. Just a third of the 415 tanks deployed were available the next day. When Lieutenant Bion was ordered to take the 5th Battalion's serviceable tanks into action in a divisional assault near Méaulte, only four of the unit's thirty-six tanks were on hand, and none was from his own section. For this reason Bion would not be in a tank himself but on foot. Much was being asked of this experienced officer for he was also going into battle feeling decidedly ill and in the knowledge that a pass was in his pocket giving him leave to England.

Lieutenant Wilfred Bion, 5th Battalion, Tank Corps

I remember little except feeling ill and tired. … I was vomiting badly; I did not know till the day before the attack that I had contracted the influenza which had appeared as an unknown pandemic inflicting all armies. I was at divisional HQ trying to absorb my orders when a medical officer saw me looking ill and diagnosed the infection. He advised me to take a couple of bottles of champagne into action – 'Your runner can carry it.' 'And if it makes me drunk?' 'Then he can carry *you*.'

Luckily the orders were simple – drive from our starting point towards the enemy and go on from there; then stop. At least, that was what I thought they were as I contemplated my trembling hands; not fear this time – fever.

It was a hot day. The rolling devastated region of Méaulte shimmered in the heat. I sweated and trembled and staggered about till I found myself back with the camouflaged tanks.

This time the action was to start at 'dawn'. ... All watches were precisely synchronized. We all – tanks, gunners, infantry, the whole division – attacked at the same moment.

The first thing of which I have any recollection is sitting in an infantry trench, pausing before making an advance. The sun was hot. The camouflaged tanks at which I had arrived the previous evening were somewhere in the battle. I could not see them. My two runners had one bottle of champagne for which they showed some solicitude though they seemed more concerned for me. ...

Someone was blowing a whistle. We all scrambled out of the trench, my two runners shoving and pulling me.

Time to advance. I felt extremely fit; it seemed queer but unmistakable that the battle was doing me a lot of good. There were a number of wounded, ours, not German; I thought it strange that they were in grotesque positions.

The enemy had gone, leaving the position to be held by a small rearguard with high velocity guns whose shells had [an] unpleasant quality – the whizzes arriving after the bangs. So one could not duck as one heard the shell approaching. This explained why the infantry lay about in grotesque attitudes and groaned.

A tank lumbers forward near Monchy-le-Preux, Arras. Note the crashed aircraft in the middle distance.

Gun-laying inside a Mark IV British tank. During action, the hot, stinking conditions inside made life nigh intolerable for the six-man crew.

At last I saw one of the tanks. It had stopped; the petrol feed had broken down.

'Come on!'

'Where to, sir?'

'Where to? In, of course. We'll ride the rest of the way.' They probably thought I was drunk. I told the tank commander to carry on as before when he had got it started again. Just then it *did* start, so suddenly that he was hurled against the sharp edge of the ammunition racks. The blow was on his temple and he lay there unconscious. I took command of the tank.

The summer weather and the heat of the tank's engine, the stench of petrol and petrol fumes made conditions inside the vehicle almost unbearable.

Lieutenant Wilfred Bion, 5th Battalion, Tank Corps

Nobody was about, certainly no enemy. Even the lack of mud gave a nightmare quality to the drive, for in real battles one did not travel fast and easily across rolling downland unopposed. Nor did one go for rides in tanks if one felt ill and bright-eyed.

I turned to shout to the driver. 'Lots of sausage balloons up.' I pointed to the long array of dark shapes looming almost overhead. Funny the way German observation balloons always looked so dark compared with our silvery shapes. …

I tried to be jocular. 'Do you know,' I shouted, 'I get the feeling we are being fired at!'

The driver looked tense and pale. He must be tired, I thought.

'It's those balloons sir.'

Of course – it had not occurred to me! We were under direct observation; they must be concentrating on us. But in that case why were there no shells bursting round us?

'Get out!' I shouted. 'All of you! Walk close behind.' They tumbled out. I took over driving the tank, meaning to drive a zigzag course with the escape hatch over me open. Then I realized that with no crew I could not steer the tank and could not drive anywhere but straight ahead. I had no sense of fear. I opened the throttle so that the tank was at full speed.

Before I knew what I was doing I had left the driver's seat and joined the crew behind. It was difficult to keep up with the fast-moving driverless tank. Then, only then, panic overwhelmed me. Suppose they were not firing at us? Suppose they did not hit us? A fully equipped tank in complete working order would have been handed over to the enemy, abandoned on my order by its crew.

I could not catch up with it; as I stumbled and tried to run to the door I fell. Then mercifully the shell hit, pierced and burst. The tank stopped, flames spurting everywhere. In a moment it was a total wreck.

I felt bemused, unable to grasp what had happened. I only knew that I had failed in my desperate resolve to get back to the tank. Had I succeeded I could not possibly have survived. Every course I had initiated had almost immediately seemed to be an irretrievable blunder. …

We worked our way back through the high velocity area, through the zone of shelled men, back to… And then I remembered I had on me my leave pass which the Colonel had caused to be dated as valid from 4.30 that day. I was to be picked up by a box-body car at the crossroads of the village from which our attack had started. Such a point, well marked, easy to refer to by map reference co-ordinates, would be the focus of attention by enemy gunners. At that crossroads I was to remain till picked up – alive or dead.

The sun was still high. I leant against the warm brickwork and waited. The shelling was not heavy but it was accurate and monotonous. It blasted the houses of that crossroads; they were rhythmically blotted out. I did not want to miss the box-body. I sat down on a chunk of masonry.

The gun – I decided that it must have been a single one – was firing at extreme range or I would not have been able to hear its shells coming. I decided to lie down to save myself the bother of throwing myself flat each time. How boring it all was. I thought I heard the box-body coming. The driver was driving like hell. I also heard the shell coming – like hell. I thought it would be a dead heat.

As the smoke and rubble dust cleared I saw the box-body, stationary, with racing engine. I scrambled into the back. 'Home, John!' I bawled. By the time the next shell arrived we were clear of the crossroads and a hundred yards away on the road to Boulogne.

By good fortune, Bion's trip to England was uninterrupted. Indeed, the journey was so seamless and efficient that by four-thirty the next afternoon he was in London and 'in the terminal stages of a Turkish bath near Russell Square'. The abrupt departure from the battlefield with all its accompanying horrors to a world of public gentility was impossible to adjust to and the 'chatter' of ill-informed civilians excruciating to listen to.

Lieutenant
Wilfred Bion,
5th Battalion,
Tank Corps

It was quiet and two old fellows were discussing an item in the evening paper.

'I see,' said one mellow voice to the other, 'we've been over the top again.' There was a note of complacency, of pride in his voice.

How nonplussed he would have been if he had known that one of 'us' was listening, hot, indignant. 'We' indeed! Who the hell was he to say 'we'? Now I can understand the genuine note of sadness for the comradeship that has passed him by, though it surprises me that I think of 'comradeship' in this context at all. I have no memory of thinking of the men of my crews in that action. I must have told them to report back to Company HQ. I remember joining with another crew who were going out of action with their tank – the only one, as it turned out, to survive the action – because I had to refuse a terribly mangled infantry soldier a lift. He was grotesque. ... He should have made me laugh if only I had retained my prep school sense of humour about physical deformity. 'Hullo, fig-ear,' we said – if we were big enough to be safe from retaliation – to a boy whose ears bore a striking resemblance to that fruit. Or, 'Look sharp Hobson!' to a boy whose features were so distorted that he was known as 'hatchet face'. What fun, what wit! If only one could have seen the funny side of a grown man with his trousers full of faeces because his leg had been blown past his ear! Of course all that had been at four-thirty yesterday. At four-thirty today I was very comfortable in my Turkish bath.

'Mother, Mother... You will write to my mother, sir, won't you?'

'No, blast you, I shan't! Shut up! Can't you see I don't want to be disturbed?'

These old ghosts, they never die. They don't even fade away; they preserve their youth wonderfully. Why, you can even see the beads of sweat, still fresh, still distinct, against the pallor of their brows. How is it done? Like the dewdrops on the petals of Rédouté's roses. Marvellous isn't it? So, so ... death-like, isn't it? But of course it's just a trick – he's not really dead, you know. Please, *please* shut up. I will write, I really will. ...

The Turkish bath was very refreshing; I felt so clean. It's not *real*, you know; just a kind of trick. Really, of course, one stinks. They have a way of making people look so life-like, but really we are dead. I? Oh yes, I died – on August 8th 1918. We all had a good laugh about it at the Club where the rats – there was one old Chap, bald, bloated, corpse-fed, who sat on my chest one night – it made me laugh because his whiskers tickled my face. ...

'Are you all right?' I awoke with a jolt, sense of humour all gone, to find the bath attendant peering into my face. 'Excuse me sir, but I think you must have been dreaming.' I hurried. I had not left much time to catch my train to Cheltenham, where my mother was staying to be near my sister at school.

Cheltenham was very beautiful. The weather was good too. The shops were very nice. I liked the school too; that, I thought, was very nice when I went to hear a school concert. I often said so when people asked me. I think they wanted me to be enjoying my leave, not to be dwelling too much on what I suppose they thought were the horrors of war. In fact I was not dwelling on the horrors of anything. Yes, I certainly thought Cheltenham was very nice. I stressed how 'very nice it was'. But although I did my best I seemed unable to convey a convincing degree of appreciation. Once only I felt I had established an emotional contact and that with a maiden lady, Miss Collar, with whom I had stayed on my holidays from school when my parents were not in England.

Miss Collar was a stout lady who wore pince-nez which were always highly polished and added brilliance to the professional jollity – she was joint owner of a boarding house for missionaries – of her welcome to her patrons. I don't think she liked me. … On this occasion at Cheltenham she seemed less formidable though remaining physically undiminished, perhaps because her vegetarian diet had saved her from the worst rigours of rationing. She was ill at ease when she drew me aside to make a special and private request. After one or two cursory conventional questions about what it was like to be in action with tanks, she came to the point that was really exercising her.

'What was it like,' she asked, 'when you drove your tank over people?'

To this I had to give some thought. Certainly I had been very afraid, when I was leading a tank from in front, outside, by signalling to the driver through his front flap. But I had never driven over anyone; I had to admit that the experience had so far escaped me. I thought she seemed disappointed when we rejoined the banalities of more general conversation.

As many soldiers had experienced in the past, there was hope and expectation in the anticipation of leave, and so much disappointment in the experience – and a lingering desire to return to those who understood.

Relations with anyone I respected were intolerable, notably with my mother; I wanted nothing except to get back to the front just to get away from England and from her. I can only hope she had a similar wish to be rid of me.

Lieutenant Wilfred Bion, 5th Battalion, Tank Corps

At last I had said goodbye and was leaning out of the train window. 'Mind the door,' I warned her, 'it's filthy.' 'Everything,' she said, near to tears, 'is dreadful … I mean nothing is really cleaned up nowadays.' And so we parted.

It must have been a very strange experience to return home on leave from the Western Front; one of the older men described it on his return to the battalion as a short visit to another planet where he found it impossible to communicate with the natives.

Corporal Frederick Hodges, 10th The Lancashire Fusiliers

Sometimes the conversation in a dugout or a barn turned to Civvy Street, to places and events that now belonged to a past that was a closed book. We accepted this philosophically and quite cheerfully; we knew that many of us would never experience life there again.

RFA officers having a pause and a drink.

Second
Lieutenant
George
Atkinson, 91st
Field Company,
2nd Army, Royal
Engineers

22nd August: Beastly hot day and was tortured to death in the evening by mosquitoes – during this warm weather one usually knocks about in the day-time in one's shirt which becomes saturated with sweat, and then dries off again in the cool of the evening – the mosquitoes love the stink and after dusk they feed on us in millions – there is no respite, you grow tired of killing them and dawn finds you on the edge of insanity, swollen like a long-dead mule. It is these things which constitute the horror of war – death is nothing.

Wrote a cheerful letter home saying that I am very well and happy.

So great were the casualties that those who possessed obvious intelligence and who could handle responsibility were offered promotion. Lance Corporal Frederick Hodges was elevated to the rank of corporal and made Battalion Gas NCO after a short course at the Gas School; he was also told to take over the duties of orderly sergeant of the Headquarters Company and put in charge of the regimental police. He had just passed his nineteenth birthday.

Corporal
Frederick
Hodges, 10th
The Lancashire
Fusiliers

Taking over so many responsibilities at my age was abnormal, but so were the times. So many experienced NCOs, mature men, had been killed, wounded, or taken prisoner in the German spring offensive, that responsibilities far beyond our years or experience were suddenly thrust upon us. Another 19-year-old was promoted to corporal and put in charge of the battalion's machine-gunners.

Training for responsibility is usual and very desirable, but in such an emergency, with no more mature soldiers available, we boys had to take responsibilities in the heat of battle. In these circumstances, it didn't take long for the boy soldiers to mature, since so much was expected of us.

At battalion HQ, I was never free with so many and varied duties; many of which were unfamiliar to me. I also now realize how lonely I was.

One of Hodges' responsibilities was to instil into the men a greater respect for the enemy's gas shells, encouraging comrades to wear their respirators. He knew how much they hated pulling them on, how claustrophobic they felt inside and how they made breathing difficult.

A gas shell seemed innocuous compared with high explosive shells, which arrive with a roar and burst with a crash, scattering fragments. The blue cross shells now being used were Jerry's latest tactical weapon, and were often mistaken for high explosive because there was no wobbling noise as they came over. The danger was that some men were unwilling to wear their gas masks, and then, if Jerry switches to a lethal type of gas such as phosgene, this can irreparably damage the lungs or kill outright. I constantly warned men of the danger, telling them that the irritation of the nose and throat, which many of them did not think was a sufficient reason for wearing their respirators, was only the first stage. Pain in the stomach and severe vomiting could follow, plus numbness of the limbs. They would then be sitting ducks for Jerry's lethal green cross gasses.

I had learned at the gas course that most of the types of gas shells used by the Germans contained a liquid which became a gas on exposure to the air. Thus it required only sufficient explosive to crack the shell case although it sounds relatively harmless.

When I became Battalion Gas NCO, one of my responsibilities was to ensure that men realize the danger from a quiet gas shell, and to urge them as well as order them to wear their gas masks. Sometimes when we were sitting waiting for orders to move on, I would give a short informal talk about the various gasses and their awful effects when one was exposed to them without a gas mask. My constant warning about the deadly effects was confirmed later in civil life when I knew of men who died prematurely after years of ill health coughing their lungs away.

Corporal Frederick Hodges, 10th The Lancashire Fusiliers

Went to Mericourt to get some water. There was a strong smell of 'sneezing gas' (blue cross) everywhere. It was especially strong in the village, which had no doubt been saturated with it. No civilians in the village, which was badly ruined by enemy shellfire. Five of the big 'supply' tanks were camouflaged near the quarry – they had come up during the night. Later in the day they went off up to the line, loaded with water (in petrol cans), barbed wire, ammunition, etc.

Heard that the battalions were getting on very well. Saw several batches of prisoners coming down – Wurtemburgers, No.448. They were placed in the old 1916 prisoners' cage near Mericourt.

Private Sydney Fuller, 8th The Suffolk Regiment

A wrecked German AV7 tank. These were first seen on 21 March, north of the St Quentin Canal. Only twenty were ever produced, the Germans using more captured British tanks than this cumbersome machine.

Near the Somme village of Thiepval was Reginald Kiernan. Thiepval was a village in name only, having been obliterated in 1916; almost nothing tangibly man-made remained, other than trenches.

Private Reginald Kiernan, 7th The Leicestershire Regiment

We have been in here [Thiepval] some days. The trenches are very shallow and open, stony and falling away, as though the earth were too tired to stick together any longer. All night, and especially at 'stand-to', Jerry puts over a 'whizzbang', strafe. There is hardly a warning: there is a 'zip', then a burst and a shower of stones. It is jumpy and nerve-wracking, because you never know when Jerry will start again: odd ones, then three or four all at once. He will throw just one over, right in the middle of the night.

Down in front of our trenches there is a railway line, all torn and mangled, at the foot of a slope; there is the Ancre River, too, with a bridge flush with the water. Nowhere is there any solid ground, but shell holes, shell holes, shell holes, bits of aeroplane and old iron. There are no trees. In front is the brow of Thiepval, brown and yellow, scarred with trenches.

22nd August: We were advancing in the open, across the 1916 battlefields. In our advance we passed the remains of woods with well-known names, now only shattered tree stumps. We crossed old grass-grown trenches which had been blown in and smashed by the 1916 shellfire; we saw the rotting remains of old sandbagged parapets, belts of machine-gun

Corporal Frederick Hodges, 10th The Lancashire Fusiliers

German prisoners carry away the wounded from the battlefield.

Preparing the guns of 218 Siege Battery, late summer 1918.

ammunition, rusty bayonets, cartridge clips, and, among the flourishing weeds, groups of old graves.

It was a desolate scene; lifeless, a place of death and decay and neglect, with a history which seemed far more remote than two or three years. Was it possible, I thought, that it is only two years since my old school mates had fallen on these slopes?

The names of these villages and woods were familiar, they were a part of British history, and now we were fighting for them again. I remember passing Pozières where thousands of troops had died in 1916, but saw only a rough notice scrawled on a piece of wood near some grass-covered ruins. They were foundations of houses with cellars choked with weeds in full flower. Nature unaffected by the war.

Private Reginald Kiernan, 7th The Leicestershire Regiment

The desolation is terrible – there is just nothing – only flat, grassless fields, and holes at every yard. Even the roads are pocked and blown up. I can't get away from it, and it is before me whenever I sleep for a few minutes, though I can't sleep much. As we go on we see names on the boards that make one think of all those fellows who have died here in the real fighting long ago in 1916 – 'Nach Courcelette', 'Nach Flers', 'Nach Guillemont', 'Nach Ginchy', 'Nach Longueval', all those names that I have read of when I was in the Upper Fourth – and we have slept in a field where there was no straight earth – all holes and a lot of dead Welsh. … Everywhere there are German signs and the air is full of the heavy smell of Germans.

Private Sydney Fuller, 8th The Suffolk Regiment

25th August: Heavy gunfire in the early morning. At 7 am we were roused and ordered to pack up for moving, at once. Had breakfast, and then moved up through Morlancourt (now reduced to ruins by our guns), across the Bray-Albert road, to the old 1916 German front line, on the crest of the hill south of Fricourt. Saw two abandoned enemy field guns – one concealed near Morlancourt, the other on the Bray-Fricourt road. Most of the enemy's gun pits were west of this road. On the road were several dead German horses and wrecked wagons, the results of our shells and bombs. Saw a few dead Germans and British. … Our front-line troops were somewhere near Mametz, Fritz having retired. Our own guns were moving forward, the 6-inch howitzers being already in Fricourt. Saw one prisoner, a guardsman of some kind. Very hot. One of our balloons was brought down in flames by an enemy plane near Albert, and it was rumoured that the enemy had mined the town extensively before leaving it.

28 August: Our troops attacked again, the barrage starting at 3 am. … Our headquarters cook was slightly wounded by some cartridges which exploded in the ground under his trench fire. Saw a German bicycle, a queer-looking affair, with not a scrap of rubber on it. The saddle and tool-bag were made of paper. The 'tyres' were bands of steel, covered with leather on the outside, and having numerous small spiral springs between the rim and the 'tread', in place of air.

Corporal Frederick Hodges, 10th The Lancashire Fusiliers

? August: It is well on in the month, but I do not know the date. I have been 'over the top' for the first time. We lay out all night near the railway, and just before dawn our machine guns put up a barrage over our heads. It was a terrifying sound – like a thousand winds all whistling at once, carrying the sound of a million little threatening hammers, striking a thousand strokes a minute. At dawn we rushed over the bridge, and three German machine guns fired down the ridge and sent up high fountains of water. The air was singing with bullets, and fellows were dropping and lying still, all spread out. A hand grenade burst on a man's helmet 20 yards in front, but only cut him slightly on the neck. We took cover in a shell crater, and along the sides of the bridge near the water, which is a dirty green, and filled with iron and wheels, and helmets and rifles and boots.

Private Reginald Kiernan, 7th The Leicestershire Regiment

The firing stopped. But when we moved it started again. We crawled back as best we could. The Welsh, Dorsets and West Yorkshires have come up. At dusk the Welsh went through our trenches very quickly and quietly; they were all very experienced troops. The West Yorkshires were laughing and joking. One man said, 'I've got to wag this 'ere flag when I see the bloody Tanks. What 'opes.' The Dorsets were very silent and white. They were all very young, and terribly tired, and had brand new uniforms, with clean divisional marks.

The Welsh are to cross the river at night and lie out on the other side; then rush the German posts and carry on with others.

Two men, possibly signallers of the Duke of Wellington's Regiment, lie where they fell in a hastily prepared position. In the foreground is a Lucas Daylight Signalling Lamp box.

29th (?) August: The day after Thiepval was taken, the Boche counter-attacked. Going up the road to stop it, a mine went off under our feet. It is as though a hammer had hit you on the back of the head, then everything is shut out by the smoke. It is only a little mine, but some men were wounded, and a big labourer in front of me has been hit all over the back with bits of road. We went forward along a very deep sunken road which ended in a crossroads. The sky was dotted with shrapnel high above it, looking beautiful with its white puff against the deep blue sky. Men were hit on all sides, and leaned against the banks of the road with grey faces. We halted a moment and crouched near the side of the bank. A man lay beside me on his side, with a clean cut triangle taken out of the rim of his tin hat. There was the exact triangle on his left temple, bright red, and wet. The splinter had driven the bit of tin hat into his head. He was warm but quite dead.

From the sunken road we filed out onto the open fields left and right on each side of the road. The bullets were sending up little spouts of dirt everywhere on the ground. It was a miracle, but no one was hit then. We lay down and an officer said, 'Over there, half right, 300 yards, rapid fire.' I fired like blazes, but I could see no one.

After stopping the counter-attack we lay out all night. It rained like a waterfall, solid and heavy. Just before the rain started a young officer just out from England stood up to stretch himself, as it was dusk, and I suppose he thought he was safe. He just crumpled up. He was very tall and broad. He lay dead about 10 yards away. Another man in a shell hole nearer me raved all night. His leg was blown off. He used terrible language, blaspheming and cursing and groaning. His voice grew quieter just before dawn. I crawled across very carefully at daylight. He was dead, with a terrible angry look on his face.

1st September: We were very hard up for water, being now in a district where no artificial water supply existed, and all wells, etc. had been destroyed two years before. What water we did get was bought up by the water-carts, probably from Bray. I had another walk round when off duty. On the hill above us, towards Hardecourt, the enemy had tried to hold up our advance a few days before. They had hastily dug a shallow trench, and packed it with men and machine guns but were unable to check our men. One or two of the machine guns still stood at the top of the trench as they had been captured. Being a new trench, there were no deep dugouts, but merely small funk-holes in the trench sides. Many of the enemy dead still lay there as they had fallen. In one funk-hole I saw a dead German, in the act of throwing off the covering of waterproof sheeting under which he had been sleeping. He had evidently been killed by a shell or bullet as he was awakening, and had stiffened in that attitude. He looked as if alive and posing for a photograph or picture. The packs left lying about had all been rifled by souvenir hunters. I found that practically every one of the dead enemy's water bottles was full of black coffee – they had evidently not been in the trench long when they were killed. Being very thirsty I sampled some of the coffee, and found it still very good.

Private Sydney Fuller, 8th The Suffolk Regiment

Driver Sydney
Burridge, Army
Service Corps

Sunday, 1st September: Not 50 yards from headquarters is a family vault and erected over it is a stone monument [that] can be seen for miles, so I walked across to look at it. But it had been hit by a shell and twisted halfway round off the foundation. The slab had almost been removed and a wooden beam put across with a rope onto it so you could lower yourself down. I should say it was about 15 feet deep. Being nosy, I had to let myself down and explore. When I reached the bottom, my foot hit against something and when I struck a match, I found it was a coffin that had been broken open, showing the remains of a body. Everything looked weird as only a little daylight was coming in where the stone slab had been partly removed. All over the bottom of the vault was nothing but broken coffins and partly decaying bodies. In one recess a coffin still lay only partly open. This desecration – the open coffins – was no doubt the work of Germans, looking for valuables.

Historians have long debated whether the advances made in the war's last months were the result of a series of tactically astute, even brilliant, decisions or profound German war-weariness. Even amongst the soldiers themselves, some took a rather more jaundiced view of the reasons for operational success than others.

Private Stephen
Graham, 1st
Scots Guards

The exploits of the autumn of 1918, whilst they redound to the heroism of our soldiers, did not seem to show great military genius at work behind us. We had a good cause and our morale was good, and we had large numbers and many guns, but did not trust the brain. The organization of the transport was obviously weak and the enemy was never pressed. On the German side there was a bad cause, a weakening morale, not large numbers, and comparatively few guns, but a good organization of transport and plenty of brain work. The whole autumn campaign was Brain versus Cause and the Cause won. No matter what blunders our leaders made, the common soldier always felt the cause was good. But the German did not believe in his cause, was not ready to suffer for it any more and lapsed into indiscipline. There was a steady decline in discipline throughout September and October.

The infantry were prone to argue that supplies came too slowly, that the transport could have been better organized, but those driving the limbers did not agree. They perhaps better understood what it took to resupply an army on the move.

What impressed us most was the efficiency of the army's organization and the marvellous control of all the services in the rear. … Now that a battle was being waged, and the line was moving forward on a front of 40 miles, the wonderful organization that had gradually been built up justified itself and worked like clockwork. Not a unit possessed a horse, a vehicle or a lorry which was not put to good use in the next few months. All the light and heavy railway material needed in the advance was not only handy but provided with men to lay it. Wherever a captured road needed rapid repairing, a Labour battalion mysteriously appeared for the purpose. Whenever a sausage balloon was brought down in flames, there was another on the spot with observation officers to man it. And so on, right through the branches of the service. Even rations were better than they had been in far quieter times than these. Oh, that everything had run so smoothly in those Somme days [1916] when the traffic problem seemed insurmountable, although the offensive was carried on on a much shorter front! It had taken four years to get to this pitch, but it was consoling to have lived to witness it.

Driver Aubrey Smith, 1/5th The London Regiment (London Rifle Brigade)

2nd September: Went into St Omer with Day and had tea at the club – succeeded in obtaining some butter at 15 francs per kilo – verily the French are a hospitable people! Returned to the mess to find the rumour about Kemmel is confirmed – apparently the Boche are evacuating forward positions with a view to consolidating their line for the winter. This is all very cheerful and no doubt makes good reading in the clubs at home, but unfortunately it necessitates our return to the line tomorrow. … Transport and pontoons started on their return journey tonight.

Second Lieutenant George Atkinson, 91st Field Company, 2nd Army, Royal Engineers

3rd September: Entrained at 8.15 am and detrained at railhead about 12 noon. Marched forward past our old billets and eventually took over very comfortable billets from a company of American Engineers. The line seems to have gone far forward, all the old gun positions are empty and the sausages [observation balloons] are well in front of us now.

After all, I think that the ability to park our transport in the open in full view of Kemmel will do us more good than the 'rest' could ever have done. The shadow of that ghastly hill has been over us for so long that our relief at having regained it is out of all proportion to its practical value. The effect on the men has been little short of miraculous, and already they are joking about the possibilities of Christmas at home – or at the worst in Berlin! Once more we look forward to the possibilities of a semi-victory, and the dog-like fatalism which upheld us through the weary summer is gradually changing to something like Hope and Confidence in the Future.

Cavalrymen with a Hotchkiss gun in action in apparently untouched fields.

Driver Aubrey Smith was east of Arras, beyond a formidable part of the German Hindenburg Defensive Line, known as the Drocourt-Quéant Switch. This was ground that appeared largely undamaged, a step change from anything encountered before.

In the farm grounds were some German Army huts – the first we had seen in the course of the war – and it can be understood that the sight of buildings still standing upon ground recently captured made quite an impression on our minds. All the familiar traces of war were on every hand, and yet we moved in an environment suggestive of back-area surroundings. The ground had been well shelled and debris lay about, yet there were large stretches of green grass in places.

Driver Aubrey Smith, 1/5th The London Regiment (London Rifle Brigade)

The spring crisis was long past, permitting the British Government to reintroduce its rule forbidding overseas service for anyone aged under nineteen. What would happen to those lads in the front line still aged eighteen was less clear. Would they be removed from the line?

I'd been out in France for several months when there was a campaign, I believe in the *Mirror* newspaper, about 18-year-olds going into the line, and the Government was worried because so many had been killed or injured. The tide had clearly turned against the Germans and it was felt that boys of my age should not be sent to fight now that the enemy were falling back. In response to the pressure, someone in the regiment decided to remove me from the firing line. Being born in 1900 made me one of the younger ones in the battalion, and so I was given a job with the regimental police, but, to be honest, that was the worst job of the lot. Behind the lines, when the men were out on rest, they were often difficult to control. These buggers in cafés or estaminets might be killed the next day, and they didn't care a damn for the likes of me or anybody else.

Private Doug Roberts, 7th The Buffs (East Kent Regiment)

If we had to turf them out of a place, the first thing the men used to do was shoot the light out, making the place inky black inside. There was a corporal with me from the Durham Light Infantry, or Devil's Last Issue as we called them, and he was a good chap. He said, 'All right, Doug, you stop there, you count them as they come out.' He went into this café. Next moment a chap comes flying out the door into the night air, landing with a thump. 'Don't start counting yet, it's me,' and it was this corporal. They'd physically picked him up and thrown him out.

The new rule would not help that small band of soldiers whose youth had gone undetected. In September, 18-year-old Reginald Kiernan took part in the fighting at Épehy. After six months in France, his attitude to the war had profoundly changed and he craved release from the fighting, though he apparently never chose to reveal his real age.

Private Reginald
Kiernan, 7th The
Leicestershire
Regiment

Most fellows at the front are inclined to be a bit religious. Once a fellow said to me, 'What's this 'ere confession?' But I could not interest him, and he was soon bored. Another fellow, rather a big, windy, stupid man, said, 'I'd bet I'd make the bloody priest sit up.' There was a shout of protest at this. Another fellow said, 'Well, I've nowt against the Catholics.' …

I know why these fellows defended the Catholics. It's because they're afraid of Death. It's because of the Somme. Here, Death seems to hang in the very air. We live in it, and it's always heavy around us, even when one is thinking of something else. Before our little attacks, whilst we are lying out in the grey of morning, just as night is passing, the men do not look in each other's faces. Every man seems to be living in a small life of his own, and I know that Death is talking to them all. We all know it, and we know that each of us feels it spreading over us, like the sky at that hour, all grey and uncertain, as though it were uncertain of the coming day, and what it holds. How terrible is the sky at dawn. So we do not talk, and we keep our eyes down. At these times if a man looks at you he looks stealthily, or if he looks straight in your face you feel as though he was keeping something back – inside his head – which he would never show you. As though he were ashamed of you knowing.

It is afternoon and warm and sunny. Last night we lay out in front of a village called, somebody said, Beaulencourt. He knew we were there, and lashed the ground with machine guns, and sent up all sorts of lights, white, yellow, red and green. …

The big Fear is off my back once we start forward. It is just before that it is strongest and stops the flow of blood in me. While we were lying again before going through the village, there was a red flash and a roar right above me, and a thud on the man lying next to me. He did not move. He was dead. He had been telling me that he was a tram driver in civil life, and that he had three children, a boy and two girls. He had been staring along the ground into the darkness, anxious and excited. When the lights went up I could see the sweat still trickling on his face.

We went through the village before dawn, and the Germans came up out of the cellars and surrendered. But the village is on fire now. We have been shelled and swept by machine guns in the little trenches we dug, but all is quiet now.

I never feel any emotions now, except the great terrible desire always surging up to get away, away back out of all of this, from the toil and the horror of it all, and from this landscape, and the awful spirit over it, and to shake off this awful Fear which is leaning on me, pressing me down, like a big, brown, shapeless shadow that I can't hold off. …

A soldier with a strong spirit would be certain to get killed. I think all the bravest men are killed. After every action we've had, the best fellows, the ones you could rely on, are gone.

Battle fatigued: Lieutenant Alexander Gallaher, 4th (Royal Irish) Dragoon Guards, had been on the Western Front since August 1914. Wounded four times already, he was to be wounded a fifth time in October 1918.

Captain Charles Farley, 4th (Royal Irish) Dragoon Guards, taking a well-earned break during the advance in August. Captain Farley had been with the regiment on the Western Front since January 1915.

But what I've thought of most today, and it has been running in my mind all the time, for we had to learn it by heart, is Rupert Brooke's *The Soldier*. I cannot feel like that. I do not want my body to rot away under the field, with its yellow earth and thin, pale grass. Perhaps Brooke could feel like that because he's *had* something in this world. He'd been to Berlin, and he'd had lovely warm afternoons in Cambridgeshire, beside decent, quiet rivers; and he's had time to *think* and enjoy things. *I* have never had time to think. I have had *nothing, nothing*. I want to get back from all this, back out of it – and sit and think, and look at clean things, and hear my people's voices again.

Rupert Brooke had *seen* England, and England had made him love her. I have seen nothing, I have *had* nothing from England. Rupert Brooke had longer than I've had to see things and enjoy them. He was ten years older than I am now.

Corporal
Frederick
Hodges, 10th
The Lancashire
Fusiliers

Emotion was numbed; we ignored the dead as machine-gun bullets hissed and cracked past us, some cutting into the ground in straight lines. Although I saw men fall right and left of me, and passed by some horrible sights, I had no thought of death for myself. No one stopped to help the wounded who groaned as we passed; the one overmastering impulse in all who still lived was to keep going. We youngsters had, in a few short months, become quite acclimatized to the fact of life and death on the Western Front.

We accepted the fact that it was a very dangerous place; that death or wounds were its natural, constant and its inevitable state, and, that we were all, officers, NCOs and men in it together. Individually, everyone was afraid sometimes; but morale was always maintained by firm leadership. Even when nerves were frayed, a good leader can overlay men's fears with his own determination and quick positive orders. These, and example, always produce instant action by trained soldiers.

Personally, I am neither by temperament, nor upbringing, the tough physically courageous type; but in dangerous situations I often experienced exhilaration instead of fear.

I faced the facts of life and death, and they are that the moment the fear of death made a man try to avoid it, he ceased to be a soldier.

16th September: I do not know any of the officers we have now. One is a captain from the Transport Lines. They are sending up yeomanry in riding-breeches who do not even know how to take cover, and men from baths and stores.

Private Reginald Kiernan, 7th The Leicestershire Regiment

The platoon sergeant has been wounded, a little bit of shrapnel in the back. I have been trying to trace why my Fear has so increased. Now I know it was the sergeant. I am sure it was the sergeant.

He was sent up from Battalion Headquarters and was new to the line. He came just after Thiepval. He was terribly windy and showed it in his face, a thing I had never seen anyone do. Before we did our little stunts against the machine guns, the officers would meet and talk to the NCOs. When he came back to see us the sweat would roll off his face and a little black moustache. A real parade sergeant – and a bully if he dared be. He would say, 'We're going over,' and I would feel a wave of fear pass from him to me, though I hated the sight of him.

When he was wounded it was just daylight. The officers were walking about on the top, though the machine-gun bullets were singing everywhere, and the shrapnel was bursting low down with a splitting crack and flash. One of them said to him, 'Wounded? Why the hell don't you go back?' The sergeant said, 'I'll stick it, sir.' The officer said, 'Get to hell out of it, do you hear, now!' The sergeant went off, crouching and stumbling. An old fellow sitting near me said, 'Trying for the DCM, the windy bastard.'

Fear! A little wounded man, a man about fifty, spoke to me when he was going back. He said, 'These fellows who are afraid – it's 'cos they can't face their God. They've got something on their minds, they have! Daren't die, that's what I say. Daren't die! Daren't face their God.'

But there is more in it, though that's true. It's the lying like those fellows we've passed – on your side with a fixed grin on your face, or on your back with your eyes turned up – and no one caring! And it's the thought that you don't die like a hero. That would help. There are no heroes here. No one cares. A man is forgotten in the next moment. We don't even know each other's names, or our officers' names, and our officers don't know us even by sight. We don't know what we are going to do, or what we are making for when we attack. We don't know where Jerry is, whether he's 300 yards or a thousand yards away. We don't know anything at all, and

A German gunner lies dead beside his abandoned gun. The picture was taken by an officer serving with 218 Siege Battery, Royal Garrison Artillery.

we just go forward – every man for himself. Everything is unknown and unthanked, unpraised, and there is no pity anywhere – not even a 'Poor sod', as we pass the men who've been killed.

I can't die like that – that is what I fear, I think, more than death itself. But it's Fear, Fear, Fear, all the time when you are not doing anything, and who can describe Fear? He is with you, by your side, round you, over you, in your mind and your body, even when you can sleep.

Corporal
Frederick
Hodges, 10th
The Lancashire
Fusiliers

One's life was not one's own; instead there were onerous duties, strict discipline, a chain of command and instant obedience to orders. There was comradeship and battalion pride; everything was shared, whether rations, duties, discomforts, or dangers. Death was always hovering, but trench life was not lived in tension or fear; it was lived in top gear. Physical health was excellent, and the high spirits and humour which are normal in young men were always evident.

The infantry of 1918 was young, fresh and strong; inexperienced, but quick to learn and act in changing circumstances. There was a strange enthusiasm to being an infantryman, with everything you possessed attached to you; one was always ready to move at a moment's notice. Life was uncomplicated, and the nearness of death sharpened one's awareness of life; there is exhilaration in danger, and courage is contagious. …

The soldier lived in a real world, close to nature; his past life irrelevant, his future uncertain, and the present moment is his life. Small pleasures please; they give a satisfaction out of all proportion to their old values; a hot drink of tea or a clean pair of socks; regular rations or a rest from duty; a letter from home, or even an opportunity to wash and shave.

17th September: We have been relieved by the Queen's with full companies. There's only a few of us, and we thought the Queen's would never stop coming into our trench. Queen's, Queen's, Queen's, endless files of them. They looked very white and strained in the dark. The way up is through a deep railway cutting, and shells have dropped on the Machine Gun Corps dugouts in the sides. There are patches of blood here and there all over the place, and bits of head in tins hats, and lumps of grey and red body, with pieces of khaki sticking to them. The Queen's had just come from Ypres. They said it was quiet there. … We have a number of new officers, some of them in their twenties. Some of them were all right at first, but seem to be shaken now, and some of them appear not to get on well together. But we have some grand captains.

In our platoon there was a short, fat lad, who, we all thought was 'not quite right'. Some time since, perhaps a week ago, he came out of a dugout just after a German shrapnel shell had burst very high above us. He had his boot loosened and told the sergeant he had been hit in the foot with shrapnel. But there was no cut in his boot or sock, though his foot was gashed. The sergeant made him show his jack-knife, and there was blood on it. He went back, but the sergeant said he would be marked SIW (self-inflicted wound) and would get five years.

Private Reginald Kiernan, 7th The Leicestershire Regiment

It would be so easy to shoot oneself in the leg or foot when in action, and then one could get back out of it. But I cannot do it. There is no burn to give you away if you put your water bottle across the muzzle of your rifle. But I could not do it. The thought of it has always filled me with disgust. *Someone* has to do the fighting. Nor would I go sick again and go through the repeated examinations to prove I was not malingering. The doctor is a decent man, but he has to be wily and adamant because so many try to 'swing it'.

17th September, night: I am writing this as we wait to set off. When the attacking stuff, Mills bombs, smoke bombs, etc., were being given out nearly all the fellows disappeared. They don't want to carry it on the march up. Three of us have got the whole lot to carry. The sergeant who has issued it will carry nothing. He is a hound. A huge man, a professional footballer, they say. He has kept our rum all the time we have been in the line here, and those who wanted it have had only an occasional spoonful, yet his water-bottle has been full of it, and he kept to his dugout all day and all night – the big, white-faced hound. There is another sergeant who is fairly sound, but his nerve is going though he tries to look as usual. He must have been a good sergeant once, though I believe he was only a Derby Scheme man.

I have been thinking of how queer everything is in the world, how great and wide it is; so that one seems utterly small and lost in it all. … Just now in England there will be trains rumbling in the darkness, and there'll be lights in the houses. People will be coming out from the picture palaces, and hurrying back to warm kitchens. Some will be having supper in brilliant hotels, and others will be pressed for money, and others starving. Mothers will be writing to their sons over here, with little stubs of pencil, under the gaslight. Men and women will be gliding away from the theatres in long, closed cars, wrapped up and warm. They'll have white furs, and there'll be flowers in little silver brackets in the windows, and the men will be in evening dress, black and white, they'll be tall people with soft voices and clean, decent conversations.

But out here it is dark, with a warm wind that is sighing as it comes over the fields, making me feel I want to stretch my body up to the sky,

and throw out my arms, and drink it right into me. Yet I will never see the lighted tramcars again, or the bright streets of shops, or people hurrying along and laughing loudly in the daylight. Oh, God, I have done nothing very wrong. Cannot I live on, just a little more?

18th September, 4 am: We have come up and are 'lying out' to 'go over'. The air is alive and shaking with fire. It is hardly dawn yet, just grey and black. Along the railway line our barrage is down, a great wall of grey smoke covered with yellow flashes. It is the first time I have seen a barrage from behind. It is raining and very cold.

Waiting for business: prepared wooden crosses lie in a heap beside the track.

Everything is banging and roaring, and there is the steely shriek of hundreds of shells, and that great wind overhead. There's the big whistle and 'shee-ing' and hammering of the machine guns, firing over us from the railway embankment.

I do not feel at all afraid. A boy is lying near me on his back in the rain. He was tall and lanky and K-legged, and had a very small, grey face. He looked like a stalk a minute or two since, when he was standing up with his groundsheet round his shoulders. I noticed him suddenly then, and remembered I had seen him before, somewhere. He is on his back now, and his legs are wide apart. He has been killed by a stray bullet. No one knows who he is, or what his name is, or where the bullet has hit him, and no one has bothered to notice him. He looks quite natural, gazing up at the sky. But he is dead.

I think, myself, that he was always tired; tired beyond anything anyone can know, and that he is resting now.

I have come to write this in a little dugout, cut in the railway embankment. I have made an Act of Contrition, and I think that this time it was perfect. Before, there has always been fear in it.

The roar is greater outside, and the machine guns are madder and madder. The grey light is getting stronger and is creeping along the floor, whitening it. We shall go forward soon.

They are shouting outside. I must go.

Reginald Kiernan was wounded, ending his fighting days. He had taken part in operations amongst the forward outposts of the Hindenburg Line, a line refortified in the summer months and the last significant obstacle for the Allies to overcome.

The Germans were being pummelled at every turn. On 26 September, French and American troops advanced to the south between the river Meuse and Reims while on 27 September the British First Army attacked at Bourlon Ridge. Meanwhile, the Third Army advanced towards Le Cateau. The next day, the Second Army, helped by French and Belgian troops, attacked at Ypres, surging over the Passchendaele Ridge. Then, on 29 September, after eroding German positions around the Hindenburg Line, an all-out assault by the Fourth Army, aided by Australian and American troops, was launched, rapidly breaking through what once seemed an impregnable defensive position. The attack, aided by fog and overwhelming artillery support, said much about the growing capabilities of the Allied infantry: the victory said even more about the crumbling self-confidence of German soldiers who surrendered in vast numbers.

By 3 October, Allied troops were through into open country. The end of the war was getting close, though few would guess just how close.

Overleaf: *Second Lieutenant John Lawrence (left) with a fellow officer of 218 Siege Battery and German souvenirs at their feet.*

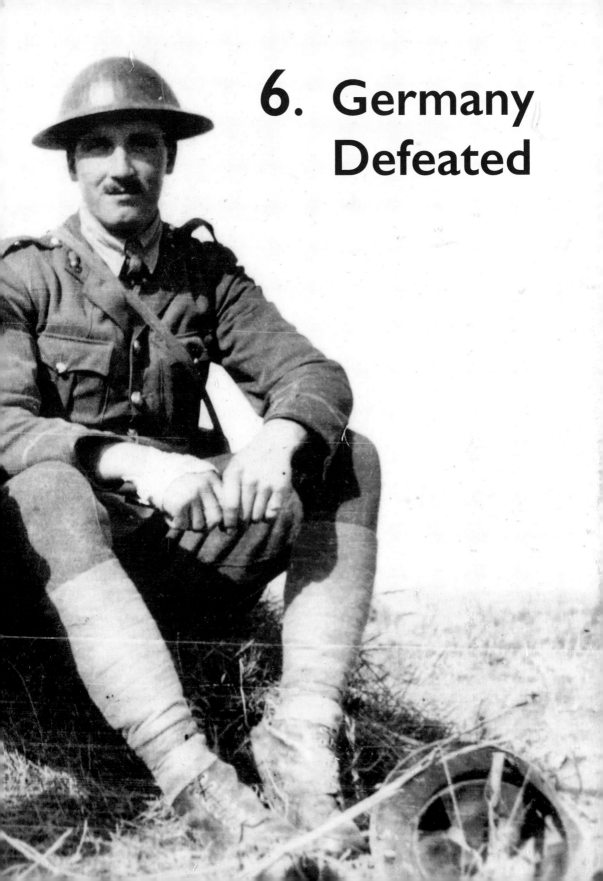

6. Germany Defeated

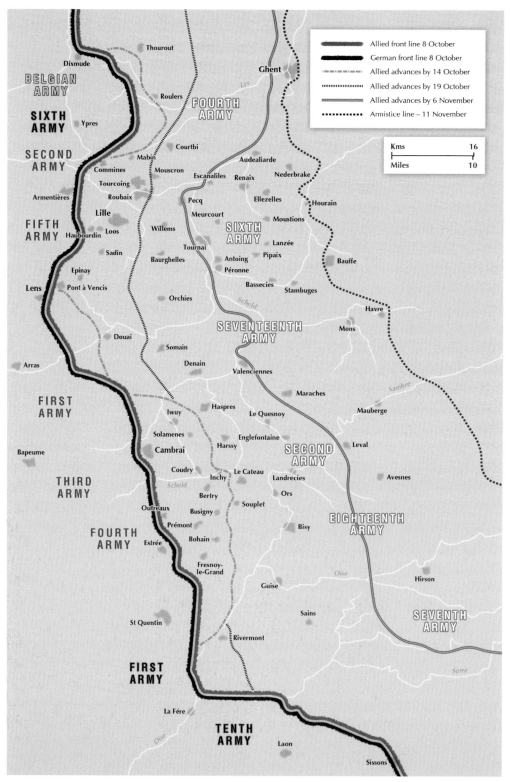

Advance to the Armistice, October–November.

'I went into a large empty house and found a blackboard on an easel standing in the middle of the main room. On the blackboard was written in German: "You are chasing us away now, Tommy, but we shall come back."'

Lieutenant Alan Thomas, 6th The Queen's Own
(Royal West Kent Regiment)

––––––––––

We are without definite news, but apparently the whole show [at Ypres] has been a great success, and the army is only waiting until we can get the roads through. I can never forget the great change which seemed to spread like wildfire over the spirit of the army on the evening of the 28th–29th [September].

We were in the midst of the worst of the mud area, miles of transport wagons were bogged along our single road, it was raining hard, and few of us had eaten anything for twenty-four hours. Nobody was looking forward to the dawn. But from somewhere behind us a rumour came through that Bulgaria had asked for Peace. There was no cheering, no demonstration of any sort, but the news seemed to put new spirit into the tired troops. The weary mud-caked horses were lashed and spurred again, men put their aching shoulders to the wheels, and once more the limbers lumbered forward. All night long the wagons toiled painfully up those fateful ridges where scores of thousands of our finest infantry had died, and in the drizzling dawn they saw their reward at last – behind them lay the dull, dead plain, with its memories of misery and mud – before them, they looked down upon a new, unbroken country, and the spire of Ten Brielen church, untouched of shot or shell, beckoned like a winning post against the eastern sky.

2nd October: Heavy rain again last night, but it hasn't damped our spirits. We could meet almost any call again now. At 5.30 am an orderly came in

Second Lieutenant George Atkinson, 91st Field Company, 2nd Army, Royal Engineers with orders from the CRE saying that we are to work from six to nine on the divisional main road. By dashing off without any breakfast we were able to start at 7.30, and returned for a meal at noon – our first since yesterday evening. In the afternoon, Day worked the sections on the road while the Major and I brought up the heavy transport. Artillery horse-lines just forward of our own were heavily shelled for about five minutes and a lot of horses were knocked out – about 100 of the poor beasts stampeded, and it was a pitiful sight to see some of them dragging their entrails along the ground.

This incident made me realize that if the Germans have any fight left in them at all we are in a very precarious position. Several divisions are herded together with the river Lys in front of them and an impassable belt of swamp and mud behind.

At night many fires were visible again where the enemy is burning villages along his retreat – many of these appear to be very far off, which looks as if they contemplate a big withdrawal – a favourite theory is that they will withdraw as far as the Meuse for the winter.

An officer and his servant of the Royal Irish Rifles sitting in the Ypres Salient as men move up in the background.

3rd October: Company commenced work on a new plank road to relieve the strain on the main road. I went forward with three wagons to a dump on the Menin road to get material, but it took us all morning to get there as the roads were blocked with artillery limbers – we want ten times more transport and ten times more labour than we have got if we are to make any reasonable progress. The Field Companies are quite inadequate to cope with any serious road-making in an advance like this.

In the afternoon scouted round with Cooper looking for what had once been a first-class road, clearly marked on our maps. We couldn't find a stone, a tree, or any single thing that would indicate where the road had been – we couldn't even fix it from our maps, as farms, houses, and landmarks of any description had totally disappeared. We had some difficulty in getting back, and once Cooper's horse went down to her belly in the mud – we nearly lost her, but got her out eventually.

British troops were pushing out of the devastated Ypres Salient, while to the south, men were beginning to move over open country after breaching the Hindenburg Line. These men included troops of the 10th Lancashire Fusiliers, 17th Division, who passed through villages where civilians had lived under German occupation for four years.

One afternoon the HQ Company was approaching a small town through some cultivated fields on its outskirts. The men were moving forward in a long line across a turnip field. We were following up the advance and ahead of us we could see enemy shells bursting at the crossroads just outside the town.

Corporal Frederick Hodges, 10th The Lancashire Fusiliers

We saw the Colonel and the Adjutant sit down with their backs to a large tree in the middle of the turnip field. They were looking at their maps. Since it looked as if we were not going on for the time being, we all sat down amongst the turnips and some of us cut one up to see if it was edible – it wasn't.

Then some men walked over to the left to a farm, and I decided to go too. The farm was old and in bad condition; shellfire had destroyed some of the barns and other outbuildings. On the farther side a muddy road led towards the town. When I reached the back door of the farm, I found a

An officer and his Artillery Board identifies 218 Siege Battery's latest targets.

small queue of men waiting, and saw inside an old Frenchman pumping up water from a well under an old stone sink; it was very primitive. Soon I moved into the stone-floored kitchen and as I waited my turn, I studied his old wrinkled face; grey hair spouting out from under a peaked cap. Outside enemy shells were bursting, some quite near, but the old man was completely unconcerned as he pumped up water. … Life must go on; British boys were thirsty, so he filled our water-bottles.

The 1st Scots Guards were also crossing into unspoilt land. In early October the Guards took ground south-west, then south, then south-east of Cambrai, forcing the Germans to evacuate the town on the 9th, or risk encirclement.

Private Stephen Graham, 1st Scots Guards

Havrincourt, near which we spent the night of the 7th [October], was complete desolation; Ribécourt was no better, but Marcoing was a trifle less smashed, and gave the impression of having been a rather pretty town in peace-time. We spent the night of the 8th on the ridge between Marcoing and Masnières. It was very cold, with a hoar frost on the grass, and the men, expecting to go into action on the morrow, slept as best they could in old machine-gun emplacements and ditches. On the 9th we heard that Germany had accepted President Wilson's fourteen points, and on this day, too, we began to see new types of landscape. We had passed through the zone of destruction, and were emerging into the comparatively unharmed regions which had remained in German hands since 1914, where the fields were ploughed and harvests had been taken, where the villages had red roofs, and the spires were on the churches.

The last village to show signs of being badly battered was Crèvecoeur – Heartbreak Village – and there also were many German and British dead, the latter being chiefly New Zealand men. All the way to Séranvillers there had been hard fighting, and the German gunners lay piled on their machines. On October 10th, however, we swung clear of the old desolation altogether, coming to Estourmel. We learned that Cambrai had fallen and that the whole campaign was going well, and the enemy was on his knees seeking for peace. The battalion did not need to go into action, for the tentative object we marked out for them had been abandoned without a shot. It was billed for the next day instead. The hour of setting off for the line was fixed for one in the morning. But, housed in a jolly village, the men made a most joyous night of it with feasting, singing, and merriment. Lights shone in all windows, and from end to end of the village was music

Trees felled by the enemy across the path of the Allied advance.

and hilarity. Indeed, out in the middle of the main street one fellow was sitting at a piano, and a crowd was round him singing catches. Nearby the pipers were playing. In another billet there was a whistling chorus. Those who wished to rest reclined on mattresses on spring beds. Supper in the cottage with a section of a platoon round a regular family table, the fire burning merrily in the stove, the wall-clock ticking and striking, the faces of French villagers looking out from faded portraits on the walls, made a strange impression, but a good one.

Lieutenant Alan Thomas, 6th The Queen's Own (Royal West Kent Regiment)

It was about this time, about a third of the way through October, that we first began to feel that the war was nearing its end. Various rumours were reaching us – such as that Austria was on the point of collapse and that Turkey was giving in – and some official announcements were circulated warning us that on no account were we to imagine that peace was in the offing. It was clear to us then that the end was not far off.

Private Stephen Graham, 1st Scots Guards

Germany had accepted the fourteen points of President Wilson [a road map to peace originally offered by Wilson in January 1918], and had agreed to evacuate France and Belgium by military arrangement. Not that due weight was attached to such news. Incredible rumours of the kind and of other kinds were always in the air, and were indulgently received: Germany had accepted the peace conditions, yes, and also Hindenburg was dead; the Kaiser had committed suicide; 16,000 German soldiers had broken the neutrality of Holland, and the Dutch had declared war. The Americans had taken Metz. With all that was unlikely, the prospect of peace did not obtain much credence.

Second Lieutenant George Atkinson, 2nd Army, Royal Engineers

10th October: Went forward into the outposts to reconnoitre tracks and ways forward for the guns. We were in absolutely virgin country, and it was a new experience to think of death lurking behind these green hedges and quiet farm buildings.

At night took the section up and did a lot of work – filled in several ditches, cleared a ride through a wood, and chopped down several trees with which we made a small bridge – took the floor out of the farm kitchen to cover it with.

[12th October] Neuvilly near Le Cateau: The whole front was constantly moving forward; we rarely spent two nights in the same place. If we were not in action, we were following up battalions that were, and then leap-frogging them into the next battle. New drafts came to make up the numbers, no one was indispensible or irreplaceable; and I began to be regarded, and to feel, one of the old soldiers of the battalion that I had joined myself only six months earlier.

Many of the boys I had known had gone; only very occasionally did I see and speak briefly to one of the boys who had come out to France with me. Three of them were Norwich boys – Griggs, Hoddle and Guymer, who were in the same hut with me in the big camp at Mansfield; they had been put into the East Yorkshire Regiment when we arrived at Calais.

One day, as the Lancashire Fusiliers passed through the East Yorkshires during a leap-frog, I spoke to Giggs, who told me that Hoddle was still alive but Guymer had been killed. Another day I waved and smiled when I saw Corporal Hammond, another East York, as we marched through a village, and he touched his stripes and waved back.

The sheer scale of this final Big Push was enormous; the follow-up of supplies, ammunition and Mills bombs; the battalions leap-frogging past one another, gave us a sense of purpose and a confidence which the men who fought in the earlier fruitless and bloody battles of 1915–1917 never experienced, despite their persistent courage and self-sacrifice. …

It was a strange experience, after months in trenches and fields, to pass through a town occupied by civilians. On one occasion when we were following up other troops who were in contact with the enemy, we halted in a main street of a town, sitting on the kerb for a few minutes' rest while waiting for orders. As we moved on down the street, I glanced into shop windows; it was a glimpse of another world; a far away world which we had almost forgotten.

Corporal Fred Hodges, 10th The Lancashire Fusiliers

The Germans were capable of defiance and small-scale counter-attacks, but while some units – some men – fought bravely, there were others who understood the hopelessness of the overall situation. German soldiers might defend the Rhine and their homes, but the fact was they were in France and Belgium, and increasing numbers were not prepared to give their lives for a lost cause.

These images are part of a collection pulled from a skip in 2012. They were taken by Acting Major Oswald Riley, 79 Brigade, RFA, in the summer and autumn of 1918.

Brigade casualties lying in Varennes Cemetery. The brigade suffered a number of deaths during the fighting in April.

A British 12-inch railway howitzer apparently 'resting', September 1918. It could fire a high explosive shell over 8 miles.

Artillery dug in near the village of Hermies, west of Cambrai.

Officers of 79 Brigade RFA snapped outside their dugout.

Wounded being evacuated by barges.

We were now advancing over country abounding with small villages and large farms. I particularly remember a large farm which we captured soon after dawn one October morning.

The farm buildings were well built of red brick and extended all round a large farmyard which we entered by an arched gateway in a high wall. As I entered, the Germans had just surrendered; about twenty stood with their hands up or clasped on their heads; others lay dead or wounded.

I went straight across the farmyard and entered a long open-fronted shed on the far side of the yard. It had a manger running all along the back wall, and on the floor there were half a dozen German dead and some badly wounded who had been carried there by their comrades during the fighting; there was one German Red Cross soldier attending to them.

My investigations were suddenly interrupted by the RSM whose voice I heard bellowing, 'Corporal Hodges! – Corporal Hodges!' As I hurried out of the shed and across the yard, I saw that more Germans were pouring through the main gate where the RSM stood just inside the farmyard. They all had their hands up, and the RSM was pushing and poking them with his revolver into some sort of double rank. 'Come on,' he roared at me. 'Get them out of here!' And added with a grin, 'We're outnumbered in this yard. Lead on, Corporal, I'll make them follow you. Take 'em to the POW cage.'

As I led this untidy looking double line of prisoners out through the gateway, I could hear the RSM's rasping voice counting them out, 'Two-four-six-eight-ten…'. When I was about 50 yards from the farm, I stepped to one side, motioned them to keep going, and looked back to see what I had got. I estimated that I had about fifty prisoners, and at the rear, one Lancashire Fusilier. Seeing, about 60 yards away, another Fusilier driving another half a dozen Germans before him, I shouted across to him to join us. A few minutes later we were also joined by another small group, which to my great surprise, included a German officer. …

We were approaching Poix-du-Nord and were meeting troops marching to the front. They were fresh and full of humorous quips; in a very different state from we Lancashire Fusiliers who had been on our feet in fighting equipment for about fifteen hours without food or rest. As these troops passed us on the road, they shouted insults at the Germans, and one of them, seeing the German officer by my side, shouted as he passed, 'Make that bloody bastard Boche carry your pack!' I made no

Corporal
Frederick
Hodges, 10th
The Lancashire
Fusiliers

reply, and reflected that the nearer one is to the battle, the less hate there is. Some of these boy soldiers going up to the front had probably not been in action. I felt a certain kingship with my prisoners.

Uncertain where to take the men, Fred Hodges marched the prisoners several kilometres, engaging in stilted conversation with the German officer – mostly in schoolboy French. Eventually Hodges located the cage.

Corporal
Frederick
Hodges, 10th
The Lancashire
Fusiliers

It was about 10 am when I finally handed over the prisoners to the Military Police, who counted them, and to my great surprise, gave me a receipt for them as if I was delivering cattle.

The receipt was for one German officer and fifty-eight other ranks. I noticed that they detached the German officer from the rest, led him off into a building and expertly sorted the other ranks by regiment, penning them like sheep. They were only too ready to lie down on the straw in the cattle pens.

Hodges returned to the farm where he had picked up the prisoners. He was little more than 25 miles south-west of Mons where the war had begun four years before. Having searched for the POW cage, Hodges now searched for his battalion, which had vacated the farm. Within a day both would enter Mormal Forest – a great woodland through which the original BEF had retired during their famous retreat in August 1914.

Corporal
Frederick
Hodges, 10th
The Lancashire
Fusiliers

There was not a soul in sight on this deserted battlefield; the battlefront had swept on and left the dead lying where they had fallen. We came to a group of nine Lancashire Fusiliers; they lay on, and just off, the track in grotesque attitudes, just as they had fallen when a direct hit from a German battery had caught them as they marched. We stopped for a moment or two to see who they were; I forbade any pocket rifling, but we took some of their iron rations, i.e. 'bully' biscuits and tea in a white canvas bag.

Further on, we saw a British soldier, on this otherwise completely deserted area, coming out from a farm shed standing by itself half left from us. He pointed to the shed and shouted, 'Have a look in there! Some of the poor blighters in there need help badly.' We went across to the shed,

St Quentin Canal tunnel, Bellicourt, captured in bitter fighting at the end of September.

The entrance to the tunnel: on the left a door led into a room in which were found a number of bodies and several large cauldrons. A rumour grew that the enemy were boiling down the dead for fat.

ducking our heads to enter by a low doorway. There was a manger along the back, and on the ground, lying quite close to one another in a row, were about twenty men. Some were British, some were German. Some were dead, some dying; about half were able to talk.

As I walked along the row of men, eyes in ashen-pale faces looked up at me. I spoke to several young Lancashire Fusiliers but knew none personally. It was midday and some of them had doubtless been there since dawn, or just after. We gave some a drink from our water bottles, and offered to re-dress their wounds, but they said, 'No. we'll wait for the RAMC.'

We promised to report where they were and left them; there was no more we could do. Often there was this gap of a day or more in a rapid advance. Wounded men unable to walk to a dressing station were bandaged by the stretcher-bearers or by their mates, and left behind as their comrades pressed on to consolidate their position or continue to attack. Later, the ancillary services come forward, tend the wounded, bury the dead, collect weapons, ammunition, picks, shovels, petrol cans and generally tidy up.

We passed the farm from which we had escorted the German prisoners, and then after crossing more fields, began to approach a large village, I think it was Englefontaine. It had evidently been strongly defended, for as we passed through orchards of apple trees between us and the village, many tree trunks were scarred white by machine-gun fire.

Under the trees lay several groups of Lancashire Fusiliers; all dead. Amongst them lay a young officer; I went close to see if I knew him, but his face was so disfigured I could not recognize him.

Looking up, I saw one of my men trying to remove from the sleeve of one of the dead, a Lewis gunner's badge, and I ordered him to leave it alone. I realize now that we were all mere boys and how understandable it was at the age to covet a nice brass badge, even in those grim circumstances.

15th October: Our colonel called all his officers for a conference. Sitting on the edge of a makeshift bed he read out the day's work ahead. It was the intention to take Courtrai. Information had come in to the effect that the Germans were preparing to make a stand but that for some distance the ground was clear. B Company – my company – would form the first wave and I was to be the direction officer. I was given points on the map and compass bearings and had it impressed on me to keep well ahead so that a good line could be maintained.

Second Lieutenant Harold Jones, 2nd The South Wales Borderers

Zero hour was at 9 am. We took up our positions, the barrage duly dropped. It was to be a creeping barrage and at the first alteration of range I was to move forward. Patrols had reported there were no Germans immediately in front of us but as soon as we showed ourselves we had proof that the patrols had not done their work properly, if they had done it at all. A terrific burst of machine-gun fire accompanied by artillery opened out on us and before I had covered 100 yards I was lying on the ground with my right leg shot off above the knee and my right shoulder badly smashed! My runner was lying on top of me shot through the stomach. Jerry was there in strength waiting for us. He got 50 per cent of my company alone, some of the men who had been right through the war. Although so very badly wounded and apparently bleeding to death, incredible as it may sound, I did not lose consciousness. As wave after wave of the attack passed I called for stretcher-bearers. Quite properly they would not stop. A few fellows tried to cheer me by telling me I had a 'Blighty' but I had great doubt as to whether I should see home again.

Notwithstanding my apparently hopeless state I was quite interested in the progress of my comrades. I can visualize now the grey strained faces that passed me and how they all avoided a second look at me and my runner who were no doubt a ghastly sight. One boy, bless him, did stop and give me a sip of his water bottle. I saw my colonel pass with his little staff of runners and he had a look of grim determination on his face doubtless engendered by the heavy casualties we had received. At long last a stretcher party came along. They put my runner on one but I would not allow them to touch me! I wriggled onto the stretcher myself. My bearers were two lusty Scotchmen. After carrying me some distance they put me down and seeing my eyes closed argued as to whether it was worth while taking me any further. I was too weak to join in the argument but fortunately some German prisoners came along and were commandeered to carry me and very gentle they proved to be. We reached the dressing station safely and I was soon sent on to the field hospital where the amputation of my leg was completed. Thanks to wonderful surgery my arm was saved. This day's fighting was the last in which my battalion took part and notwithstanding our heavy casualties was a great success. It was very hard luck on me to have come right through only to be knocked out at the end but I have no grouse. I realize that I had been exceptionally lucky to have lasted so long.

Driver Aubrey Smith, 1/5th The London Regiment (London Rifle Brigade)

The transport travelled by road on the 15th, and a very memorable trek it was. As a matter of fact, it was the last occasion in the war on which we journeyed *away* from the firing-line, and all the details of the familiar, desolate landscape over which we passed for mile after mile were like a panorama of past incidents being brought before our eyes. Chérisy, Wancourt, Neuville-Vitasse – it was the first time I had been in the village since April 1917 – Beaurains, Achicourt, Arras – all these places filled one with melancholy and gave plenty of scope for philosophizing. Overgrown trenches, almost obliterated German and British graves, relics of barbed wire, scenes of old horse-lines and memorable dumps once visited by night, passed by us as though the Kaiser were taking us for a tour of inspection from end to end of this abhorrent wilderness and saying: 'See what I have accomplished.'

The Germans in retreat with what appears to be looted material stacked high on their wagons.

Second
Lieutenant
George
Atkinson, 2nd
Army, Royal
Engineers

16th October: Company moved forward at 10.30 am to battle areas and took over billets from a company of our left division. There are no signs of war here, and almost every man in the company has a bed to sleep in – splendid grazing for the horses and lots of vegetables in the fields for ourselves. It is all like fairyland, and we walked out solemnly this afternoon to look at a large green field without a single shell hole in it.

Reports state that we have taken Courtrai, and streams of refugees coming back along the roads indicate that it may be true. Unfortunately, they are all of the very lowest classes, and as they only speak Flemish we were unable to get any information out of them. It is a heartbreaking sight to see them trudging through the rain – old men, women, and the tiniest of children. Sometimes they wheel a barrow containing a few of their goods, but most of them are without anything except the miserable rags they stand in.

Private Stephen
Graham, 1st
Scots Guards

The great adventure of this stage was the entry into the village of St Python, in which three platoons participated. Towards midnight on Saturday a railway bridgehead was taken without the enemy knowing it. Another patrol surprised and captured a machine-gun post in silence. Various sentries were disposed of silently, and an entry into the village was effected.

It was found next morning that the sleeping and silent settlement which they had wandered about by night was full of Germans and of French civilians, and our men therefore marched into a melee of mingled hostility and hospitality.

A cheery old Highlander, called 'Fergie' by us all, one of my original squad, told me how embarrassed he was by the women trying to throw their arms round his neck, whilst he, with fixed bayonet, crept forward, watching every corner of a wall for the shadow of an enemy. The villagers were entranced by our appearance on the scene. It must be said these were the first civilians we had seen for two months. The enemy had been evacuating the French population with his guns and his ammunition, and now, because we had come further than he had expected and had surprised him, we came upon civilians en masse.

Whether these, during their four years' stay with the enemy, had been ill-treated or not, it would be difficult to say, but they were well fed and cheerful, and at the same time extremely joyful in greeting us. A captain and a sergeant major entered one of the houses and received a very warm greeting, and sat down to have coffee, whilst the women asked question after question about the advance. Wherever our men went indoors and encountered the French, they were regaled with coffee and eggs and soup and what not. But the clearing of the village proceeded all day under heavy machine-gun fire, and much sniping by the enemy. The German commanded nearly all the streets, with his machine guns posted in the houses on the other side of the river.

We were now approaching the village of La Jonquière. The Germans were still holding the place (but not, we gathered, in any great numbers) and were covering the road leading to it with machine guns. We crept along the ditch at the side until we came opposite the first house in the village. The house, unlike any that we had seen up to now, had the appearance of being occupied. Awaiting our chance a sergeant and I dashed across the road. As we reached the other side the machine guns in the village opened up again. The door of the house was bolted and we hammered on it. Presently we heard footsteps inside. A moment later the door opened a couple of inches and an old French peasant's wizened face was staring out at us. It was plain that he had no notion we were there. Instead of flinging open the door and letting us in, he continued to stare at us through the chink.

Lieutenant Alan Thomas, 6th The Queen's Own (Royal West Kent Regiment)

'Come on, mister!' exclaimed the sergeant, preparing to put his weight against the door.

'Nous sommes les Anglais,' I announced, hoping that my accent would not be too obscure for him.

'Les Anglais!' he repeated in astonishment.

It was difficult for us to realize that he did not recognize our uniforms.

He opened the door wide and then went hobbling to the head of the cellar stairs, where he stood shouting down. There was something very like exultation in the old man's voice. A moment or so later we found ourselves surrounded by women and children, all speaking at once. Even the sergeant made out that they were glad to see us. …

It was in this village that I went over a house that had been ransacked by the Germans an hour or so before. The coffee was still hot in the pot

out of which they had been drinking. It was a better class house than the others, and had been decently furnished. But now most of the furniture was smashed (presumably to prevent the English from using it) and in one of the bedrooms the contents of a chest of drawers containing mostly lingerie had been strewn over the floor. It was as if burglars had been searching the place for valuables.

Private Stephen Graham, 1st Scots Guards

The homes of the exiled villagers were unreservedly in the hands of the soldiers, as were also the strange hoards of potatoes, carrots, and turnips, which the Germans had accumulated in every cellar. The cellars had been dug out marvellously, and contained considerable supplies, which the enemy had been unable to remove in time. Thus every evening there were unusually good suppers simmering on the French stoves, vegetable soups, strengthened by bully, and occasionally by the presence of a rabbit which had been found. On Thursday, October 17th, however, the battalion marched back to Boussières, which was crowded with other brother battalions. An atmosphere of festivity and happiness reigned there also, and though rooms were more crowded, the comfort was as usual as at the former village. And whilst the men sang and gossiped of the war, the chiefs were busy with the details of the next advance. On October 18th a practice moonlight attack was carried out, and on the 19th the battalion marched forward to its new battle positions for the next stage of the advance.

The 19th was a Saturday, and that evening, in a large house on the St Vaast road, a battalion dinner was given, and all the officers who were going into action after midnight sat down together and dined. The Colonel presided; Captain R. acted as host, and his cook prepared the dinner. It was a characteristic occasion, when each, even in conviviality, knew that a few hours hence he or his friend might be dead. At midnight the battalion marched out in the pouring rain to the crossroads at Arbre de la Femme, and in what was otherwise an almost bloodless advance the youngest of the subalterns met his death.

All that was encountered were rather lonely German posts and slight garrisons in little villages. Prisoners were sent down in the course of the night. The advance was generally notable because of the flaming thermite shells used to indicate the boundaries of the barrage, and also to give the signal when every four minutes the fire-curtain lifted and swept clear of a hundred yards.

Carrying on our offensive, the Second Division was now in the line, and numbers of blue-clad Germans streamed back to us along the highway. The cages at St Hilaire filled several times with Germans, strange, unwashed, ill-shaven, dirty men in shoddy uniforms, with broken boots and weather-beaten old hats – all sorts and sizes of men, Prussians, Westphalians, Bavarians, Alsatians, different types of faces, all relieved, all 'out of the war', and yet all depressed. With the failure of Germany's fortunes in the field the last vestige of dignity seemed to have departed from the faces of the prisoners; they were creatures that once were men; human beings who had suffered three successive kinds of degradation – they had been industrialized, then militarized, and finally captured by an enemy. Nevertheless, a considerable amount of curiosity reigned among us regarding them, and we lined the road in numbers to look at them come in, and crowded about the barbed-wire cages to stare at them. After nightfall friendly Tommies brought cigarettes and handed them through the wire, and talked with those who could speak any English. Such conversations were mostly friendly, but I was highly amused to listen one evening while a little fellow in the Royal Scots recapitulated in a loud voice

Opposite: *Returning refugees in Ruuval village. It would take years and extraordinary endeavour to recreate some semblance of normal life.*

all the atrocities the Germans had committed, and especially those with regard to British prisoners. The captured German kept mildly protesting that it was not true, but the Scot out-voiced him firmly and terribly.

Whilst we were billeted at St Vaast there was considerable increase in the civilian population. From the villages liberated by the Second and Third Divisions the evacuees of St Vaast and St Hilaire came slowly, with their bundles, over the shell-pitted roads, and found their old homes amongst us. They were a very quiet and humble folk, and the children much astonished us by lifting their hats to the officers, even upon occasion to the sergeants – the Prussians had taught them to. The returned villagers took over the living-rooms, and the soldiers went to the barns and the cellars, or they waited for our next move to take over their property then. Certainly those first to return to their property were luckiest. The Germans during their occupation had moved chairs, beds, tables, clocks, from house to house to suit the requirements of rank and comfort. Each officer had made up his apartment, according to his taste, from the furniture and belongings of neighbouring houses. The consequence was that the returned villagers had to go from house to house with barrows

A civilian with a mattress piled onto his wheelbarrow walks through a wrecked village. Private Stephen Graham speculated that not every item was 'claimed' by its rightful owner.

to make up their belongings. Thus, whilst having tea, two women would come in at the door of the billet and look around whilst we saluted them and addressed gallantries. They would select one chair perhaps, or throw loving eyes upon the much-scratched piano. Then our fellows would give them a hand to shift the furniture. Whether in every case these returned villagers had an unbiased vision of what was their own and what belonged to less fortunate neighbours I cannot say, but I imagine some lively disputes would eventually arise as to whom exactly belonged certain armchairs which had appeared in an unwonted way in houses that used to be more bare, and whose was the covetable wall-clock that now hung on the wall.

The new villagers, however, set to work to clear and to clean, and to render barracks and billets into homes once more. They lived on potatoes and carrots, augmented with army rations; their fires burned, their wash-tubs outside their houses steamed. For themselves they had a strange unwonted look to us, these first civilians. They were decidedly different from the French we had left behind in the old Arras and Albert regions; in their faces were reflected the German; they were more humbled and depressed than the French refugees who had lived with the French. And they did not speak the curious talkee-talkee pigeon-English which our old friends in the background used to converse with us. When we said to them 'Commang ally plank?' and 'Tout de suite and the tooter the sweeter', they seemed mildly surprised. They even brought Germanisms to us, such as the word *Kapoot*, unheard by us till then. These apparitions in black seemed like ghosts of people who had died in August 1914.

The people were anxious to do anything for us. Did we want billets? A billeting officer had the time of his life. In the past he had often experienced trouble in finding accommodation, but now he was offered it in such profusion that he was afraid of slighting the people's feelings by having to refuse some of them. One man admitted to me that he had been given seven cups of coffee in half an hour. Many of the houses still exhibit the placard in red, white and blue, which was in every window at the end of October – 'Glory to our liberators' – and some of us have kept these placards. They will serve, in years to come, when we sit around the fire at home smoking the pipe of peace, with our old carpet slippers in the fender, to remind us of the patient souls to whom we brought freedom at last.

Lieutenant Leslie Tilley, 2/6th The Norfolk Regiment

Not all civilians welcomed Allied troops. Some civilians had collaborated with the Germans, and their future in their villages was now in the balance; the Germans had gone and retribution was likely. Other civilians appeared to harbour inexplicable animosity towards British troops, not that the troops cared that much.

Private
Christopher
Haworth,
14th Princess
Louise's (Argyll
and Sutherland
Highlanders)

I am one of ten men who occupy the front room of a house, and our hosts do not appear to rejoice in our occupation. Before retiring for the night we decide to make a drink of *café-au-lait* which we were able to buy from the canteen when on rest. One of the boys approaches Madame and courteously enquires if she will provide hot water, but Madame is hostile and refuses, so we are deprived of our nightcap.

In the morning we explore the garden and discover boxes of German soda water and articles of German Army clothing, some of which we annex as souvenirs. We break up the boxes which contained the bottles of soda water, and proceed to light a fire in order to boil water for a drink. Our hosts, who constantly keep a watchful eye upon our movements, observe what we are about to do and become almost frantic with rage. The wood is lighted in the stove, and the old couple continue to run about like the proverbial scalded cats, screaming and gesticulating; but we take no interest.

A man from another platoon calls upon us and we tell him what all the fun is about, and he laughingly remarks, 'You ought to be in my billet across the street. The old girl brought us an early morning brandy to drink in bed. She's the goods and looks after us like a mother.'

Driver Alfred
Henn, 3rd
Battery,
Warwickshire
Royal Horse
Artillery

We were coming through French village after French village, and our officer halted us and said we'd got to take our canvas buckets and fill them with water to give to the horses. So we all trooped down this long street of working-class houses until we came to a gap in the terrace, where there was a pump. As we approached, we were stopped by a crowd of people who would not allow us any water.

After a moment, a woman shook her fist at us and said, to our total surprise, *'Allemands bien, vous cochons'*, 'Germans good, you're pigs'. It shook me and I can only think that some of our own troops had gone in there before and misbehaved themselves.

British soldiers must have been particularly 'bad' for the Germans had hardly been 'good'. German troops had left a trail of devastation: houses ransacked, road and rail infrastructure wrecked, factories looted for metals. They were living on their wits, and they were hungry, often leaving local people with little to eat. As a consequence, British troops were told that their own rations were being reduced in order to feed civilians, although old soldiers were long enough in the tooth to believe this a convenient excuse, as they saw it, for logistical errors and incompetence.

The people were friendly and kind to us, but they seemed as yet too dazed to realize that the German Occupation was actually a thing of the past. They were badly clad, looked sad and emaciated. What they craved was meat. They asked for the carcass of a horse that had been killed in our lines. It must have been a British horse, because all the German horses we came upon had been stripped of the best of their flesh. Seemingly every

Captain James Dunn, RAMC attd. 2nd The Royal Welsh Fusiliers

A bridge blown up by the enemy over the canal near Vendin, north-east of Arras.

German on finding a dead horse took out his jack-knife, cut himself a steak – preferably from the loin, and put it in his haversack for a future meal. The inhabitants stripped the bones; groups of old men, women and children could be seen round the carcasses.

Captain Mervyn Sibley, 9th The Gloucestershire Regiment

The Boche had destroyed the bridges and railway tracks most methodically and thoroughly. Weeks after he has left, too, delayed action mines go up, making further trouble when everything is thought to be in order. For long distances every single railway metal has been rendered useless by a small charge being exploded at every alternate join. This just bends the ends of two metals to one side, and thus they all have to be taken up and replaced. As for bridges, I have to see one railway or road, in the district covered by his retreat, which he has left intact. The Germans have driven off all the cattle on which the people chiefly depend for food. One old woman lamented that she had nothing to eat except for soup and dry bread so we gave her a packet of chocolate.

Lieutenant Alan Thomas, 6th The Queen's Own (Royal West Kent Regiment)

By degrees we went forward with more confidence. But we very soon found that though the Boches had fled they had left a lot of little things behind them. The door of a German dugout would be found shut, and the fellow who opened it would be blown to pieces. Trip wires were encountered, linked up with high explosives. Delayed action mines would be laid under houses – the kind of houses that would naturally be chosen as Brigade or Divisional Headquarters. In one house a piano (always a popular find for the troops) had been left intact. When the first chord was struck up went the piano and the house as well. We soon learnt to be careful.

Driver Aubrey Smith, 1/5th The London Regiment (London Rifle Brigade)

Events soon began to move so rapidly. ... The evening that Harbord rushed in with a paper announcing the fall of Ostend, Lille and Douai, we began to feel somewhat optimistic, and the further capture of Tourcoing, Roubaix and Bruges showed pretty plainly that we had now arrived at semi-open warfare. On the 24th we read of another big British attack south of Valenciennes; then the Italians struck, then Ludendorff resigned. Aleppo and the whole of Syria were conquered. Austria sent in a request for peace. Of course we had been so beguiled by hope of victory in the past and so steeled to face the prospect of another two years of war, that our feelings erred on the side of incredulity rather than over-exuberance. … For once we were rather keen to return to the firing line: we wanted to know the thrill of going forward, day after day, liberating civilians as they had done at Bruges and elsewhere: we wanted to know the joy of being welcomed by the French population. …

At last the movement orders arrived, and we made preparations for departure. So light-hearted were we that, when the hired piano was loaded on a GS wagon and driven over to the residence of its owner, the unloading party, with one man seated at the piano, sang ditties to all and sundry as they passed through the village, and before they reached their destination quite a crowd of civilians had crowded round to listen to the novel concert party.

We were going back to the Cambrai sector, but no longer could it be given that name. For the firing line was now close to Valenciennes, and beyond that, the distance getting shorter every day, was the town we wanted to reach more than all others – Mons!

The German Army bought time for its retreating troops: makeshift defensive positions were taken up, often behind a river, but to what end? Ludendorff knew that the German Army was beaten. An armistice was required, but there was still a lingering assumption that this could be negotiated rather than an unconditional submission. Meanwhile, the fighting retreat continued, with German machine-gunners selling their lives dearly to stall the Allied advance.

Our battalion's turn to take the lead again. A crisp morning with a heavy white mist on the ground so that you could not see 10 yards in front of you. My company formed the advance guard. The 'point' (marching 25 yards ahead of everybody else) consisted of a sergeant and one man. Half an hour after we started I joined them just to see how it felt to be leading the whole British Army in the direction of Berlin. The bite in the air had a tonic effect and the stolidity of the sergeant next to whom I marched, added to one's confidence. The ring of our footsteps on the road must have told anyone who heard them that we knew where we were going and that we meant to get there. …

Suddenly out of the mist a tenor voice challenged us.

'Halt! Wer da?'

Lieutenant Alan Thomas, 6th The Queen's Own (Royal West Kent Regiment)

Inspiration from dire necessity: the Germans were adept at clever improvisation; sham shell holes conceal dugouts and machine-gun nests near Courrières.

Sham shell holes.

Tank traps near Pont-à-Vendin.

Unfinished and abandoned German concrete pillboxes near Provin.

We paused for a second and then the sergeant spoke.

'Oo are yer?'

A shot cracked. The bullet must have passed between me and the sergeant – about the level of our heads.

'Tell the men to get into the ditches,' I said. We took to them ourselves, blessing the French for their sagacity in lining their *routes nationales* with ready-made trenches. We opened a covering fire with rifles and Lewis guns at point-blank range. For a moment or so our fire was returned by a Boche machine gun. Our men kept their heads down and their fire up. Then the machine gun gave over and a moment or so later I blew my whistle and ordered the 'ceasefire'. Gingerly we got up out of our ditches and advanced along the road. There was no more firing now and no more tenor voices challenging us. When we had gone about 50 yards we came to a farmhouse, situated at a crossroads. Three or four Germans were lying there – all dead. Fading into the distance we could hear the clatter of hooves. Of the machine gun there was no trace. The Germans in fighting their rearguard action were using mounted machine guns. They held up the advance as long as long as they could, then galloped away.

Pressure had to be maintained on the German Army so that they were forced to see, as quickly as possible, the hopelessness of their cause. No respite would be given, for a pause would only encourage the enemy to regroup. But Allied troops were exhausted by the pace of advance, which, if anything, was increasing, and the emotional toll that exhaustion took on the men was as great as it was physical.

Second Lieutenant George Atkinson, 2nd Army, Royal Engineers

20th October: Standing-to all day under one hour's notice to move as the forward division are attacking the ridge which overlooks the Scheldt. In the evening we heard that the attack was held up and failed, and we are to try our luck tomorrow. At 9.30 pm I rode forward with No. 2 Section with orders to join the Fusiliers before dawn. It was abnormally dark, raining persistently, and I had the greatest difficulty in finding our way – worst of all, I had to conquer an ever-growing feeling that I didn't care whether I found it or not – even that little responsibility was too much for me. I wanted to be alone to cry. After two hours I fell into a coma and then dismounted and walked to prevent myself giving way altogether.

We found the brigade at 3 am, and I put the men into a barn for two hours' rest. I gave orders to be called at five, and turned into an armchair in the farm-house kitchen.

For the first time since I came to France my nerves gave way completely and I was tormented with fears of the morrow. I had just been told that we were to go forward with the Fusiliers against the banks of a canal and help them across as well as we could – there would be machine-gun fire and no cover. Those were the facts. We have done infinitely worse a thousand times and thought nothing of it.

But I lay in that chair for two hours actually shivering with fear and apprehension. My crazy mind wouldn't rest, and I saw myself killed in a dozen different ways as we rushed for the canal bank – at one time I had the wildest impulse to run away and hide until the attack was over. I knew that was impossible, and then I thought I would report sick and pretend to faint. I was ready to do anything except face machine-gun fire again – once we got so close that I could see a German's face leering behind his gun and the familiar death rattle was as loud as thunder in my ears. I sat and watched my hand shaking on the edge of the chair and had no more control over it than if it had belonged to someone else. Somehow I pulled together when the orderly corporal came, paraded the section, mechanically inspected

A bridge destroyed by the Germans that spanned the dry bed of the Canal du Nord.

the tools, and then marched off. In ten minutes I was myself again and at six-thirty we reached the Fusiliers. At seven the advance commenced in drizzling rain and we moved forward over the sodden fields.

21st October: It was very misty at first. … Scattered groups of men worked steadily forward over the open fields and occasionally a nervous civilian would take a peep at us from a farm-house window – there was no sign of war except, perhaps, an unnatural stillness which seemed to hang over the countryside like a mist. It gave one an uncanny feeling, this blundering forward in the mist across an unknown country – the only certainty, that Death was in front and that we must walk on until He declared Himself.

By eleven we were within 1,000 yards of the canal and could dimly see the general line of the banks in front of us. Here, at least, we knew that there would be resistance, but as yet there came no sound from the rising ground in front. The ground between us and the canal was very open, so we rested some minutes behind the last thick hedges and took the opportunity of reorganizing the units. Then we went forward again, a long straggling line of crouching figures who cursed and panted as they toiled over the swampy ground.

At last the storm broke, heavy machine-gun fire but at rather a long range. The line flopped down into the mud, and groups of men began to work forward in short rushes to a ditch in front which seemed to offer cover. We reached this with very few casualties, but the fire was too hot for further progress. Sniping continued all day, and in places we pushed two or three hundred yards nearer the canal. No. 2 Section took refuge in a farmhouse and awaited developments.

After dusk I crawled forward with Jennings of the Fusiliers and got through onto the canal towpath – there were a lot of Huns around the canal and their outposts were fully 300 yards on our side of it. After some difficulty we got within about 50 yards of the bridge and I noticed that the Huns could still crawl across, although it was badly damaged – allowing for further demolitions I didn't think we should have much trouble in getting a foot-bridge across the ruins – we were nearly caught once, and lay between the water and the towpath while a party of about ten Huns walked along the path not 10 feet away. Got back safely in the small hours and had a short rest in soaking clothes on the farmhouse floor.

I am too exhausted to feel tired.

22nd October: Apparently some of our people have got across the canal farther to the north, and at 9 am the attack was resumed on that side with a view to forcing the Huns out of their position. Our orders were to co-operate by means of a demonstration against the canal, but the machine-gun fire was too heavy and we could do nothing except waste a lot of ammunition. I only remember seeing a German once during the whole day, and yet the slightest exposure on our part was answered by an immediate burst of fire – they stuck it very well, because the fighting on their right flank was very heavy and they would all have been taken if we had got through. For several hours during the morning the rifle and machine-gun fire on our left was very heavy, and the 18-pounders were continuously in action and also some howitzers – several fires broke out in the houses, but the shells had no effect on the concealed gunners in the canal banks, and we waited in vain for the blue rocket that was to signal us forward. About two o'clock an intelligence officer came round and we learnt that the Germans stuck very hard this morning – we made practically no progress as a result of the battle, and our losses have been heavy.

Someone's home: a building lies in smouldering ruins.

At four-thirty the attack on our left was resumed, and the Queens made a very gallant advance which brought them down almost as far as our left flank on the canal – unfortunately, there was no support, and before dusk the weary men had to retreat to their original positions.

On our immediate right there was very little opposition, and the Durhams are firmly established across the canal. Farther south, however, our right division repeated the performance of the Queens on a larger scale and had to abandon a hardly-won bridgehead across the river after a day of strenuous fighting.

At 8 pm I was informed by Brigade that owing to the retirement of the Queens I was covering a half-mile gap, and 'should take steps accordingly'. I mounted a piquet with the Lewis gun a few hundred yards forward of the farm, and sent out patrols every half-hour, but the night passed off without incident. I took out two patrols myself but could find neither our own people nor Huns.

We have had a bad day today – hard fighting, heavy losses, and no progress – people at home seem to think that we are chasing a beaten army which runs so fast that we cannot keep in touch with them. Would that it were true; but we have been badly mauled today and there is precious little offensive spirit in our 19-year-olds.

Second Lieutenant George Atkinson, 2nd Army, Royal Engineers

After a day of strenuous cleaning, the company paraded in the afternoon and looked ready once more for anything that Hell could offer. I counted the faces that I could remember from the beginning, but there were very few left – and myself the only officer. It struck me, too, that the very men left were the ones who had run the greatest risks – hard-bitten devils like Stephens, who had been in the thick of every mess the company had struck – perhaps it is true that where there is no fear there is no danger.

25th October: Spent another quiet day, but was rushed into the war again at very short notice in the evening. Out all night with two sections assisting forward company to put a trestle bridge across the canal lower down. There was an enormous German timber dump close at hand, and although most of the yard was burning fiercely we saved enough material to make an excellent job of the bridge. The German engineers are very thorough in their demolitions, and have made a perfect ruin of miles of this canal – apparently their explosive charges are much more liberal than we use ourselves.

26th October: At four-thirty received orders to move company to billets in a farm far behind us and near to Courtrai – obviously to undergo a fattening process for further slaughter. After our arrival in the evening I had another of my black fits for no reason whatever – they occur more frequently now, and I must surely break up soon. The sober truth is that I am about as much use here now as my grandmother would be. But even if I am a wreck it is sweet to feel that I have wanted ten times more smashing than any of the others – I have given the Fates a run for their money and I believe I blew them once or twice.

27th October: I have been in the saddle all day and feel like a king tonight. Silence and peace over the whole quiet countryside, and, as I rode home in the twilight, a touch of frost in the air to catch the horse's breath and make my blood tingle. Oh! It was good to be alive, to feel the power of the horse beneath me, to feel the strength returning to my own shattered body.

I got down with the ration party, for we are short of men. As we return with the rations, an enemy plane hovers above, and as we expect a shower of scrap iron when the enemy gunners receive the signal from the plane, we quicken our steps and break into a lively trot. We have to jump a number of ditches, each between 3 and 4 feet wide. It is troublesome work footing it over the soft earth, but unavoidable, for the roads are being shelled, we are being wise and make our footprints among the turnips which is safer but lumpy. Another ditch, and we sling the bags across the first and then hop over ourselves. At the next jump something goes amiss: my arm is painful, the sack fails to arrive at the other side and has to be fished out of the water. This incident proves rather amusing, for the corporal is under the impression that I carry the tea and sugar and other perishables, and is quite excited. Fortunately it is the bully beef and tins of milk, and no harm is done.

Private
Christopher
Haworth,
14th Princess
Louise's (Argyll
and Sutherland
Highlanders)

At risk of getting too far ahead of themselves and outrunning supplies, Haworth's company stopped at a farm.

Private
Christopher
Haworth,
14th Princess
Louise's (Argyll
and Sutherland
Highlanders)

In the shelter of doorways we post two Lewis guns, each with two men overlooking the river Scheldt. The corporal and four remaining men of the section, including me, seek the shelter of a substantial cellar: here we are favoured with five barrels of beer, which works out at half a barrel each and half a barrel over. This quenches our thirst, and is less likely to cause dangerous illness than water drawn from the pump.

In the morning the air is still and silent after the violent concussion caused by the trench mortars during the night. The corporal and I venture to explore the farmstead in the hope of retrieving something in the nature of food. The larder is empty so we ascend the stairs to a bedroom, a corner of the wall being exposed to the elements, the result of a shell. We search the room for a souvenir of our memorable visit to a bedroom in the front line when the whistle of a shell sounds, and without further ado we vanish from the room like dew before the morning sun. Bricks fly fiendishly, and with one leap we land at the bottom of the stairs. We get out of the house and meet an officer who tells us that there are no Germans for miles. What a story! I think we have heard that one before. The officer wants us to go through the gate and scout round the river bank, only he does not think it worthwhile to accompany us. He orders us to risk our necks for nothing, and as the corporal is an expert soldier, we win, for we have no doubt whatever that the enemy is on the other side of the water, and the officer goes back to reconsider, and obtain expert advice.

Driver Aubrey
Smith, 1/5th
The London
Regiment
(London Rifle
Brigade)

Prospects of seeing home again grew rosier, whilst the desire to protect one's skin and carry through to the end naturally increased. What extra bad luck it would be to get killed or mutilated now – having carried on so far!

It was critical to impress upon the troops that they must not slacken in their resolve to harry the enemy, although not all exhortations to fight were inspirational. All the same, winter weather would soon take its toll on men fighting in the open as they scratched around for shelter, while rain, sleet or snow made life miserable. The end felt near, and nobody really wanted to be in the field come the New Year.

29th October: We are getting near the end of the war and the prisoners we take now won't have very long to do work for us and remember we shall not get so much value from them. Kill the Germans so that they will not be able to come up against us again. Don't think about anything else but knock the blighter out and see the end of it.

General Cameron Shute, GOC V Corps

It is dark, and as I stand behind a Lewis gun, I wonder if we are as near to the end as we believe. I shudder as I think of spending a long winter out here. It is freezingly cold tonight, and I cannot feel my feet. If this is a sample of the winter, and it is only just beginning, then there will be plenty of work for the 'trench feet curers'. I am wearing as much clothing as possible: winter underwear, leather jerkin over my tunic, great-coat and a thick woollen scarf. Oh for the smell of a fire!

Private Christopher Haworth, 14th Princess Louise's (Argyll and Sutherland Highlanders)

Operational pauses were necessary to allow supplies to catch up and for units in the line to be replaced or reorganized. It was just a matter of catching breath before going on again.

Feels familiar: officers of the 4th (Royal Irish) Dragoon Guards resting near Le Cateau, October 1918, close to where the regiment had seen action in August 1914.

Private Stephen
Graham, 1st
Scots Guards

At dawn on November 4th we set out for the line, passing out of the village with pipers playing. The sun rose over the misty valleys and ridges below, and fresh breezes and clear skies enveloped the first morning of the fight. We made our first halt, and rested below our batteries, most of the men with their fingers in their ears, whilst the gunners, with their 60-pounders and 8-inch howitzers, kept giving us the warning to 'hold tight'. When the march was resumed we began to see the first wounded. We passed a dead German lying with his head in a pool of blood, and then batches of German prisoners carrying stretchers. The wounded of our own comrades began to come down, and told of an easy progress, stopped now and then by isolated machine-gun posts of the enemy.

In the afternoon we marched into Villers-Pol, and most men, after sweeping and cleaning the billets, lay down and rested a few hours before the march to the line. Hot suppers and rum-rations were dished out after midnight, and then at 2 am, with all the extra fighting impedimenta of shovels and bombs and sand-bags, and what not, the battalion marched cautiously on, scouts reconnoitring each stretch of country in front, and reporting all clear before we crossed it. It was a dark and windy night, and crossing the scenes of the day's fighting, we remarked here and there in the dark the vague shapes of the dead.

Corporal
Frederick
Hodges, 10th
The Lancashire
Fusiliers

At a crossroad in a business area, right in the town centre [Berlaimont], was a huge crater caused by a mine exploded by the retreating Germans. The Royal Engineers were examining the crater as we passed by and went on to explore the possibilities of billeting our troops in one or two of the factories in the town.

We split up and I went into a factory and saw that all the machinery had been destroyed by some form of explosion. I was very doubtful about using it for fear of delayed action bombs or concealed booby traps among the wreckage.

I reported back to the officer, and after some discussion we decided to put the battalion in some old warehouses and large old houses along the banks of the [Oise] canal. On my way back to the outskirts of the town to guide the HQ Company to their billets, again I passed the blown up crossroads, and saw the REs had just stopped a passing pioneer company. The REs set them to work filling in the huge mine crater by the

A German mural left on the wall of a destroyed church.

simple process of demolishing the damaged houses, offices and shops at the four street corners. Crashes and clouds of brick dust filled the air as I passed. This ruthless work was necessary to enable the huge flow of oncoming traffic to pass through the town.

In Berlaimont I noticed that each building had a notice-board at the entrance, which listed with typical German thoroughness, the names, ages and descriptions of the official occupants. The best rooms, on the ground and upper floors, were for the German troops, while the French civilians were relegated to the kitchens and cellars. The town had been occupied for four years, and all the many public notices on door or walls were, of course, printed in German, and usually contained the favourite word *VERBOTEN* [forbidden].

It is usual on night marches for the officers to practise map reading in an endeavour to find shortcuts. This practice has often been the cause of more bad language amongst the expeditionary force than anything, except perhaps plum and apple jam. The enemy artillery leads us down a railway where there is no railway, the permanent way having been destroyed by the enemy to retard our movements, until a large mine crater looms before us, barring further progress. Another halt; another thousand curses; still the whistling of the shells overhead.

Private Christopher Haworth, 14th Princess Louise's (Argyll and Sutherland Highlanders)

Every crossroads had a huge crater blown in it, 20 or 30 feet and more deep, [and] it was obvious that horse traffic was going to have a difficult time and that motor lorries would be held up entirely.

The full extent of the disorganization caused by these obstructions was apparent. Losing my way on the way back to Angreau through taking a new route which was supposed to be more direct, I wandered miles out of my course along roads over which endless convoys were journeying and meeting with accident after accident at various huge mine craters. It

Driver Aubrey Smith, 1/5th The London Regiment (London Rifle Brigade)

was so dark that the leading horses, coming upon them without warning, tumbled right in. At one crossroads, in a village of which no one knew the name, lanterns were being frantically hurried to an enormous crater in which a whole wagon and team had disappeared and the drivers, pinned underneath numerous horses, were supposed to be drowning. Some of the crossroads were impassable and vehicles had to turn back.

Nobody could tell anyone else what road he was on, what village lay ahead, or how to reach his destination. Even officers I spoke to hadn't the least idea where they were, and if a civilian gave them the name of the next village it conveyed nothing to them. Here and there a group of officers could be seen trying to read maps by torchlight in the pouring rain. Never before had my sense of direction so far deserted me as it did that night, for, coming to crossroads, I had not the least idea which of the four would be most likely to lead me to Angreau. …

Our infantry were 'away forward' right enough, but all the services they depended upon for their food and ammunition were falling out by the wayside one by one, like 'also rans' in a cross-country race. The foremost railheads were getting farther from the front, the roads available for lorries were becoming scarcer and scarcer, and the distances to be covered by horse transport had been extended to four times the normal. In other words the war had run away from us and only a small band of skirmishers was able to keep touch with it.

The Germans were retreating onto their own supplies and their reinforcements, limited though these were. They were also passing over ground they were familiar with. The opposite was true for the Allies, as Aubrey Smith knew all too well, and finding the right route forward was difficult and occasionally nigh impossible.

Driver Aubrey Smith, 1/5th The London Regiment (London Rifle Brigade)

We went down a steep hill – there had been a heavy German counter-attack at this point – then over a river by a rough-and-ready bridge where artillery columns came into evidence with all their usual bustle, past some trenches, up a slope and straight on for a long way across flat country without much sign of it having been a battlefield. And then we were forcibly reminded once again of the horrors of war, as we had been on many another scene of battle, though this momentary glimpse impressed itself on my mind perhaps more than any other.

We suddenly descended a small slope so as to cross a sunken road, the banks of which were perhaps 5 feet high; then we passed straight across, up another slope and continued our course in the direction of Saultain. But in the momentary glance to right and left as we passed from one side of that road to the other, was enough material for any artist who cared to portray what warfare really meant. Strewn all about the road – as far as the mist would allow to see – in all kinds of attitudes, lying with their faces downwards, huddled up in fox-holes, flung backwards with hands raised as if to avert a blow, were scores of dead bodies, British and German. In addition there were rifles, equipment, overcoats and stretchers in profusion. It was the Preseau-Marly road, the scene of bitter fighting, attack and counter-attack, on November 1st and 2nd, and nothing had been touched since the battle. The spot was now behind us, but its impression was on our minds and caused us to shudder. Were not hundreds of wives and mothers waiting for news of those who had fallen there? Was not the whole of the Western Front a similar scene of butchery? Come, put such thoughts aside. Think of the glorious peace to be achieved by all this sacrifice! Over there is a German aerodrome, hangers and sheds complete. Just ahead is the village of Saultain, captured yesterday afternoon, probably full of civilians ready to welcome you. Forget all about that sunken road and live in the present.

[5th November]: The men wallowed in mud all night, and it rained and rained, never ceased raining. The German artillery was very active, though firing largely at random. There were a number of casualties from stray shells. The last men to fall in the war fell, as it were, by accident; strolling back from the line towards headquarters; they were being brought back to Bermeries for a few hours' rest, and were lighting cigarettes and chatting in little knots when two heavy shells came in their midst, tore one man's face off, ripped up another's stomach, and the like.

Private Stephen Graham, 1st Scots Guards

Seems like the end of the war to me; it's a proper breakthrough at last. And then, most glorious sight of all, the cavalry. How we cheer them as they trot past. This is the first time I have seen mounted cavalrymen so near the front and in full war-paint, tin hat, spare bandoliers of ammunition round

Private Thomas Hope, 1/5th The King's Liverpool Regiment

November 1918:
Germans killed
in the last days
of the war. The
man on the right
lies in a shallow
ditch close to
Le Cateau. The
photograph
was taken by
Lieutenant
Harold
Bebington, Royal
Field Artillery.

their horses' necks, swords and rifles, everything complete. The creak of leather and the jingle of harnesses sound, to my ears, almost like the bells of peace. They canter over a rise in the ground and are lost to view, and I have an uncomfortable feeling that I won't be in at the death after all. If this advance continues, with cavalry streaming through, the war will be over within a fortnight. It's a great feeling chasing the Boche, even at a distance.

Driver Aubrey
Smith, 1/5th
The London
Regiment
(London Rifle
Brigade)

8th November: We had been hoping for some really good peace news for days and now a rumour came round which, although difficult to believe, was confirmed by several people at brigade. General Hull, who paid HQ a visit during the afternoon, said that German delegates had come through the French lines to receive the Allied Armistice terms and he gave the war two more days to run. While we were prepared to accept the news about the delegates as truth, nobody, so far as I know, had much respect for the General's opinion as to the duration of the war. We had heard optimistic staff utterances before and, with all due respect to the General, we thought he was somewhat extravagant in his talk of the war being over in two days. Two *months* perhaps – if we were lucky!

The Colonel explained that we were to go up the line. Where was it? Well, he was not yet sure. The line was moving now and he advised us not to think too much of the line.

'If I were you I shouldn't even think too much of advancing or retreating either. I keep on having orders as if the whole British Army were moving forward in one piece. That means that if the Boches hold on, or try to disengage, or counter-attack, everyone always thinks their titchy bit of battle is the whole army falling back or defeated or winning. All I can tell you is – we are supposed to be going to Mons.'

A rustle of papers amongst the officers as if a breeze passed over some tall grasses, or scabious flowers by a fresh country road, or a long-meadow in far-off England. …

Lieutenant
Wilfred Bion,
5th Battalion,
Tank Corps

*A concealed
position hastily
evacuated by the
enemy, leaving
a helmet and a
MG 08/15 light
machine gun.*

'Isn't it Bion?'

Oh God, what's he saying? 'Oh yes sir.'

'I don't believe you are listening!' Still, he had a kindly expression.

'About Mons sir. We end up where we started.'

'No, where the Expeditionary Force started.'

'Yes sir. That's what I mean sir.'

Lieutenant General Sir Claud Jacob, GOC II Corps

9th November: From a speech to 34 Division on parade at Courtrai

The appearance of the men of this division on parade today is as fine as anything I have ever seen. Indeed, the whole British Army is in excellent form at the present moment – particularly its morale, which has never been better.

This can be largely attributed to the magnificent success we have now gained after four years' effort.

The enemy is now beaten and is very nearly cleared out of France. He actually sent delegates with the white flag to Marshal Foch to ask for an armistice.

The conditions of the armistice have been handed to them and they have been told that they must either accept or reject them within seventy-two hours, i.e., by eleven on Monday next.

The conditions of this armistice are so severe that it seems at first sight scarcely possible to imagine a great and proud nation like Germany being able to accept such humiliating terms. If they do not accept these terms we shall have to continue beating them until they are compelled to accept them, but it is doubtful if that has not already occurred.

In either case, it is almost certain that there will be a cessation of hostilities at a fairly early date and we shall then have to occupy Germany and see that the conditions of the armistice are strictly adhered to and carried out.

When this time comes and also during the subsequent period of Demobilization following the Declaration of Peace, many of us will be anxious to get back to our homes at once without further delay; remember, however, that though every effort will be made to demobilize us as quickly as possible, it will not be possible for every one of us to return to civil life immediately and we shall all of us have to exercise much patience, for an army of four million men cannot be demobilized in a few days.

During this period every one of us must continue to set an example of conduct, behaviour, and bearing, both to the people of the country and the troops of our allies, French, Belgian, and American. We must continue to uphold the traditions and fair name that the British Army has always held in the traditions of the world up to date, and more particularly during the present war.

Remember, you belong to a very good division. It has done magnificently. You have a first rate divisional commander and good brigadiers and it is largely due to their able leadership that you have been able to accomplish what you have. Remember that there is nothing which a division with good leaders cannot accomplish.

You are now going to hear the names read out of the recipients of honours. Every one of these men has done something especially worthy of reward and has set an example which every one of us should try to follow. I congratulate you on having such men in your division.

10th November: A temporary [road] blockage caused us to halt beside a long line of lorries facing eastwards like ourselves and a few of us thirsty for news, got into conversation with the drivers.

Driver Aubrey Smith, 1/5th The London Regiment (London Rifle Brigade)

'The war over tomorrow at eleven o'clock,' said the one nearest to me.

What a typical ASC rumour!

Seeing the cynical look on our faces, the driver proceeded to state that he had come straight from corps HQ, where he had heard that the delegates had accepted the terms.

'You see if I ain't right,' was his parting remark as we moved on again. Nobody believed him, but it gave us an excuse for feeling optimistic, and that night we lay down to sleep in a civilian cottage with rather lighter hearts than we had had for some time.

The rumour was persistent. Hobson, the great rumour-monger who could be trusted to trot out some fresh item of gossip at a time like this, came up and asserted that a notice had been posted up at brigade HQ to that effect. Where he had heard the news I don't know, but he was so convinced of its truth that he offered to take any odds on it.

Private
Frederick Voigt,
Labour Corps

Above: 'The
final allied drive'
says the caption.
Officers and men
of the 33rd MGC
pause by the
roadside.

It was Sunday, the 10th of November. We had no work to do and wandered restlessly round the town. An official communiqué was posted up outside the mairie, but it contained nothing new. There was a crowd of soldiers round a Belgian boy who was selling English papers. We bought the last copies, but they were of the previous Thursday and did not add to our knowledge. The suspense was becoming unbearable. My conviction that the Germans would reject the terms of the Allies was shaken – not by any further evidence, but by the general atmosphere of excitement and hopeful expectation which communicated itself to me. I kept on repeating to myself, 'They will not sign, they will not sign', and intellectually I believed my own words. And yet I was continually imagining the war already over and what I merely thought seemed unessential and irrelevant. The stress of wild hopes and mental agitation became almost a physical pain.

'All services suspended!' Valenciennes railway station.

A large number of Allied prisoners taken in 1918 never reached registered camps in Germany but were held in France to work behind the lines, repairing the infrastructure, unloading supplies and, against international law, being forced to ferry munitions. As the Germans retired, so did the prisoners, walking miles in deficient clothing and with insufficient food or water. Many died in the days before peace came.

We were passing through Charleroi and a lot of the local people seemed to be very excited, a few flags were waved, but we didn't think much of it. As the Germans retired we preceded them, sleeping anywhere, anyhow, sometimes by the side of the road, sometimes on the floor of a building, we had no option.

Private Walter Humphreys, 1/15th The London Regiment (Prince of Wales's Own Civil Service Rifles)

We arrived in Fleurus [east of Mons] and made preparations to stay the night outside the town in some open sheds. In the morning, after spending a terribly cold night, they placed us in a factory with other prisoners to await further orders. Early in the evening, some Belgians rushed up the

Private George Gadsby, 1/18th The London Regiment (London Irish Rifles)

stairs with some hot soup and we were surprised to find them wearing English and Belgian ribbons. They told us the war was over and needless to say, we shook the dust off the ceiling with cheering.

The next morning, the Germans took us to Namur where we were escorted to a small church on the outskirts. During the evening the Germans raided a barge containing wine, bringing several cases into the church. All the Germans were drunk, and some threatened to throw their own sergeant major into the canal which lay on the opposite side of the road. Several broken bottles lay on the church floor and the stench of wine was awful.

Early the following morning, the Germans wanted us to renew our journey to Cologne but we refused to go any further. At the first opportunity we all left the church and went on our own, the Germans eventually leaving us, pulling their own carts.

We stayed in Namur enjoying the pleasure of watching the defeated German Army retire. A donkey and a calf shared the pulling of one wagon, and all the German soldiers wore strands of red ribbon proclaiming revolution against the Kaiser. Some of them, as they came out of the estaminets drunk, were singing the *Marseillaise*.

Rifleman Robert Renwick, 16th The King's Royal Rifle Corps

We were in Waterloo Church on the night of 9th/10th November. Next morning, we were put on the move again, pushing the wagons, and after doing a few kilometres were halted for a rest when a high ranking officer came galloping up on horseback. There followed what seemed to be a serious discussion and two officers tore off their badges from their uniforms. We sensed that they were admitting defeat at last and that night we were put into a POW camp for the first time. Next morning, we were informed by their interpreter that an armistice had been agreed and if we pushed their wagons a few more kilometres, we would be set free to make our own way back to the British lines. We objected to this and insisted on our release at once. A few of us made for the gate but the sentry up in his box pointed a rifle towards us, turning us back. However, finding a weak place in the wire at the rear of the camp, we made our escape to freedom at last. It was a white frosty morning and we stood there stunned; you were free but you didn't know exactly where you were or what you were going to do or where to go. It was a strange feeling, standing there in rags and

Two British prisoners photographed, according to the accompanying caption, on the day of the Armistice.

tatters like tramps with no visible means of support. I remember seeing one lad with tears of relief running down his cheeks.

We were in a farm without food or water, then late in the afternoon a German officer walked into the yard and said, 'As an armistice has been signed, you can do as you like as we have no food for you. You are free. We are going back to Germany.' And he walked out and left us there. Everybody scrambled outside to make sure they were free, where they intended to go when it was nearly dark I don't know. Four of us who were great mates decided there was no point going anywhere so we climbed up into a barn and got a good night's rest, sleeping on the hay.

Private Walter Humphreys, 1/15th London Regiment (Prince of Wales's Own Civil Service Rifles)

Back in May, Private Percy Williams had been captured during the German Aisne Offensive. He had been in Germany less than six months, but he was in a bad way and knew he would not survive much longer.

Private Percy
Williams,
1/5th The
Northumberland
Fusiliers

I was in a little hospital in Bremen. I had gone down from 12 to 6 or 7 stone, my leg was giving me trouble, and my head was covered in sores from malnutrition. I was cold and I was hungry and my one thought was how much longer was this going to last. I was desperate to get away, to get home.

One night I heard some noise, it sounded like rifle firing, and I asked a German guard what was going on but was told it was nothing, *'nichts, nichts'*. It wasn't until later that a doctor came round and I noticed he was no longer in his army uniform but in civilian clothes, I asked him and he said, 'There's been an armistice, but it's only for a few days, it'll start again, you'll see.' …

So many men were ill, a lot of them were dying from the influenza epidemic. The clothes used to hang off them and their faces, arms and legs were thin. There was an Australian called Wheatley, he was a big chap, 6-footer, an engine driver from Sydney, and he was in the next bed to mine. One day I asked the German orderly where Wheatley was and he said he was *'kaput, kaput'*. He'd died and they'd buried him already. That upset me terribly. He's been a prisoner for a couple of years and was as thin as a rake, coughing all the time. In the end he couldn't breathe.

In anticipation of the armistice in France, men began to clock-watch. There was a feeling both of tension and of waiting; no one could predict how they would feel once peace arrived. At the stroke of eleven, they would become 'survivors', permanently distinct and separated from their fallen comrades.

An image of no distinction except that it was taken at 10.00 am 11 November, showing a battery moving forward one hour before the end of the Great War.

11th November [early morning]: Trendell tried to create an atmosphere of rejoicing by throwing his hat across the room and hitting Sharpe in the eye; Dixon bemoaned the fact that there was no beer in the place with which to celebrate the events, while Greene declared that he would end up the day 'blind' if he had to steal rum for the purpose. The astounding piece of news had left Figg speechless at first, but it was not long before he recovered his articulation and pronounced it to be a staff dodge to cheer the brigade up preparatory to being ordered 'over the top'; and his facetious question: 'What's the betting we shan't hear a gun fire at five-past eleven?' put rather a damper on the assembly.

Towards eleven o'clock we constantly looked at our watches to see how much longer the war had got to last and it was a difficult task for Watkins to walk up and down the lines urging men to erect harness racks in breathless moments like that. At about ten minutes to eleven a gun sounded in the far distance and we wondered whether any poor devil had 'gone West' as a result of that shot.

Then the minutes ticked on and a clock struck eleven. Immediately the bells of the village church rang out and women came to their doorsteps literally weeping for joy; a feeble cheer went up from the section and men gathered in knots to discuss the turn of events. We were really too stunned for much gesticulation. … We strained our ears for distant gunfire. … Silence!

Driver Aubrey Smith, 1/5th The London Regiment (London Rifle Brigade)

6 November, near Le Cateau. German officer dead hastily buried and photographed by Colonel RD Perceval-Maxwell.

Canadians of the 42nd Battalion, killed on the eve of the Armistice, lie under black crosses in Mons Communal Cemetery. Around them are the dead of many nationalities, including British infantry killed in August 1914.

If only we were in England now! Just picture the enthusiastic crowds in London, in the offices and restaurants and streets! Just picture the shouting and singing and waving of flags! What celebrations! What lovely girls would be blowing kisses to all and sundry! What crowds there would be round the bars!

Erquennes! Fellows repeated the word contemptuously, as though there existed in the universe no more benighted spot in which to celebrate the occasion.

'To think of being stuck here,' wailed Rayner. 'No champagne, no vin blanc – only about ten widows and a cow.'

By some of the men the fact of our being sent to Erquennes was regarded as a deliberate move on the part of the army authorities to deny them their wish to get dead drunk. Now if we had been a few miles ahead in Mons!

As 11 am approached, I left the village and walked back to some of our guns. The field across which I walked was littered with the usual debris of war. Especially noticeable to me were the groups of German rifles, bayonets plunged into the soil, with German coal scuttle helmets hanging from them by their chinstraps. I had seen this many times before and knew that they marked the hastily dug graves of our enemy in the last battle, but now it came home to me that these graves were the graves of our former enemy.

Corporal Frederick Hodges, 10th The Lancashire Fusiliers

11.11.18 ARMISTICE DAY

We were anxiously awaiting orders when about eight-thirty the 'Sounder' started to tap. Campbell was the divisional operator on duty and as the instrument ticked I read off 'Hostilities will cease …' That was enough. I had to suppress the jubilation in the office in order to give Campbell a chance to get his message off. Before he had finished the office was crowded with enquirers. Mr Bell came in and took the telegram while I appropriated a copy. The excitement among the troops was not great; indeed, except for a little spasmodic jubilation here and there no difference in the ordinary behaviour of the men is to be observed. It is just taken as a matter of course. The two old ladies of the estaminet hardly know where they are. For the past week they have been living more or less in a state of terror, not understanding what was happening and spending sleepless nights because of the noise of the guns. When we told them the good news they broke down and cried. We gave them jam and cheese, luxuries that they had not enjoyed for years, and in return they gave us some apples which they had kept hidden from Fritz.

Sapper Albert Martin, 122nd Signal Company, Royal Engineers

The language of the neighbourhood is Flemish but one of the old dames can speak French so we are able to make each other understood. Their chief concern last night when we arrived was whether they would be able to get a good night's sleep without the disturbance of shells and bombs. We did our best to calm their agitated feeling and they did get a good night's rest for everything was very quiet. Our orders for the day were merely to remain where we are but the 123 and 124 brigades had to push forward as far as possible and not halt until 11 am, securing, if they could, the passage of the river Dendre. From information that has come

Stripped and destroyed: a Belgian factory abandoned by the retreating Germans, leaving a trail of destruction in their wake.

through during the day I doubt if they have got quite so far. There was not much gun-firing this morning and what there was ceased at 11 am except for an isolated gun that kept banging away until 3 pm. I understand that this was an Australian battery that had got out of touch with headquarters and consequently had not received the 'ceasefire' order. But I have my doubts. I fancy they were having a little bit of 'own back'.

At 11 am the guns stopped firing, and a strange, almost uncanny silence lay across the battlefield. I was silent too, feeling no desire for any conversation with the gunners, who began to clean their guns and tidy up the gun sites. The occasion was too big, too poignant, for words, and I walked slowly back to the village, mind and spirit strangely numbed.

The weather was fine and cold and still.

I looked again at the German graves as I passed, and I thought of the relations of these men in Germany. I thought too of the many 'Men of 18' who also would never return home to their families.

Corporal Frederick Hodges, 10th The Lancashire Fusiliers

Jerry had stripped the town of every bit of brass for ammunition for their guns, and left the population starving. Anyway, the local people rushed out and we gave them what food we had, and the Colonel said, 'Come on, we must get on,' so we pushed them away. On the far side of the town, we could see Jerry getting away in railway trucks. We started to run and we could see them leaning out, sticking their two fingers up at us, and this dark staff car came up and a chap said, 'War's over, boys, war's over now, an armistice has been signed.' It had just passed eleven o'clock. And the language! 'Get out of it!' We wanted those blokes for what they'd done to the town. We told him to go and have a look at it. But the war was over, and we muttered and cursed. The Captain told us to shut up and said we could go and find a cup of coffee. Finding a bar, we went in and there were an elderly man and woman. She got on with the stove, and we told them the war was over. They were delighted and the old man ran into the stables to get something and there was a bang and he was killed. The Germans had left a booby trap as they'd pulled out. This couple, they had gone all through the war and to be killed on Armistice Day like that! Oh, there were hardly any words from the boys, they couldn't speak, they were so upset.

Private Percy Johnson, 21st The London Regiment (First Surrey Rifles)

Private
Frederick Voigt,
Labour Corps

So the war was over! The fact was too big to grasp all at once, but nevertheless I felt an extraordinarily serene satisfaction. Then someone said: 'The people who've lost their sons and husbands – now's the time they'll feel it.' The truth of this remark struck me with sudden violence. My serenity was broken and I looked into the blackness beneath it. I knew what I was going to see, but, nevertheless, I looked, in spite of myself, and saw innumerable rotting dead that lay unburied in all postures on the bare, shell-tossed earth. A horror of death such as I had never known before came upon me – a crushing, annihilating horror that seemed to impart a fiendish character to the shouting and singing in the camp, as though millions of demoniac spirits were howling and dancing with devilish glee over the accomplishment of the greatest iniquity ever known. At the same time I felt ashamed of not joining in the general jubilation, and bitterly disappointed that my own thoughts – always my worst enemies – should obsess me at this supreme hour. But I knew that the war had lasted too long. ...

As I lay in my tent amid the shouting and singing I again felt that bitter thoughts were gathering, but I was distracted by a man sitting two places from me, who said: 'It's a bloody shame we can't get any wine or spirits and get bloody well drunk tonight.'

A man lying near him, who had kept very quiet all the evening, suddenly sat up erect, glaring with fury, and shouted: 'That's all you can think about, getting drunk – you dirty little blackguard! You don't deserve to have peace, you don't! Bloody lot of fools – all shouting and singing and wanting to get drunk! They ought to have more respect for the dead! The war's over, and we're bloody lucky to get out of it unharmed, but it's nothing to shout about when there's hundreds and thousands of our mates dead or maimed for life.'

'Don't talk bloody sentimental rot – call yourself a soldier? You ought to be a bloody parson!'

'I don't call myself a soldier – it's a bloody insult to be called a soldier. I'm not a bloody patriot either – I reckon patriotism's a bloody curse. I kept out of the army as long as I could, but they combed me out (that's their polite way of putting it!), and shoved me into khaki, but they never made a soldier of me! I've never been any use to them! I only worked when they forced me to. I've been more expense and trouble to them than I'm worth. I haven't helped to win this wicked war, and I'm proud of it too! Sentimental rot be damned – if everyone had been my way of thinking there wouldn't have been a war, no, not in any country. The war's won, I know, and I'm sorry for it. But Fritz has come off best, not us. He's lost the war, but he's found his bloody soul! I'll tell the civvies something about war when I get home — I'll tell 'em we rob the dead, I'll tell 'em ...'

'For God's sake chuck it ...'

Left and overleaf: *The moment the fighting stopped: two pictures taken of the excitement in a provincial town in England.*

'All right, I'll chuck it – I know it's no bloody good talking to fellows like you. Go and get drunk, then, do as you bloody well please. That's all you're fit for …'

He flung himself back into bed and wrapped himself up in his blanket and did not say another word.

[Anonymous author, England]

11/11/18

Hurrah! Hurrah! Hurrah!

'*Der Tag*' Peace at last.

I think we have all gone mad. Such a day! It seems too good to be true. Of course in a way we thought that the Armistice would be signed but now that the deed is done we can hardly realize that the war is over. I was dressed ready to go to the Red Cross today but the news came just before I started from the house and all the sirens commenced howling so of course I could not sit working all day. I went into town instead and Aunt Tilly followed later. I wish you could have seen Liverpool. All shops and offices closed immediately and the streets were thronged with people, you could walk on their heads.

Soldiers in gangs, munition girls, American Red Cross nurses, all sorts and conditions. We met Misses Harrington and after meeting Aunt

Tilly thought we would try and get some tea and watch the streets from a window. We went to Boots' café but all the waiters had gone so went to Kings. We waited some time but no one came to attend to us – they said that waitresses had taken French leave and gone. We went to the kitchen downstairs to see if we could wait on ourselves but they would not allow us to do so. So upstairs we went again to watch from the windows feeling very hungry. Just after we entered the café they closed the doors so that no one else could enter so we were fortunate to get a view. After a while we noticed a soldier carrying tea for his party at one of the tables so I went foraging again. There is another kitchen upstairs so we had a try there – only the kitchen girls were there but they were awfully good and we had such fun. We had to forage for cups and they washed them for us and made us some tea. We raided the tables for eatables and got some buns and bread and butter and altogether had a jolly picnic. You never saw anything like the streets. Everybody seemed to have downed loads as it were. All motors and carts seemed to have been left for anybody who liked to occupy, they were filled with all kinds of people. Flags were flying, drums going. One man was playing the drum with wine bottles. The medical students marched past in their overalls. We heard one of the Yanks make a speech from the Town Hall. This is the Lord Mayor's first day in his new office and the first day of peace.

I fired my first shot in anger about eleven o'clock of the morning of 23rd August [1914] near St Ghislain on the Mons Canal. When the final whistle went four years and a bit later, where do you think I was? Two hundred yards from where I started.

Sergeant Harry Bell, 1st The Queen's Own (Royal West Kent Regiment)

Overleaf: A happy crowd of British troops in an open cattle truck in Cologne's main railway station.

ROLL
ON
"DEMOB"
(SOME HOPES)
COLN-DEUTZ
"EXPRESS"?
(DOUBTFUL)
TRAIN GUARD

7. The Blessed

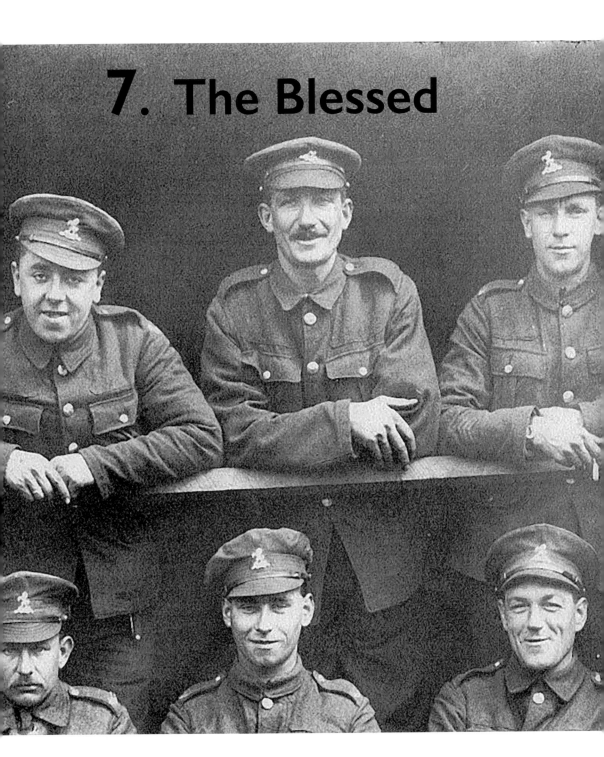

'I wouldn't have missed this march for anything. I feel it is a fitting finish to the long war. To march into the enemy country is second only to smashing it up!'

Captain Eric Bird, Machine Gun Corps

––––––––

My Dear Douglas

I am sitting by the fire on a cosy Saturday evening, Father in his chair doing the same as I am; writing to you. I have been meaning to write to you ever since the wonderful news came and tell you how it was received in this corner of the world. I kept on saying 'How I wish Donald was here! Wouldn't he be happy!'

Well we were waiting all that weekend in a kind of breathless silence for the news of Germany's answer; you could feel it everywhere you went. On Sunday morning came the news of the Kaiser's downfall, which was staggering enough although we expected it. Edgar Leslie, the Cottayers and I walked up to Crayford in the morning and one of the ordinary Psalms was the 51st, which seemed almost uncanny. Well, the news didn't come and on Monday morning Jessie and I were doing our ordinary work and the clock struck eleven, and suddenly the whole world seemed different! Sirens were blowing, guns booming and one began to realize that fighting in France had ceased! Jessie and I did a bit of rejoicing and then as people must have meals and a house must be kept clean I started off with my shopping basket and she went on with her work. I had got no farther than the gate however when I saw that Dartford Road was different. Little flags were appearing at the windows and children were running about with Union Jacks on sticks. I remembered our flag and came in and hoisted Leslie's Union Jack with due ceremony with Jessie's help; we saluted it as Guides should and marched back to our work again. I caught a tram which was cram full of munition workers all beaming with two days' holiday – everyone was smiling. It was just like one big family.

Muriel Strickland, sister, Captain Douglas Strickland, Army Ordnance Corps, 34th Division

Opposite:
An unknown Engineer captain in jovial mood stands by an unexploded shell on the Messines Ridge shortly after the Armistice.

In the afternoon I went up to London to meet Father at Westminster Abbey. The train was full but the family feeling was getting stronger still, everybody obliging and kind and smiling. I had not the remotest idea what to expect in London and made my way out of Charing Cross Station just expecting everybody to look very happy I suppose, but I had not got down the slope past the fruit shop when a roar made itself heard from the street below, a <u>continual</u> roaring with crowds and crowds of people seething like – well I don't know what it was like. I was soon a speck in it getting whirled about with the rest. Funny little impromptu processions with flags and anything that would make a noise were laughing along, cheering and shouting and tootling on tin trumpets and combs and things – motors were swarmed all over by people having joy rides. I saw one girl ringing a little bell and shouting 'how then one for the boys! Hurrah 'h 'h 'h 'h 'h' went up from the crowd in a roar. 'and another one! Hurrah, 'h 'h 'h 'h 'h…' 'And another one!! 'Hurrah, 'h 'h 'h 'h 'h 'h 'h 'h 'h…

Then she was swallowed up in the crowds and another joy ride would come along, all doing the same thing. Well I wanted to get to Westminster and as the buses could only go at a snail's pace I easily got into one and found an easy seat inside because the thing to do was to go on top and wave a flag and shout to everybody.

It was grand at Westminster. The bells of St Margaret's were clashing and clanging, <u>Clang!</u> <u>Clang!</u> And people were streaming into the Abbey. I saw one thing, a great big Tommy with his kit on his back, his helmet, and all with the dirt of the trenches on him still, cap at an angle, pipe in his mouth mooching along, utterly unconcerned, as if it had nothing to do with him: a girl on a motor pointed at him and cheered but he took no notice. What he wanted to do was to get home I suppose.

It <u>was</u> quiet in the Abbey! And dark <u>too</u>, but the service was beautiful and the sense of relief everywhere! One could almost see it!

I tried to keep a seat for Father but it was no good and I was thankful to find him afterwards coming from another part of the church. The road outside was still there and I wondered if I should get squashed on my way back to the station – Edgar and Leslie were there too and we tried to get some tea but it was no use. We got into such a crowd that I wondered if we should ever get out again.

However, we did and the next evening we went up again to a theatre in a party. We went into Trafalgar Square first and it was a sight to be remembered.

Crowds of people waving white flags processing cheering, shouting, letting off little squibs and <u>cheering</u> them! as if they'd set the Thames on fire. If anybody got a rocket he was a hero and had to be cheered by the whole square. Everybody had suddenly turned into a baby. Then they began to light four bonfires on each side of the column and the old lions stood out against the sky with people swarming all over them, their faces red in the glow of the fire (the people's faces I mean!). When we came out of the theatre, the Australian soldiers were putting the seats from the square on the fire and tearing up blocks from the paving and getting as wild as Australians do, so we thought we'd come home which we did and weren't in bed till two! Well, I'm quite excited just remembering it. It's good to be alive in these days.

Your letters have been a great pleasure to read. To think that you will be in Germany soon! It is <u>great</u>. Congratulations dear old boy and oh my dear we're proud of you.

Very much love xx
From Muriel [Strickland]

Not everyone could celebrate. Too many people had lost close friends and relatives to take part in the carnival scene. War had deprived the author Sir Arthur Conan Doyle of several members of his extended family, including his son Kingsley, who had been badly wounded on the Somme and had just died of pneumonia. He understood that people must celebrate peace, but not as some wished to do.

Sir Arthur
Conan Doyle

I was in a staid London hotel at eleven o'clock in the morning, most prim of all the hours of the day, when a lady, well dressed and conventional, came through the turning doors, waltzed slowly round the hall with a flag in either hand, and departed without saying a word. It was the first sign that things were happening. I rushed out into the streets, and of course the news was everywhere at once. I walked down to Buckingham Palace and saw the crowds assembling there, singing and cheering. A slim, young girl had got elevated on to some high vehicle, and was leading

'The Beast of Berlin', says the sign: an effigy of the Kaiser is strung up in Richmond, Yorkshire.

and conducting the singing as if she was some angel in tweeds just dropped from a cloud. In the dense crowd I saw an open motor stop with four middle-aged men, one of them a hard-faced civilian, the others officers. I saw this civilian hack at the neck of a whisky bottle and drink it raw. I wish the crowd had lynched him. It was the moment for prayer, and this beast was a blot on the landscape. On the whole the people were very good and orderly. Later more exuberant elements got loose. They say it was when the Australian wounded met the War Office flappers that the foundations of solid old England got loosened.

Those who would now 'feel it', as Private Voigt's comrade had put it, chose to stay indoors. How could they be part of the revelry? Phyllis Iliff's fiancé, Lieutenant Philip Pemble of 213 Squadron, RAF, had been killed in June 1918.

Phyllis Iliff

So it has come – the day when this war which has wrecked my life and altered my whole character [has ended] and what does it mean to us, us, who have lost our all in this fight? A fight which is not won. It is wickedly unfair to our dead, you dear boy are the only one I think of, of course, but very soon will England have to answer for this base piece of treachery in which millions of brave lads like yourself went 'West' only to have been sold as the English Government would sell anybody or anything. But England's day is over, the Throne shakes, Ireland openly hates England and will soon be out of their power, Scotland silently hates the English and is working swiftly and silently for the time when they will be free also. France and Italy and all other 'allied' countries turn away from England to – America, the country which will in a few years head the world. How America despises England which pretends to be so clever, while with her bad ruling, petty strikes and pigheadedness is losing trade and every other thing which makes a country famous.

And here – on the night when all are laughing and enjoying themselves, left alone, I sit and think of what it would have been had you not been taken away and my heart were not slowly breaking. This night when 'everyone is happy' as people say. Dear Lord! Have mercy; it is not in human nature to stand so much.

Germany had capitulated: no other conclusion could be drawn once the armistice conditions were accepted in full. There was no equivocation, no negotiation. The demands of the agreement were punitive, as victors will impose on the defeated. Germany would withdraw from all occupied territory, ceding the long-disputed regions of Alsace and Lorraine to France. The German Army had to pull back east of the Rhine and leave vast quantities of war material behind. All Allied prisoners had to be released without delay. All this and more, to ensure there was no resumption of hostilities.

On the Western Front, soldiers' thoughts turned quickly to home and the critical question: how soon would they be permitted to return to civil and civilian life?

That night [11th November] the picket kept up a glorious fire, and were able to flash their lamp about freely without fear of Hun aeroplanes, occasionally pinching themselves to make sure they were living in a world of reality. The civilian room in which we prepared for a good night's rest was filled with talk about one subject only: demobilization. And when we lay down on the floor eventually, the last thought before we dropped off to sleep was not the eternal 'When will my turn come?' But: 'When shall I be in civvies again?'

Driver Aubrey Smith, 1/5th The London Regiment (London Rifle Brigade)

We parade for a thanksgiving service at which the CO disturbs our peace by remarking, 'Do not think that armistice means you will be able to return home. On the contrary, it will be months, even years, before you are able to leave. It will be years before the army is demobilized.'

Tactless or ungenerous – I know not which – but the phrase 'It will be years' is the signal for bitter dissent, and cries of 'Oh!' followed by general uneasiness and suppressed hissing in the ranks, which causes the RSM to bellow, 'Silence in the ranks!'

Private Christopher Haworth, 14th Princess Louise's (Argyll and Sutherland Highlanders)

The battalion march past the CO, and on the command 'Eyes right!', Higson, who is muttering imprecations upon the military people, refuses to salute by turning his head and eyes to the right. The RSM thunders, 'Eyes right!' but Higson makes no response and the RSM leaves the CO, rushes madly to Higson and forcibly turns his head to the right. Company Office for Higson in the afternoon, and he returns smiling, having escaped punishment by pleading that he had a stiff neck and was unable to salute.

Driver Aubrey Smith, 1/5th The London Regiment (London Rifle Brigade)

Every day we spent in uniform now counted more than ever as a day wasted, and we were more impatient to get away from France. … The news of the Kaiser's abdication and the publication of the severe armistice terms did not arouse such enthusiasm as the announcement, a few days later, that employers could apply for men previously in their service. How feverishly did we write home, one and all, drawing attention to this

scheme and requesting our employers to urge our claims, or, in the case of unlucky ones who had no jobs, beseeching friends to pretend they had employment for them!

What enthusiasm could the companies put into road-mending or the drivers into harness-cleaning when such duties were regarded as an objectionable means of passing the time until one's papers came through and one was finished with such manual labour forever. The pettifogging attempt at 'poshing up' made everyone fed up to the hilt. The inspiration for this came from higher quarters than battalion, for we received notice that we were to be exceedingly smart, as we should shortly be marching proudly into Germany. …

At Harmingies the mania for 'poshing-up' developed with redoubled fury, and matters reached a climax when Frampton won the much-talked-of money prize from Division for the smartest transport turnout. The gift proved to be a five-franc note, which was only rivalled in generosity by the bottle of pickles presented by Lieutenant Russell.

Two days after the signing of the Armistice there was a men's concert in one of the many French steel works. There was a platform on which were ranged our instrumental band and pipers. In a vast shadowy hall the troops were accommodated. Quartermaster sergeants were dishing out rum punch, which the officers had afforded us. A new good humour had come into men's voices. The verity of victory had suffused the surface of all minds. The soldiers sang in chorus to the band, they sang even to the pipes. Singers had an unprecedented reception, and when as answer to encore the band struck up *Take me back to Blighty*, the whole vast audience of Tommies seemed to melt and fuse in its enthusiasm. The theme of going back home touched their hearts as never before. For now suddenly, after years of hope and hopelessness, it had become a practical matter.

The day after the concert there was a lecture by a Divisional Staff officer on demobilization, on that first scheme of slip-men and pivotals and one-man-business-men which proved so slow and worked so ill. Said the officer, 'I know perhaps you won't agree, but I'd like to say to you men that you might do worse than think of going into the army as a means of living after the war. Conditions of service will be much improved.'

Private Stephen Graham, 1st Scots Guards

Opposite: *The huge work of reconstruction begins: workmen rebuilding a river crossing.*

Whereupon there was a roar of laughter throughout the whole audience, and we felt somehow that was the best joke of the whole Armistice time.

Allied troops must look victorious on their march to the Rhine and that meant spit and polish. Where polish was in short supply, brick dust was used as an abrasive, which, with a dab of water, cleaned steel and even buttons and buckles.

Driver Aubrey
Smith, 1/5th
The London
Regiment
(London Rifle
Brigade)

The necessity for extra hands to enable us to bring our vehicles and harness back to ceremonial state caused the transference of several men from the companies to the transport. Our own numbers were below strength, and we should in any case have to get extra men if we were to leave shortly. So one fine day a contingent of some twenty to thirty men, mostly recently recruited miners, found their way to the section, with whom they had not even language in common, let alone any other bonds of sympathy. … With such an accession to the transport strength as these new-comers represented, the small muster of old hands became more pronounced, and it was reasonable to suppose that as soon as demobilization started our little band would practically cease to exist, since our claims to rapid demobilization were assuredly paramount.

But exactly the reverse was the case. Foremost among the starred occupations was that of mining, and it was laid down that the miners should be sent home before anybody else, irrespective of their period of service. It was incredible that these men, who had been conscripted for the most part at the fifty-ninth minute of the war, thrust into khaki and sent out as reinforcements in September and October, should be the first to go home, while men who had volunteered in the first months of the war and seen years of active service remained in France to watch their departure. The troops in France had the additional grievance that men in camps at home who had not even left England's shores were reported as being demobilized in big batches because they were at a convenient distance from the various demobilizing depots. Can it be wondered at that the temper of the older soldiers was at boiling point? Was it not natural that there should be rioting and turbulent scenes in various quarters owing to this very unfair treatment?

Mons. 15·11·18

Apart from the desire to go home, these would-be civilians felt that jobs would be offered on a 'first come, first served' basis and that those left floundering in the army would miss any chance of getting a decent job. Even those who knew they could go back to a career were conscious of the fact that experience in their chosen profession had been retarded by years of service in khaki and all that meant for settling down and starting a family. Freedom would be months away for many of these men, especially those chosen to march to the Rhineland.

In the secular mind the question of the future was uppermost, and a new crop of rumours arrived, the most widespread being that we were going to Paris to be reviewed by Joffre and were then going to London. But the simple fact was that we were detailed for garrison duty in Germany, and must first fulfil a long march – through Belgium and the Rhineland to the banks of the great mother river of Europe, the Rhine. The battalion

Scottish troops march through the packed town of Mons, four days after the Armistice.

Private Stephen Graham, 1st Scots Guards

commenced to do practice route marches. The men had to wash their equipment and shine up brasses and clean boots in their old training barracks style. Discipline became more severe, and we understood that we had got to dazzle the Belgians and impress the Germans by our smartness and by the austerity of our fulfilment of duty.

The first week after the Armistice therefore was one of ardent preparations to shine. New clothing was brought up and the old discarded. All kits were revised, and if any man was short of anything which he could not make up from the supplies he was warned to pick it up somewhere, and if anyone of any other unit left the desirable thing about 'looking spare', he had better 'see it off'.

It was bright, frosty weather, and the battalion in a new glitter of peace looked very well on the march. It was not too unpleasant an ordeal for the men, though some were ready to criticize when they saw they had still to carry gas masks and steel helmets and 120 rounds of ammunition as well as heavy packs and well-oiled rifles and equipment with every brass a-glitter. But most of the sensible ones understood that it would be best to enter Germany in full fighting trim, and with all the reinforcement of moral influence which training and discipline and style could afford.

The load to be carried was heavy, and so a medical inspection was ordered, and men likely to fall out on the march were separated off

Packing up: guns of a heavy siege battery are hauled onto a train for departure, ultimately to England.

and kept behind. Bad characters who might be expected to run amuck in Germany were also ordered to be held back, but I do not think our colonel found any bad enough for that. General Rawlinson's manifesto was served out to each of us, and we read that whereas Prussian discipline was founded on fear, ours was founded on mutual trust between officers and men, and we wondered if that was so, but we did not wonder much. A cartload of new boots was brought up for the torment of our feet should our soles give way; all the last preparations were made for departure, and on the morning of the 18th November we set out from Maubeuge.

We are starting almost immediately on a march of 200 miles towards the Rhine. Everyone has got rather dirty and shabby during the last two weeks, but we are now desperately trying to improve our appearance, so that we shall be suitably impressive and properly represent the majesty of the British Empire. The march will take nearly a month. Last night it almost seemed as if the war had started again. A large ammunition dump must have been gradually burning a mile or two away, the violent explosions shaking the houses.

Lieutenant Riseley Tucker, 9th The East Surrey Regiment

As the troops marched east, they came across parties of Allied prisoners stumbling west. The British authorities had sent strongly worded recommendations to camps that it was better for prisoners to stay put than to attempt a long tramp, but some prisoners, particularly those in western Germany, around Aachen and Cologne, could not wait and set off in the direction of 'home'. For prisoners in France and Belgium, often in unlisted camps, there was nothing to do but start walking. These men had never received relief in the form of Red Cross parcels as their whereabouts were unknown to the authorities and they appeared in a decrepit state, close to collapse.

It was misty and frosty, and it threatened to snow as we marched out in our long files, keeping studiously to our right on the way to the last village of France, Villers-Sire-Nicole. The road was hard after several days' frost. We were all provided with gloves, which kept our fingers from being chilled, and the march was pleasant. We must have afforded a strange contrast, all rosy cheeked, well equipped, well set up, marching with decision and

Private Stephen Graham, 1st Scots Guards

style, we and the returning British army of prisoners we met on the road, the haggard-faced soldier, worn out and emaciated, who in fives and sixes came straggling in from Namur and Charleroi where they had been liberated in accordance with the Armistice conditions. They were dressed in parts of old German uniforms. Some had black trousers with broad white stripes, some were wearing shabby Prussian blue; nearly all had German caps decorated with little Union Jacks and French and Belgian colours. They carried bits of equipment, such as gas masks or haversacks; their boots were worn out; on their chests large numbers were printed, in convict style. And they walked slowly and lamely, being absolutely worn out, their arms and legs wasted away, their eyes sunken and with flabby folds of flesh hanging beneath them. No recruiting officer, even at the hardest time of the war, would have enrolled such specimens of humanity in an army. Yet they had all been stalwart fellows when they fell into German hands. Doubtless their condition and appearance would be much improved by the time they got to England – thanks to the care of French and English in the rear – but for us who saw them as delivered from captivity the sight is unforgettable.

French and Belgian populations fêted the Allied troops along the route. And, as the battlefields were left far behind, so the normality and banality of everyday civilian life became the overriding, heartwarming, image to the soldiers.

Private Stephen Graham, 1st Scots Guards

We put down the heavy packs from our shoulders and laid aside our rifles, cleaned our boots after the long march, and still a little lame in the feet and racked in our backs, stepped nevertheless eagerly forth into the gay Belgian town hung with bunting and flags and flocking with a joyful excited populace of civilians. We were in that mood when the apparition of the first electric tram gliding into view gladdened the eyes, when the smell of locomotive smoke and steam across the grimy railway lines reminded of home, when the sight of young men in numbers in civilian attire made the heart beat faster with anticipative joy at our own coming release.

On the Friday the last German battalion without horses but with men in the shafts of the wagons passed through the town. On the following Wednesday the first British infantry arrived. The English soldier was a novelty, a hero and a saviour at the same time. There was hidden virtue in khaki, and even to touch the common soldier was good. There was magnetic contact between us and the crowd. The girls smiled on us, men shook hands with us promiscuously, and children reached up to be kissed. Great numbers of little children were in the street, some with their mothers, some without, and all were radiantly innocent and welcoming. It was common to see five or six little ones hanging on to the sleeves of one of our stalwart fellows, much to his pleasure though also to his astonishment. We had not been treated in this way before.

Always the peasants said the Germans passed through so many days before; they marched with their officers under arrest; they marched silently, no songs, no more shouting of 'Nach Paris' as of old. We began to see in nearly every village, and often along the road, effigies of the enemy set up by the inventive Belgians, regular Guy Fawkes figures, German soldiers' tunics and breeches stuffed with straw, a bunch of rags for a head, a casserole on that, and a gas mask dangling from where the ears would be. Below all an ironical inscription: 'Nach Paris' or 'Kapoot'.

'How did he pass? Was he humble?' we asked often concerning the enemy.

'When he came he was too grand for words, but when he returned he was *petit, petit,*' said the Belgians, laughing gleefully. The same Belgians were not all so happy if one mentioned the subject of cows to them. 'He drove away all our cows. The procession of his cows was much longer than the procession of his men. Whenever they want meat they kill another cow.'

We passed often the pitiful remains of but lately slaughtered cows – heads of cows with faces fresh and pleading, entrails of cows in horrible grey heaps, all along the way. And then all billets, all fields where the enemy had camped, were left in indescribable filth. There were the evidences of a complete breakdown of discipline. The country people showed us the black debris of great bonfires where the retreating soldiers had piled rifles and machine guns and stores of all kinds, and set fire to them before crossing the frontier to Germany. Over most of these bonfires sentries were placed, and the Germans were sufficiently German to shoot down any Belgian who attempted to steal from these funeral pyres of the war.

German troops
enter Cologne
to a heroes'
welcome, days
before Allied
forces arrive.

The last German troops to pull back over the Rhine. The banner above the bridge says, 'Go away proudly you heroes into the Homeland. Cologne thanks and greets [you]'.

At Bende a farmer told how a German officer received the news of the Armistice. He was sitting at the table with a bottle of cognac and a German novel. A corporal came in with the communiqué, read it out, and handed it to the officer. The latter, reading it, gave a deep groan, rose from his chair and threw his helmet with a crash upon the stone floor. Then he took a terrible draught at the cognac, omitting to pour it into a glass, but putting the whole bottle to his lips. He picked up his helmet and was quiet for a while, buried in thought. Then suddenly once more he started up, groaned again, flung down his hat and ran his fingers through his hair in an agony of grief.

A quarter of a million troops of the Second Army marched on Germany, and far more men remained on the Western Front, most moving west, recrossing the old battlefields. Without fear of sniper's bullet or artillery shell, they viewed the scenes of their titanic struggles: Hooge in the Ypres Salient, Ginchy on the Somme, Fampoux near Arras. They looked with wonderment at the damage and began – even now – to think wistfully of place names that would remain buried in their souls all their lives.

As we marched, day after day, through the battlefields through which we had fought, we were able to see, in daylight and at leisure, the war-ravaged countryside which we had previously seen only in brief glimpses from a trench or when fully occupied in an attack. This long march was an experience I shall never forget. The weather was cold and wintry. Every night we halted and slept in one of the empty war-scarred villages. We all appreciated the regular nights' sleep and I was glad to be finished with posting gas sentries.

During this long march, and particularly during the ten minutes' rest each hour, men were saying to one another – 'Cor! Do any of you remember when we held that trench?' 'Look over there, that's Havrincourt Wood, does anybody remember those comfy German huts we slept in when we were in reserve, just before his attack on 21st March?' 'Yes, but look, that's the trench we held when Jerry came over.' 'This must be where we lost Captain Sankey when we attacked up that rise and met Jerry head on and had to retire.' 'Who remembers putting up barbed wire here?

Corporal Frederick Hodges, 10th The Lancashire Fusiliers

Blimey, this was no-man's-land when we were here last May.' 'Yes, and that's where Captain Jowett was killed, he was a good 'un.' Actually, there was only one officer with us who remembered any of these scenes.

Second Lieutenant John MacDermott had been home on leave when the Armistice was signed. The fighting over, he picked up his camera and returned to his unit. He was not the only man to photograph the battlefields in that short window before nature reasserted itself, softening the outlines of shell holes and trenches, covering up the detritus of conflict.

Second
Lieutenant John
MacDermott,
51st Battalion,
Machine Gun
Corps

I had brought back a camera, which was no longer forbidden, and with it I set off on foot one free day to get a photograph of the grave of one of the officers [Second Lieutenant Archibald Mackinnon) of another MG company whom I had known slightly and who had been killed near the end of hostilities in the neighbourhood of Avesnes-le-Sac. I had the countryside all to myself and followed a route which took me over ground I had been near before, but not actually on. I could trace, in part, the way along which our infantry had attacked by the marks of shrapnel and one British soldier still lying in a kneeling position as he had fallen. Not very far away and without anything to show that it was responsible for this casualty was an object I had never seen before – a German-made tank. By comparison with ours it was immense, with plenty of room inside and easy to access. I got inside and had a good look around, to the detriment of my service uniform for the juggernaut had been in vigorous action and the smoke from its guns was thick on everything, including my clothes by the time I emerged.

In December I got leave to visit my brother Robin's [Robert MacDermott] grave at Auchonvillers. The Germans had not reached the village in their great drive towards Amiens but the village and its military cemetery had suffered from enemy shellfire and the chalk headstone, which my brother's riflemen had carved and set up, was broken in several pieces, though the grave itself seemed undisturbed. I then walked over to the nearby little village of Mailly-Maillet to see if I could find a bed for the night. Some of the inhabitants had returned and I heard that there was a prisoner of war camp just a short distance away.

German prisoners on a working party: enemy POWs would not be released until the signing of the Versailles Peace Treaty in June 1919.

I went there and was most kindly received by the OC Camp, a captain who gave me a comfortable room and a good dinner. I explained my situation and he took particulars of the grave plot and said he would get one of his prisoners, a sheet metal craftsman, to make a suitable grave marker with full particulars of identification.

Thousands of German prisoners remained on the Western Front, tasked with the job of clearing the battlefields alongside British troops. The Germans would remain under a light guard until a final peace settlement was signed.

My host was most interesting about his work. He had some 300 prisoners in his charge and their main task was to help clear up the battlefield of the Somme. There were few escapes, he said. The countryside was so devastated that food had to be hoarded by anyone planning to get away and this was why kit and hut inspections were frequent and thorough. He asked me would I like to come on parade with him the next morning and I was glad to accept. I will never forget that parade. It was handed over to a Prussian Guards sergeant major who called the prisoners to attention with a very long word of command that ended in a sharp, short, bark-like

Second Lieutenant John MacDermott, 51st Battalion, Machine Gun Corps

A British guard with his German charges. Both sides appear entirely comfortable in each other's presence.

syllable on which 600 heels came together as a single pair and with a single click.

Then we went round the ranks and, suddenly, it seemed to me the oddest of experiences, as though we had lost all touch with reality and were engaging in an act of fantasy with those who had sought to gain the rule over us by death and destruction, now behaving in complete obedience to the will of their gaolers. It was more, but that is the nearest I can get in words to what I was feeling. I could hardly keep my face straight, but just as I was on the point of laughing outright the Captain said loudly: 'You must see our new showers' and ordered the ranks to make way, which they did with alacrity.

Clearing the battlefields was fraught with danger, for vast quantities of abandoned ordnance lay everywhere. On 10 December two men of the 1/4th Duke of Wellington's Regiment were killed in an accident involving enemy artillery shells and a third, a Private Baxter, died of wounds: four other men were wounded. Those killed outright included Private George Hardy, a father of two who had served in France for more than three years. Private Percy Baxter was a father of one who had arrived in France only ten days after the Armistice.

I was employed clearing up the battlefield for two or three months. We'd go scrounging round the old trenches, picking up old rifles, bullets, boxes of ammunition and guns, all sorts of stuff that was lying about. If we found any bodies, we were to report back and we'd leave them for someone else to deal with.

Anyway, a couple of lads from our battalion picked up two artillery shells, and one was carrying them, and as they walked, one of the shells slipped off his arm and burst and killed them both. That was terrible, to go through that war just to be killed then, right at the end.

Private Arthur Barraclough, 1/4th Duke of Wellington's (West Riding Regiment)

Ammunition dumps exploded and delayed mines, set by the retreating Germans, detonated with alarming regularity for days after the Armistice.

Captain Alfred
Kirk, MC,
1/4th Duke of
Wellington's
(West Riding
Regiment)

I was in command of the party who were salvaging ammunition on the 10th inst. I gave out on parade the orders received from the colonel in command of the battalion, which were as follows: that ammunition of all description must be salvaged, that shells and grenades were to be collected into small dumps and that any duds that were found were not to be touched, and that the attention of the nearest officer was to be called to them. I also warned the men that if they found anything that looked at all suspicious they were to leave it until they received further orders from an officer. I was 200 yards away when an explosion occurred, and on getting to the spot I found two men killed and five injured. These men [Private Albert Abby and Private George Hardy], along with others, had been employed making a small dump of shells of various descriptions under the supervision of an officer.

Lieutenant
Colonel Alfred
Mowat, CO,
1/4th Duke of
Wellington's
(West Riding
Regiment)

I was out with the battalion salvaging in accordance with Para. 2 of [a] brigade letter which states: 'For the present gun ammunition and grenades will be collected into small dumps, ready for examination by the experts.' At the time when the accident occurred a small dump was being formed by the odd rounds of ammunition which had been collected.

I am of the opinion that the ammunition which was handled had not previously been fired as there were no marks on the ground which had the appearance of the shell striking the ground. At the moment of the accident I was about 500 yards away: hearing the explosion I galloped up to see what had happened. I found that two men had been killed and five injured, the damage being done by a trench mortar (shell) having exploded.

The Armistice was a ceasefire, not a formal end to hostilities. Nevertheless, men speculated that it would be difficult to resume fighting were the Germans to fail in their contractual obligations. Men fretted after freedom and increasingly questioned the authority under which they remained obligated to serve. Their rebelliousness increased when food ran short or was of poor quality.

Dissatisfaction over demobilization or 'demobi-lies' as it was quickly coined, could lead to the refusal of a direct order and occasionally to full-blown rioting.

'What's Churchill's Game?' ask these men as they board a graffiti-covered train. Many soldiers were angry at the slow pace and unfairness of the demobilization process.

In the middle of this large farmyard was a huge midden, with a solid crust of old drier manure; it was quite inoffensive, we just walked round it to and from our billets. Captain Rhodes came round one day with the CSM to inspect the billets, and when he saw the midden he ordered some men to clear it 'Completely!' As soon as the crust was broken a penetrating odour pervaded the whole area, and the men refused to continue to disturb it.

Captain Rhodes was determined to have his way, which of course was usual when an officer gave an order; none of us had ever seen an order disobeyed. He picked on two of the men and said, 'Now, you two, pick up those shovels and get to work.' After a nervous glance round to the assembled troops, they both refused. 'Arrest those men and take them to the guardroom,' said Captain Rhodes. One of the NCOs marched them off under escort in true military style.

This scene was repeated several times as other men refused to pick up the shovels, and I began to wonder when it would be my turn to march

Corporal Frederick Hodges, 10th The Lancashire Fusiliers

some men to the guardroom, or whether we could run out of NCOs! It was really a very serious situation, but there was an element of comedy about it too. Then the company sergeant major reported to Captain Rhodes that the guardroom was full! Eventually Rhodes stamped off looking shaken and frustrated. We never saw him again. He was posted to a job in education.

We all felt a bit shocked at this semi-serious, semi-comic minor mutiny. Never having seen an officer disobeyed before, we wondered what the outcome would be. However, the CSM, who had gone off with Captain Rhodes, eventually brought back the men who had been arrested and dismissed them to their billets.

Driver Alfred Henn, 3rd Battery, Warwickshire Royal Horse Artillery

At Le Havre, some miners were being sent home to the pits in Wales. They were fed up with the war, everyone was. They'd gone down to the sergeants' mess asking for more food. I heard that there was a lot of argument and shouting and this sergeant told them that if they didn't clear off, he'd fight anyone amongst them, so they lynched him. I didn't see this but they said the body was there all right, an officer told us. There was a riot then, they all started. We could hear guns being fired all over the place, they were stealing rifles from everywhere, then a fire engine appeared, coming down from the town, and went inside the camp but the drivers were forced to get out and they ran back home. I was with two mates in a bell tent and we put our kit bags down and lay down behind them to stop the bullets hitting us. Everybody was firing at one another and the canteen, a huge place, got raided. It was full of food. Some Aussies were sent down in a truck with fire extinguishers to put the fires out and they asked us, 'What's this all about?' and my mate said, 'Oh, it's all about grub, you know, food', and they said, 'Oh, we're with you then, cobber.' They just chucked the fire extinguishers out of the truck and loaded up with food and wine and drove off.

The riot lasted a day, and by the next morning the officers were cooking up their own breakfast for the rioters just to keep everyone quiet. There was no punishment at all as far as I know; they just moved the troops that had taken part in it. I don't know if anyone else was killed but I certainly saw some wounded.

Opposite:
Those who did not endure the march to Germany were left to find their own entertainment in the winter snow.

The riot took place, though what caused it was clearly a matter of wild speculation.

At Le Havre there was a real mutiny. There was a strike about money the men wanted to spend. They got into the guardroom, set it on fire and picked up rifles and all sorts of things. There was firing all over the place, a terrific night. One or two officers tried to calm the rioters down but it didn't work. It was a hell of a night, machine guns, you could hear them, and bullets were whistling over. It was never in the papers, never reported, but it happened. There were casualties and we heard that some were killed, what did they put that down as, I wonder? Me and another bloke were nosy and went to have a look. There was a shallow trench and my mate said, 'Keep your bloody head down.' The guardroom lit up what was going on. We were 500 yards away and watched it from a hill. We could see people running around. We could see one officer standing up and waving his arms about, trying to stop it, but it didn't work.

Private Fred Lloyd, Army Veterinary Corps

Disaffection was less marked amongst those marching towards Germany: an obvious purpose remained in their work. There was excitement amongst men who were curious to know what it would be like on enemy territory and in a modern city like Cologne. Occupying enemy territory made victory seem real. Most units marched or rode the entire way to Germany, the first cavalry passing into Germany on 1 December and into Cologne six days later.

One man, Corporal Alfred Speed, 1st Leicestershire Regiment, left a record of his battalion's efforts. The men had left Bohain, north-east of St Quentin, on 13 November and reached Germany on 23 December: 'Record of march. 230 miles in 93 hours 35 minutes. 22 marches [at] 2½ miles per hour approximately. 10 miles per march full marching order.' This march carried out over six weeks may seem like a stroll, but it was far from easy.

The first weeks of our journey were punctuated by long halts, but the last ten days in the wettest of the weather were continuous marches. They made the most trying time of our experience. Boots wore out, clothes got wet through and could not be dried. Rations were often delayed, and from continuous wearing of our heavy

Private Stephen Graham, 1st Scots Guards

packs our shoulders were galled. But the curiosity to see Germany, the sense of an adventure, and the music kept our spirits up. At each new turn of the road the evenly pacing Highlanders in the vanguard of our column felt the way, explored the new way, playing as they went.

Not everyone took to the roads. Lieutenant George Timpson was in charge of the regimental band and they took a train, though they may have wished, albeit briefly, that they had marched.

Lieutenant George Timpson, 1st The Northamptonshire Regiment

We eventually steamed out of Tournai at 3 pm, having accomplished the remarkable feat of taking fifteen hours over 3 miles.

I must confess that there was a certain excuse for that train. It only had one German engine, considerably the worse for wear; there were on it a German driver and a Flemish stoker and a French cleaner, so that they can never have understood each other; and the train consisted of a quarter of a mile of heavy coaches and goods wagons, which had probably seen very little oil since August 4th 1914; moreover the French and Belgian officials could have given even an Irish MP points in the matter if holding up business. In fact, they were more to blame than anyone, and once across the German border, we went along as well as an English goods train.

Life on that train resolved itself into a struggle for existence, a struggle in which, as usual, a mixture of slyness and quickness brought the best results.

A cattle truck does not sound inviting, but it can be made very comfortable if the inhabitants thereof have the knack of acquiring the necessary commodities. Having been a messing officer myself, I know something about getting what is going, but our RE corporal did the really good work. He had been out ever since Mons, and during four years in the army had reduced to a fine art the making of himself – and others – comfortable. He started by acquiring a first-class stove, complete with pipe, which we fixed up on one side of the wagon, the pipe passing through the slightly opened sliding door, and the gap being skillfully covered by a mackintosh sheet. Where the stove came from I do not know. I know the rest of the train had to be content with braziers made from petrol tins and buckets, which, for lack of draughts, would only burn when swung by a rope from the door or window – thus adding to the picturesque appearance of the train, but not affecting the internal temperature of the compartment to any singular degree.

Fuel was easily obtained, as we constantly stopped near goods trains filled with coal – in fact, our only approach to an accident on the whole journey was when R., in a fit of unnecessary enthusiasm, tried to pick coal off a train as we passed, and got left behind on the other truck. Needless to say, he had plenty of time to catch us up, though he was a little shaken.

On the morning of the 12th December, parading in the wet before dawn, all in our waterproof capes, we left the last forlorn village of the Belgian Ardennes and climbed out to the mysterious line which we all wished to see, that put friendly land behind and left only enemy country in front. One asked oneself what Germany would be like. But only an hour was needed to bring us to the custom houses and the sentry posts. We marched to attention, the rain streamed off our capes and trickled from our hats, but the tireless pipers played ahead, and by someone's inspiration the word went to the pipe major, play *Over the Border*; so with a skirl that no weather could suppress we came up to the line to the strains of

> *March, march, all in good order.*
> *All the blue bonnets are over the Border.*

Then the pipers separated from the main body and took up their stand in a phalanx by the side of the road beside the familiar figure of our brigadier, and they played *Highland Laddie* whilst we marched past at the salute. Thus we entered Germany with no formalities and no enemy in view. We felt much cheered though the time was cheerless, and we were full

Private Stephen Graham, 1st Scots Guards

Above:
A historical moment: the 12th (Prince of Wales's Royal) Lancers halt for a picture as they cross the German frontier, 1 December 1918.

of curiosity to see the people we still called Huns, and men still talked of bayoneting and cutting throats. Presently we began to pass cottages, and we stared at them, but could see no people. Some of us shouted, 'Come out and show yourselves' and 'Come out of hiding', forgetting that Jerry was hardly likely to be properly awake yet.

Not all soldiers were willing to forgive or forget, not yet.

A troop of the 4th (Royal Irish) Dragoon Guards cross the Hohenzollern Bridge in Cologne to take charge of the east bank of the Rhine.

The first village we came to in Germany, I'll tell you what we done, we were naughty. We came to a café. The Horse Artillery went there first, they smashed the door down 'cos they couldn't get in, the owner had locked it.

We drank everything, whisky, schnapps, we just grabbed the bottles, didn't pay for a thing. Then when we'd finished, we lined up all the bottles, and smashed them on the floor, and smashed all the glasses.

When we walked in, the woman and two of her daughters were there, thinking we might want to buy drinks, but as soon as a man of the Queen's Bays [2nd Dragoon Guards] jumped over the counter, she scarpered with her daughters and bolted the doors, so we saw nothing of them any more. The rumour was there had been a man there as well but he'd slung his hook as we'd approached the border, and he'd gone off back into Germany somewhere.

It wouldn't have done for a man to have been there, we would have beaten him up, course we would, that's war, isn't it? Why? Are you going to let them off? Ask them if they'd like a bar of chocolate? Is that what you'd do? No, come off it, you'd do the same as your mates are doing, you'd be drinking their ruddy beer, course you would. The officers kept out of the way and I heard, after we'd gone, that they paid for the damage. Officers, that's the difference between us and them.

Private Albert 'Smiler' Marshall, 8th Machine Gun Squadron, Machine Gun Corps (Cavalry)

British troops march down a street in Cologne as a former German soldier rides past on his bicycle.

Private Stephen
Graham, 1st
Scots Guards

The Germans seemed to be rather afraid of us, and servile, but very poor. Tottering old men insisted on shaking hands with us. The girls of the place seemed to be carefully kept out of our way. Billets were wretched, and the men, still fire-eating, hunted for better ones which, when found, they intended to take by storm. Those who had revolvers expected to have to use them. But we only discovered that the native inhabitants slept in worse places than we had, and that everyone was of the mildest disposition. …

I had serious misgivings before entering Germany. My comrades vowed such vengeance on the people that I anticipated something worse than war. In theory, no treatment was going to be bad enough and cruel enough for the German. We were out to wreak on him four years' war-weariness; we were ready to settle all the old scores of treachery on the field and mischance in the fight. What, therefore, was my surprise to find, after two or three days in Germany, all our roaring lions converted into sucking doves.

It was an extraordinary lesson in psychology – how, without too much prompting from officials, a whole nation comported itself to a victorious enemy army, and how that army, without any prompting whatever, took up an unexpected attitude of friendliness after vowing intense and everlasting hatred. Our authorities certainly expected a different attitude, for commanding officers had been asked to leave behind any specially bad characters who might be likely to get out of hand in enemy country, and we were all warned to stick to one another and not quarrel amongst ourselves, as we should need to preserve a united front in the country of the enemy. Every man in a billeting party was obliged to carry a revolver. Some units, I believe, made their entry into all towns and villages with fixed bayonets. But public opinion and atmosphere was different from what had been expected.

Staff Sergeant
Archibald Davis,
2nd Corps,
Royal Engineers

At Duren, we made our first all-night stop in German territory, and we naturally wondered how the people would receive us. German Civil Guards paraded the streets with rifles, and did not look very pleased with our appearance. We had strict orders to go about the streets in parties, and always to carry our bayonets. An order which I disobeyed entirely. For myself, I felt much safer unarmed; as my friends were very busy, I went about entirely alone, and although I was in the streets till late at night, I was never once molested or insulted.

There did not seem to be that shortage of stuff one would have expected, but the Germans were experts in putting up a good appearance and so covering up their poverty. Sweets seemed plentiful. I spent the day after our arrival looking round the shops and the place generally. We had no cause to complain of the way the people treated us, although they sometimes looked at us a bit sheepishly. I soon found out, however, that the people were living almost entirely on substitutes. There was a poor substitute for butter, the bread was like brown sand or sawdust, and horseflesh was the chief meat. I saw frocks made of paper, much like the German sandbags, but dyed in various colours, also underclothing and shirts, the shirts having linen fronts. There was a substitute for leather; coffee was made of oats of corn roasted and ground. 'Marmalade' (German for jam) was made of vegetables coloured to look like jam. The 'coal' used was made up into briquettes of a brown colour which, when burnt, went to a powder and dropped through the bars. Soap was exceedingly scarce and dear.

The tobacco was abominable-looking and smelling stuff, made from leaves. Razor strops, string, handbags, and puttees, etc., were made of paper. The great majority of the boots were made of canvas blackened over to look like leather, and were soled with wood with saw cuts so that they gave to the bend of the foot; others were made up of small pieces of leather (about the size of a shilling), neatly fitted together – the heels only being made of wood. … I saw here, for the first time, what I saw frequently afterwards rattling through the streets of Cologne; the various substitutes for bicycle tyres, which the Germans had devised in place of India-rubber tyres.

I did not realize how hungry some of the people here must have been, until I saw the children fight like wild beasts for the refuse from the sergeants' mess, which was thrown away just before we moved off – it was terrible to witness.

The effect of the blockade on German ports: a German car 'tyre' made out of wooden blocks.

Pleasant and relaxed soldiering in Cologne for this Royal Engineer.

Unfortunately, while we were at Duren, considerable trouble was caused by the behaviour of the Scotch troops. Not only did they demand and obtain without payment drink and jewellery at the point of a revolver, but they also smashed up some of the cafés and disarmed some of the Civil Guards who were quietly parading the streets armed with rifles to keep order.

Private Stephen Graham, 1st Scots Guards

The German's strongest feeling was one of relief that the war was over – on any terms. Our coming in was a secondary evil only. Then as regards his sensitive national pride, was he not able to nurse in secret the remembrance that he had held the world at bay, and had only given in at last because the odds were too great.

When we entered into the German houses we saw on many walls and shelves the photographs of German soldiers, and as we asked of each we learned the melancholy story – wounded, dead, dead, wounded. Death had paused at every German home. The women brought out their family albums and showed us portraits of themselves as they were before the war, and asked us to compare that with what they looked like now. And they showed us portraits of many German girls of whom we asked, 'Where are they now?' and nearly always received the answer, '*Todt, grippe*' (dead from influenza); so every soldier realized that German families had at least suffered equally with British families, and the thought rested in the mind.

We were soon seated at table with young German men who but a few weeks before had been enemies in the field. They were cold to us at first, but our engaging warmth soon cheered them out of their apathy. Though our fellows knew no German they set to work to make Fritz understand their questions by expletives in pigeon French, and all manner of gestures and mimicry, punctuated by guffaws of laughter and asides to one another.

We were all agog to find out where Fritz had fought against us, where we had faced one another.

'You at Ypres?'

'Moi aussi at Ypres.'

'Compris Bourlon Wood? Moi at Bourlon Wood.'

'Bapaume? Yes, I know that fine, M'sewer. He's been at Bapaume. Wounded, M'sewer? Twice? Moi three times.'

Our fellows would unloose their tunics and show the scars on their bodies. The German boys would do the same. Then, being unable to express themselves, both would grin in a sort of mutual satisfaction.

At Hellenthal we talked till late at night with ex-soldiers of the Kaiser. I found a young man who had fought on the Russian front, and we compared places we both knew, the German diving into his memory for the Russian phrases he had picked up, such as *chai peet* (to drink tea); *nitchevo* (that's all right); and *Ya ne poni mayu* (I don't understand). At Call, near Schmidtheim – terrible name for a place – we met a young man who had actually been opposed to our very unit in the Cambrai fighting of a year before. Wherever we went we made our exchanges, and, if anything, we found the private soldier of the German Army had had a more adventurous career than we had, and any man who had served any length of time had seen Russia and Macedonia, as well as both French and British battlefronts in Western Europe. This testified to the mobility of the German Army, and to its restless energy in the devil's dance of conquering Europe. At Mulheim a demobilized [soldier], in answer to our persuasions, put on his uniform again to let us see what he looked like as a soldier; but the uniform was a new one, and he seemed to look too smart to be the real thing. We had never seen German soldiers in the smartness which no doubt they possessed well back behind the line, but were familiar only with the down-at-heel misery of prisoners, the sinister greyness of the enemy in front of us, or the shabbiness of the look of the dead.

Before the arrival of Allied troops, small numbers of British prisoners were passing through Cologne, to a very mixed reception. Private Robert Nisbet, along with two friends, had left a camp at Mainz on a steamer and they now found themselves in the Rheinish capital hoping to take a boat down the Rhine and into Holland.

Private Robert
Nisbet, 22nd The
Northumberland
Fusiliers

It was the third week in November, and the nights were cold – we had no kit, not even a blanket between us, so at nights, when the steamer always tied up, we huddled as close to each other as we could on deck for warmth. By the time we reached Cologne, we had got tired of these chilly nights, and as we had a small amount of German currency, we decided to engage rooms at a hotel. We secured rooms at the Dom Hotel [and] afterwards we took a stroll through the narrow streets where brightly lit shop windows made the place look quite gay.

This was nearly our undoing. We were spotted by a crowd of German 'Fritzes' – most of them fighting drunk – they gave a blood-curdling yell and drew their trench daggers and made to set on us. We decided discretion was the better part of valour and sprinted for the Dom as hard as we could, the rabble hard at our heels – we could all run pretty well and we reached the hotel about 40 yards in front of the pursuers.

Horrors! The great wood door was tight shut. We hammered on it for dear life. Thank God! It was opened just before the crowd reached us – we were let in – the big door was bolted again and we had the satisfaction of hearing the angry rabble, baulked of their prey, hammering on the stout oak panels with their daggers.

The next morning we rejoined our steamer. On the 'Konig Wilhelm' [road] bridge, above us the first contingents of the German Army were marching across – they looked indeed a broken army – only the officers marched in a soldiery manner, the rank and file kept no step. Hundreds of them broke ranks and hurled their rifles over the parapet into the Rhine.

That night we tied up at Wesel Quay. We could find no hotel but came across a German railway official who introduced us to the stationmaster, a typical Prussian with rolls of skin at the back of his neck. He not only made us up beds in the first class waiting room but treated us to a magnificent meal, and only after we had finished did he inform us that the steak we had enjoyed was elephant from Cologne zoo.

After the meal he locked us into the waiting room, in which a magnificent fire had been lit. Our steamer was due to cast off at 7.30 am – when we woke up we found to our horror it was already ten past seven. We hammered on our locked door and at last the stationmaster let us out – a cab with a broken down old nag happened to be at the station

– we tumbled into it, and I told the driver to drive like hell for the quay – that horse's trot would not have disgraced the most sedate funeral, and when we reached the quay we saw with dismay the steamer – *our* steamer – rounding the bend in the distance. There we were in enemy territory, by this time with no money left and no means of rejoining our only refuge, the ship. Back we trudged to the station and told our tale of woe to our friendly stationmaster. There was still hope – a train was leaving for Emmerich almost at once, and we should reach there before the steamer, which would also stop there. The stationmaster supplied us with free tickets, and off we went to Emmerich.

At Emmerich the revolution had broken out and soldiers with the white armband of the 'Soldaten und Arbeitenrat' met us on the platform and arrested us. I saw a chance still. I noticed 'Manner' written on one wall of the station and guessed that there might also be an exit from it direct onto the street. I told the guards we had to answer the call of nature and they grudgingly told us to get on with it – in we went – sure enough, there was an exit onto the street – out we sprinted and made for the river – we had got a hundred yards away when our escape was evidently noticed, for shots rang out and the whine of bullets came uncomfortably close to us – we dived into a side street and so onto the river bank – hurray! There was the steamer, but just about to cast off again. We yelled and waved – luckily we were spotted – the jolly old Dutch skipper ordered the gangway to be put back and in a minute we were safe on board.

The British hastened to Cologne, encouraged to arrive as soon as possible by the city's mayor, Konrad Adenauer, who was concerned about unrest amongst militant, demobilized soldiers and youths. Civil strife following the abdication of the Kaiser made the authorities fear for the stability of the city. British troops would be accepted without protest or hindrance.

Those of you who knew Germany before the war, when every porter, ticket collector and postman was a uniformed official, before whom one had to bend the knee in lowly humility, will appreciate my feelings when we landed on the [Cologne] station. Every German clinked to attention and saluted as we passed; the huge station was crowded with Allied soldiers,

Lieutenant George Timpson, 1st The Northamptonshire Regiment

A moment of pride as a British soldier stands at the rear of Cologne Cathedral.

who pushed contemptuously past the ticket collectors at the turnstiles, without so much as looking at them. Civilians raised their hats, and trams stopped at unheard-of places in answer to a wave of the hand. Even that mightiest of German officials, the man in charge of a level crossing, who controls the movements of the docile Hun with stern contempt for rank and class, lifted his sacred barriers to let us through under the very head-lights of a train!

The city's population would be swollen by a quarter almost overnight and troops were accommodated wherever there was room; in barracks, and on the floors of warehouses and schools. Most officers and a minority of NCOs were billeted in the city's hotels or civilian homes, taking rooms in houses where the parents might still be mourning the loss of one son while expecting the arrival home of another. Staff Sergeant Archibald Davis arrived at his nominated billet not quite sure what to expect.

German children photographed by a British Tommy. The boy on the right wears with pride his father's Iron Cross and cap, suggesting, perhaps, that his father did not survive the war.

The door was opened by a well-built maid of not too tender years, who ran away screaming when she saw my uniform, but she soon reappeared with her mistress. I handed in my slip of paper, with the following words typed on: *'Ich mochte gern Quartier haben. Haben sie eine zimmer fur mich, bitte?'* I now keep this paper as a souvenir. To this day I do not know the meaning, but it had the desired effect, as after carrying on a conversation in broken French, broken English, and many signs, I was asked in.

I soon learned that the maid's name was Gretchen, and that my hostess was a widow with three sons – one a schoolboy and two who had been in the war.

I took up my residence here on December 9th, and was allotted a very nice bedroom (containing twin beds), heated with radiators and lighted with French casements and electric light, and everything very clean.

I was informed that there had been rioting in Cologne that morning, and in case of any trouble our troops were moving forward in battle order, the guns taking up positions commanding important points.

After three years of sleeping anywhere and anyhow, my appreciation of a beautiful bed and bedroom with every comfort can be imagined. It took me some little time, however, to get used to the German method of sleeping, with an eiderdown as the only covering, the underside of the eiderdown having a sheet buttoned on.

There was only one fly in the ointment. I had to allow a sleeping mate in the adjoining twin bed, a sergeant, who was in charge of the Post Office. He was quite a good chap, but was known as a champion beer drinker; his record as far as I know being eighteen bottles on end – not a bad record. The fact that he had had a brother killed in the war made him very bitter against Germans. This fact, combined with his beer drinking, raised many difficulties. It was his practice to come in at night and give Frau Rubens a fearful life of it, cursing the Germans. I used to act as peacemaker, but she took it all quite well, and made all possible excuses for his behaviour.

On December 12th I had one of many interesting conversations with my hostess, Frau Rosa Rubens. She informed me that she was a Bavarian, and the Bavarians were very bitter against the Prussians. I was also introduced to one of her sons, who was an Unter Officer in the German Army. He was quite a smart lad, but had been wounded in the arm and received his discharge on November 17th.

Staff Sergeant Archibald Davis, 2nd Corps, Royal Engineers

On December 15th and 16th I played dominoes with the two sons. …
During the course of conversation I learned that some of the people would
like their province to become a British colony. I was asked to tea, when I
was given some stewed walnuts. Really, it was very difficult to believe that
I was forcing myself to live with enemies.

The Germans enjoyed British protection from revolution and, indeed, protection
from likely French and Belgian retribution. Few if any would have countenanced the
idea of becoming a British colony and such a comment was almost certainly mere
flattery. Rhinelanders were nothing if not pragmatic. They knew that their best
interests lay, temporarily, with accepting the British as occupiers and received with
equanimity the presence of foreign soldiers.

Lieutenant George
Timpson, 1st The
Northamptonshire
Regiment

The family soon 'twigged' that I spoke their lingo, and crowded around.
There was a grey-haired old veteran of the Franco-Prussian War, who
stood about in a skull cap smoking a pipe which reached below his knees,
a couple of young men, a woman of thirty and a servant girl. Their views
were interesting. For one thing – and this opinion was universal – they
have not the slightest idea that they are beaten. It was unfortunate that we
allowed their armies to march back intact. They are full of pride at having
held the world at bay for four years, and regard themselves as defeated
by hunger. There is no doubt that the food situation was – and still is
– serious, but it does not seem to have dawned on them that they were
hungry because their fleet dared not fight.

The folk at the inn had no love for the Kaiser, or the ruling class, or
the war – the poorer class, who are as industrious, homely and kindly a
folk as you could meet anywhere, had no desire for the war, and were only
too thankful it was over. Nor was there any ill feeling – no one could have
been kinder to our waiters than they were, and all the men said the same
of their billetees.

Private Stephen
Graham, 1st
Scots Guards

We no longer referred to them as Huns now that we were in Germany. If
Tommies are seen marching out with German girls, both parties are put
under arrest. But in the houses and in other private places the women
are exceedingly forward. They do not display the hate or coldness or

bitterness which one would naturally expect from women towards those who had killed husbands, brothers, sons, sweethearts. The young girls are all bringing their albums, and, generally speaking, hanging round Tommy's neck, and the elder ones are fussing about fires and beds and chairs to give him comforts. For themselves, they have little food and little hope of any kind, but they are not in any way depressed. The sense of guilt, of moral wrong, is absent. All they know is they have played a game; they have lost, and they are giving up what is forfeit – that is all. And there is one great compensation – an Allied army is saving the community from revolution.

'Honour to the victors and to the liberators of Germany! That's all very well,' said a hard-hearted captain one night. 'But I must have this matter out with my host.'

So he sent for the owner of the house, who appeared suave and smiling in the mess.

British troops carefully scrutinize civilian passes on the border between the occupied and unoccupied Rhineland.

On the border of the occupied zone, Private Albert Kempsell, 1/9th (County of London) Battalion, Queen Victoria Rifles, is snapped outside his guard hut near Solingen.

Previous page: *'Don't show anyone this – we are all drunk after a dinner party,' says the caption. British officers enjoying their stay in Cologne.*

'I'm pleased to see you,' said the Captain, 'though, of course, you understand me, not really pleased in any way. But take a seat. Now, I want to ask you a lot of questions. You've been treating our army here in Cologne pretty well, I admit, and there is no complaint. But how was it that you allowed our prisoners to return home so unfriended, uncared for, unfed? How do you account for the treatment of our men in the prison camps and in the places where they were forced to work? How do you account for the atrocities your people have committed? Your women are very friendly to us, but will you explain to me the stories of what you did to French and Belgian women during your occupation of their towns? You are very polite, but how do you account for the behaviour of your submarine commanders? You say you believe in a League of Nations, but how do you account for your government's deliberate encouragement of Armenian massacres, etc. etc.?'

The German shrugged his shoulders, and grew more and more pale and taciturn. He could not answer. 'Well,' said the Captain, 'you'll have to pay for it all now, to the last farthing and the last brass button on the soldier's coat.'

The German seemed slightly relieved.

'How much will it be?' he asked.

'It is estimated at twenty-four thousand millions sterling,' said the Captain.

'Twenty-four thousand millions sterling,' said the German deliberately, and with that he stood up, for it was late at night. 'Twenty-four thousand millions – very well. We will pay it, and the account will be cleared.'

With that he waved his hand comprehensively.

'Good-night!' said he with dignity, and walked out.

'I am a married man,' I hear one of our grizzled veterans saying. 'I have four children, I've been out here three years, and it has been hell. But if the Armistice were called off tomorrow, I'd gladly go on fighting. Why? In order that we might make a clean job of it. All I care for is that my boys shall not have to go through what I've gone through. We don't want to fight it all over again in ten years' time – we want to make the world safe once for all. Else what are we fighting for at all? Germany ought to be shown that force of arms does not pay. Her army ought first to be crushed and then completely disarmed. And Krupps' factories at Essen and elsewhere ought to be destroyed. …'

How often have I listened to such talk. That is what the soldier-in-arms has thought in his heart, without prompting.

I was one of those staff sergeants who, during the three months I was with the Army of Occupation, had practically nothing to do. I only did ten days' work the whole time. All my days were alike. I arrived for my breakfast at the sergeants' mess around 10 am, much to the disgust of the Sergeant Major. After breakfast I reported to the office, then usually played patience at the mess, or walked around Lindenthal till dinner-time. After dinner I went into Cologne, and in the evening either spent some time with my hostess and her sons, or made another trip to Cologne. My staff sergeant's rank, of course, admitted me anywhere, and helped to make life a lot more pleasant than it had been as a lance corporal in the front line.

On Christmas Day, my third Christmas overseas, I commenced with a walk to the Flora Gardens, followed by a visit to all the back streets. In the evening I attended a 'Party' in the mess. The turkeys had got lost on the railway; but even with the turkeys missing we had quite a good dinner; this we could now always rely on. As with the case at these 'do's', a somewhat suggestive programme of turns was provided and, of course, the drinks left nothing to be desired. Consequently, I cannot remember a programme getting more than halfway through, as by that time everyone was helpless or under the table. As each man fell out, he was carried off and put into the nearest bed or billet. It didn't matter whose it was.

Staff Sergeant Archibald Davis, 2nd Corps, Royal Engineers

I had been given a 2-ounce packet of tobacco with a gold label on the front. You could chew it if you wanted. But I smoked fags and I'd had this packet in my pocket for six months. So I thought I'll give old Jerry a present. Well, it was Christmas Eve and we'd been heaving quite different sorts of presents at each other for the previous four Christmases, hadn't we?

So off I trudged through the snow. I went by myself, because if it turned out to be a little old lady by herself she might've been frightened if there'd been more than one soldier. I opened the gate and walked down

Private Charlie Byrne, 2nd The Hampshire Regiment

the footpath and knocked on the door. An old German with one of those big pipes opened the door and he just looked at me. I didn't know any German except *'Gut morgen'* so I said that. Then I took this packet of baccy out of my pocket and offered it to him, and I held out my hand. So we shook hands. Then he stood back and motioned me to go inside.

His wife was there and his two sons. They all welcomed me and we all shook hands. They didn't have much food, but they had a good fire and we all sat round the fire. The language barrier was terrible, but we tried speaking to each other in what bit of French we had. The old lady obviously couldn't understand anything. The two sons gave me to understand they'd been machine-gunners in the German Army. I said I'd been a machine-gunner too and we all nodded our heads. It was a pity I'd no German; we could have had a nice professional chat. I wondered afterwards if either of them could have been that gunner on the Somme in 1916 [who personally targeted Private Byrne]. I'd willingly have shaken him by the hand; he knew his job all right. …

I'd spotted a little accordion on one of the kitchen shelves. So I pointed to it and the old farmer got it down and gave it to me. I played *Silent Night* and they sang it in German and I sang it in English. They really loved that. We enjoyed it so much we sang it twice. Their national anthem is one of our hymn tunes, you know. I learned all the words of the German national anthem when I was in school – in English, of course. In those days they were sort of relations of ours; still are… Funny really.'

Staff Sergeant
Archibald Davis,
2nd Corps,
Royal Engineers

The last day of 1918 was a great day. In the first place the news came through that the turkeys consigned to us for Christmas Day had just arrived, having walked all the way from London – at least if they hadn't walked they certainly smelt like it. The best were picked out, and it was decided to have a New Year's jollification. 104 turkeys were, however, too far gone to be cooked, and had to be destroyed.

During the day I paid a visit to the Museum, which is very fine and contains a beautiful picture by Rubens. I then spent a little time listening to the German lad at my billet playing *Rule, Britannia* and *God Save the King*.

'Demobilitis' is written on the rear of the picture. Despite the ease of the Occupation, soldiers yearned for family life again.

The British Army of Occupation settled down into a comfortable rhythm. The peace treaty would not be signed before the end of June and fraternization was supposed to be kept to the minimum, but there was little chance of enforcing such an order, particularly behind closed doors. The falling value of the German Mark gave the lowliest private an economic prowess he might not experience for decades and perhaps never again. The troops bought the finest steel cut-throat razors and they bought the best seats at the opera. They had their photographs taken for souvenirs, and their boots polished in the street. They enjoyed the horse racing and the boat trips down the Rhine. Inevitably, there was trouble between soldiers and civilians, but it was low level and occasional. British troops were surprised by the co-operative attitude of most Germans who were undoubtedly glad to avoid the chaos sweeping the rest of Germany: they were also thankful to avoid a much more aggressive French occupation, whose soldiers were embittered by the destruction wrought on their home soil. Little wonder the Germans would adopt the phrase 'Island of the Blessed' when referring to the Cologne Bridgehead.

After the Peace Treaty, the number of soldiers in Germany was drastically cut while those who remained were frequently joined by their families and easy peacetime soldiering enjoyed by most. The British remained in Germany until 1929.

By contrast, life was less pleasant for those who remained in France and kicked their heels around while they awaited news of demobilization. Those who had already got to Britain were soon disabused of the idea that they were home to a land fit for heroes. Instead, rising unemployment stalked the land: the termination of 1918 did not herald in much optimism for 1919. Driver Aubrey Smith was still languishing in France.

Driver Aubrey Smith, 1/5th The London Regiment (London Rifle Brigade)

For weeks before Christmas it was dinned into our ears what a splendid feast was to be given us: extra special army rations, turkeys, nuts, oranges, figs, wines and, above all – a real surprise, which was kept a guarded secret. DAQMGs [Deputy Assistant Quartermaster General] announced the glad tidings to supply officers, who in turn passed it on to the quartermasters, who trumpeted the news abroad in the battalions, and, as the time approached, we at one time contemplated writing home to say it was not necessary to send Christmas parcels this year. At last the great day arrived and everyone waited eagerly for [Private] Hurford's return from the QM stores, bringing with him the good cheer and, above all – the great surprise. Nobody took much heed of [Private] Figg's timely warning that the army had never yet given something for nothing and that we should not utter thanksgivings before the glorious repast was set before us. We were all so confident that the grateful army would surely not disappoint us now the submarine peril was past. But our dear Figg was, as usual, right in his attitude towards army pronouncements.

The following is an accurate list of the special Christmas rations served out to each man on the transport section:

One-eighteenth part of a scraggy Turkey (No gravy).

Beef. Potatoes

Three and a half ounces of Pudding. Unsweetened Custard

Three-quarters of a Fig. One-third of a rotten Apple.

One-eleventh part of a Chestnut. (In other words, six for the section.)

And the great surprise turned out to be – PAPER CHAINS

Christmas released a delayed, hectic, hysterical excitement of celebration. Our singing had alcoholic overtones; there were too many missing faces. The jubilation of winning footballers was not greatly different from the jubilation of those who had survived fighting. Keep the men occupied; sport, trophies, 'homes fit for heroes to live in', anything to hold at bay the dark and sombre world of thought.

A mixed crowd of some 2,000 troops toiled – it could hardly be called 'marched' – up the hill to Shoreham camp. I had been demobilized immediately after Christmas. An old woman stood at the door of a respectable but dreary house, waving a Union Jack. Anxiety about the reception she would be likely to receive from a lot of 'rough Tommies' made her voice tense. 'Welcome home boys, welcome home,' she squeaked. For a moment there was astonishment at the apparition. The impulse to jeer was suppressed. 'Give the old fool a cheer,' said someone and to this invitation the succeeding files somewhat embarrassedly responded. 'They might have given us a band up this bloody hill.'

At the station the train to take us to London had no lights. In the growing darkness a man clambered onto the roof of the train to protest.

'It was the same after the Boer War. It's the same now. Ruddy heroes when you're wanted; so much muck when it's finished. It'll be the same next time as this.'

Lieutenant
Wilfred Bion,
5th Battalion,
Tank Corps

Complaints about the food that Christmas of 1918 were frequent. Driver Roberts, 130th Heavy Battery, RGA, sent a picture of his battery dinner near Roitzheim. 'They ask us to sign on after giving you a Christmas dinner like this,' he wrote. Note the food is balanced on an upturned school desk.

A day out on the Rhine: British troops relaxing on a barge as it sails away from the Hohenzollern Bridge.

I am demobilized and am twenty years of age. Behind me are four years of death, misery, and stark horror. I am dazed, and have no trade or profession. My body is whole but I have lost something that can never be regained. I have lost my youth. My father says my depression will pass, but it does not pass. At times I wish I had left my body with those who sleep beneath little crosses in France. Here I seem alone. Continually a panorama of those four years passes before me. My chums, Tubby, Johnny, and George, are back in their jobs. I have no job, and no ambition. There are thousands like me. We are young men without our youth, neither have we the stability of those more advanced in years. I see in my mind the miles of mud and shell holes. A vast grave, the little wooden crosses stand out against the sky line, the names of those beneath are marked upon them. Perhaps my name should have been among them. There at least I would *rest in peace*.

Sapper John Gowland, 50th (Northumbrian) Signal Company, Royal Engineers

*The moment,
long anticipated,
of the final
journey home
and for many an
uncertain future.*

LEAVING BOULOGNE 8. AM.

"BLIGHTY" IN SIGHT.

The war was a unique experience, a really amazing experience; we were lucky to take part, luckier still to have come through it without any serious injury. And you felt satisfaction that, if only in a very humble degree, you served your country at a very vital time. We all owed a duty to our country without any humbug, and we'd got to jump to it when the situation arose. It was part of the routine, very definitely, part of the routine. I'm being quite sincere about that.

I regretted the waste of time, of three and a half years when I should have been making my way, making some progress in life. I'd nothing to show for it, you see, but it wasn't anybody's fault. I was demobbed in April 1919 and received a bounty of £25. I spent £20 of that having a good suit made because I wanted to be respectably dressed to get a job.

Before the war, I had worked as a travelling representative for a hardware store, and at the end of the war I contacted them about my old job and they wrote to me and said, 'Don't be in a hurry back,' so I didn't bother writing again. I thought, 'Go to hell!' The meanness of it. I heard universities were giving scholarships, and I would have given my right arm to go to university, so I wrote to them asking whether there was any chance of me applying for one of these scholarships and they didn't reply, so I wrote a rude letter saying I was good enough to serve the country for three and a half years and they hadn't the decency to respond. That caused a bit of a stink.

I tried hard but I couldn't get a job. It was very frustrating, a very rough period, and then in September, I met this man, a Frenchman, and he was in the automatic machine business. He'd got a map of the Western Front, if you please, and he'd designed little bulbs which would light up and you could pick out a town, say Verdun, and information would be given about the town and the year of fighting there.

It was quite a good idea, and I was taken on to try and sell it, but who wanted to hear about the war after four years of fighting? I worked all week, evenings and weekends without a penny overtime, but in the end it was a wash-out.

Private Joe Yarwood, Royal Army Medical Corps, 31st Division

"HOMEWARD BOUND"

1914 TO 1918 WAR

Lance Corporal Victor Cole, 1st The Queen's Own (Royal West Kent Regiment)

When I went to sea, working as a wireless operator for Marconi, the men told me about the dangers they'd been through, how they'd once seen a periscope one day, the dreadful moment when they'd seen the periscope come up, and they'd turned the ship around and gone away, and somebody got torpedoed. I looked at them in amazement, with their nice bunks to sleep in and their three meals a day. In 1919 they were still on war bonus, getting an extra amount every month because there were a few floating mines. When I started telling them about Ypres and walking over the dead bodies and bones, they used to look at me in disbelief, they thought I was telling bloody lies, and they used to walk away, so I gave up speaking about it. I didn't care in those days; after the experience of that war, you learnt that. Whatever happened to me in life after that First War, it couldn't be any worse than what I'd already been through, so I didn't care.

Corporal Frederick Hodges, 10th The Lancashire Fusiliers

Mud, duckboards, shell holes, trenches, sandbags, barbed wire, dugouts, shattered tree stumps, dead mules. These were some of the sights. The sickly smell of dead mules, the fumes of cordite, the smell of phosgene lingering in shell holes, the acrid smell of burning rubbish, the mouth-watering smell of bacon frying… these were some of the smells.

The crump of shells bursting, the chatter of machine guns and the song of a lark high in the blue sky… these were some of the sounds.

Laughter, witticism, dry humour, real comradeship, everything shared, good or bad… This was the spirit in this uncomplicated world, free of essentials, life lived a day at a time with the threat of death common to all, of whatever rank.

I have always been grateful that I was old enough to go out to the front in 1918, and share those experiences.

Opposite:
Rough winter seas and the threat of mines made some journeys home more fretful than others.

Acknowledgements

I would like to thank the staff at Pen & Sword Books, who have been unflinching in their work on this book, especially Jonathan Wright, who has never failed to support me in each and every one of the books he has commissioned. I am very grateful to you, Jon. I would also like to sincerely thank Charles Hewitt for his continuing support as well as Heather Williams and Tara Moran for their work in production and marketing respectively. I should also like to thank Matt Jones and Katie Noble, who have also worked diligently on making this book what it is. As always, Jon Wilkinson has used his great talents on the book cover design and has produced something of which we are all proud. My sincere thanks to Dom Allen for the excellent maps and to Sylvia Menzies for the detailed index.

Linne Matthews has done an amazing job, casting her eye over the text and picking up every small error of mine: thank you, Linne. And finally my appreciation is due to Mat Blurton for his time and efforts in integrating nearly 200 pictures into the book and not even inviting me to 'get lost' when I asked if he could turn around some work on a Saturday night. He is exceptionally diligent and relaxed, a great combination.

I would like to thank the staff at such great research institutions as the Imperial War Museum, Lambeth, Special Collections, Leeds University and at the National Archives in Kew. I spend a not inconsiderable time at these three archives and I have always been met with great kindness and help.

I am once again in debt to my superb agent, Jane Turnbull, someone who has always been a great fount of advice and of support by email, phone or over a cup of tea at her home in Cornwall. Thank you again, Jane.

As ever, I am so grateful to my treasured Mum, Joan van Emden. No matter at what time I ask her to look over my work, she is willing to burn the midnight oil in what I can only think she still believes is a good cause. Either way, her efforts are tangible in the results, and her work and support are so greatly appreciated and admired. My thanks go to my wife, Anna: in any minor work crisis of mine she 'keeps calm and carries on', working in the City but then also looking after her two boys, one an eleven-year-old schoolboy, the other a middle-aged author! Thank you Anna, and thank you too, Ben, our wonderful son.

I am grateful to the following people for permission to reproduce photographs, extracts from diaries, letters or memoirs: David Empson, a good mate who has always very generously given me access to his great archive, and Andrew Thornton, Dan Hill, Tim Thurlow, and Helen Charlesworth for their help with images too. As always I am grateful to friends for advice and help, first and foremost, Taff Gillingham, for whom no First World War question of mine is too stupid (apparently), and believe me, some of mine are. Taff, you are always such a great mate and a great support. Thank you too, to friends Jeremy Banning, David Witzer, Michael LoCicero, Bob Smethurst, Kev Smith, and James Gordon-Cumming. Thanks also to David Blanchard, Phil Tomaselli.

Finally, I have sought whenever possible to obtain permission to use all the illustrations and quotations in this book. When this has not been possible, I would like to extend an apology and would be glad to hear from copyright holders.

Sources and Permissions

Published Memoirs

Atkinson, George Scott, *A Soldier's Diary*, W Collins Sons & Co, 1925

Behrend, Arthur, F., *Nine Days*, The Naval and Military Press, undated

Bion, Wilfred, *The Long Weekend, 1897–1919*, Fleetwood Press, 1982

Binding, Rudolf, *A Fatalist At War*, George Allen & Unwin, London, 1929

Byrne, Ginger, *I Survived Didn't I?*, Pen & Sword Books, Barnsley, 1993

Carr, William, *A Time to Leave the Ploughshares*, Robert Hale, London, 1985

Davis, Archibald H., *Extracts from the Diaries of a Tommy*, Cecil Palmer, 1932

Dunham, Frank, *The Long Carry*, Pergamon Press, Oxford, 1970

Fielding, Rowland, *War Letters to a Wife*, Spellmount Classics, 2001

Fuller, Sydney, *War Diary*, privately published, undated

Gibbs, A. Hamilton, *Gun Fodder*, Little, Brown and Company, Boston, 1924

Gowland, John, *War is Like That*, John Hamilton, London, undated

Graham, Stephen, *A Private in the Guards*, William Heinemann, London, 1928

Haworth, Christopher, *March to Armistice*, William Kimber, London, 1968

Hodges, Frederick, *Men of 18 in 1918*, Arthur H. Stockwell, Devon, 1988

Hope, Thomas, *The Winding Road Unfolds*, Putnam, London, 1937

Kiernan, Reginald, *Little Brother Goes Soldiering*, Constable, London, 1930

Martin, Albert, *Sapper Martin, The Secret Great War Diary*, Bloomsbury Publishing, 2009

Nichols, George Herbert Fosdike, (Quex) *Pushed and the Return Push*, W. Blackwood, 1919

Noakes, Frederick, E, *The Distant Drum*, Frontline Books, London, 2010

Rorie, David, *A Medico's Luck in the War*, The Naval and Military Press, undated

Smith, Aubrey, *Four Years on the Western Front*, Odhams Press, 1922

Spicer, Lancelot, D., *Letters From France 1915–1918*, Robert York, London, 1979

Sulzbach, Herbert, *Four Years on the Western Front*, Pen & Sword Books, Barnsley, 1998

Thomas, Alan, *A Life Apart*, Victor Gollancz, 1968

Voigt, Frederick, A., *Combed Out*, Jonathan Cape, London, 1920

Published Books

Baker, Chris, *The Battle for Flanders*, Pen & Sword Books, 2011

Blanchard, David, *Aisne 1918*, Pen & Sword Books, Barnsley, 2015

Cecil, Hugh & Liddle, Peter, *At the Eleventh Hour*, Pen & Sword, Barnsley, 1998

Hart, Peter, *1918 A Very British Victory*, Weidenfeld & Nicolson, 2008

van Emden, Richard, *Prisoners of the Kaiser*, Pen & Sword Books, 2000

van Emden, Richard, *Britain's Last Tommies*, Pen & Sword Books, 2005

W.A.S & J.D.N., *Wycliffe in the Great War*, John Bellows, Gloucester, 1923 (for letters of: Captain Eric Bird, Acting Captain Kenneth Jones, Captain Mervyn Sibley, Lieutenant Ivan Simpson, Lieutenant Leslie Tilley, Lieutenant George Timpson, Lieutenant H Riseley Tucker).

Unpublished Memoirs and Diaries
Cole, V., *An Englishman's Life*, 1973
Dewdney, George *'Diary'*
Foley, George. A., *On Active Service*, privately published, 1920
MacDermott, John Clarke, *An Enriching Life*, 1979
Strickland, Douglas, *letters*

Journals
Nisbet, Robert, *Reflections*, publ. The New Chequers: The Journal of the 'Friends of Lochnagar', No 2, Autumn 1995

Interviews conducted by the author with the following Great War veterans:
Private Arthur Barraclough, 1/4th Duke of Wellington's Regiment
Lance Corporal Vic Cole, 1st Royal West Kent Regiment
Private Frank Deane, 1/6th Durham Light Infantry
Private George Gadsby, 1/8th London Regiment (Irish Rifles)
Driver Alfred Henn, 3rd Battery, Warwickshire Royal Horse Artillery
Lance Corporal Frederick Hodges, 10th Lancashire Fusiliers
Private Walter Humphreys, 1/15 London Regiment (Civil Service Rifles)
Private Percy Johnson, 21st London Regiment
Private Fred Lloyd, Army Veterinary Corps
Private Albert Marshall, 8th Machine Gun Squadron, Machine Gun Corps (Cavalry)
Rifleman Robert Renwick, 16th King's Royal Rifle Corps
Private Doug Roberts, 7th Buffs (East Kent Regiment)
Corporal Ernie Stevens, 20th Middlesex Regiment
Private Percy Williams, 1/5th Northumberland Fusiliers
Private Joe Yarwood, 31st Division, Royal Army Medical Corps

Archives

Imperial War Museum: By kind permission of the Department of Documents, with grateful thanks to Tony Richards: private papers of IWM Docs: Driver Percival Glock, Royal Field Artillery, 1st Division.
IWM Docs: Captain Charles Miller, 2nd Battalion, Royal Inniskilling Fusiliers
IWM Docs: Private Edward Williamson, 17th Royal Scots

The Liddle Archive: Special Collections, Leeds University Library, Leeds.
By kind permission:
Company Quarter Master Sergeant Edward Lyons, GS0996
Second Lieutenant Michael Baines, GS0074
Private Wilfrid Edwards, GS0506

The National Archives, Kew
WO 363
Report of accidental death of Private George Hardy, 45225, 1/4th Duke of
Wellington's (West Riding) Regiment, held within his WWI Service Records, with
statements by:
Captain Alfred Kirk, MC, 1/4th Duke of Wellington's Regiment
Lieutenant Colonel Alfred Mowat, C.O., 1/4th Duke of Wellington's Regiment

Surrey History Centre: By kind permission of Surrey History Centre, Woking
Private George Fleet, QRWS/30/FLEE/1

The Regimental Museum of the Royal Welsh, Brecon
Quotations courtesy of The Regimental Museum of the Royal Welsh:
Private Charles Heare, 1/2nd Monmouthshire Regiment: 1997.139
Second Lieutenant Harold Jones, 2nd South Wales Borderers: 2001.98

Photographs
All pictures are taken from the author's private collection unless otherwise stated.

Army Medical Services Museum, Keogh barracks, Aldershot.
By kind permission of the curator, Rob McIntosh: the pictures of the 34 (1/1st
West Lancashire) Casualty Clearing Hospital. RAMC/730 P.76

Australian War Memorial, Canberra
By kind permission:
P10688.039.009, C04095, H15988, P01546.011, P01546.001, H04583

Herts@War Archive
By kind permission of the curator, Dan Hill
Images: pages 18 and 20/21

Imperial War Museum, London
By kind permission of the picture library of the Imperial War Museum:
Q Q56268, Q56269, Q91198, Q91351, Q91376, Q93858, Q94003, Q94134,
Q94139, Q94205

Photographs from the collection of Second Lieutenant John Lawrence 2012–05–73, 218 Siege Battery, RGA

National Army Museum, Chelsea, London
By kind permission:
Pictures of the Worcestershire Regiment, 1918
Accession Number:
NAM 1997-12-75-85, (103604), NAM 1997-12-75-87 (103605), NAM 1997-12-75-99 (103607), NAM 1997-12-75-101 (103608)

The Royal Dragoon Guards Regimental Museum, York
By kind permission: the pictures of Lieutenant Gilbert Cattley, pages 3, 13, 23, 37, 39, 113, 128, 234, 237, 283, 334

The Wardrobe, Museum of Wiltshire and Berkshire Regiment, Salisbury
By kind permission:
SBYRW 25019, 1st Royal Berkshire Regiment advancing, 21st August 1918

I should also like to extend a huge thanks to friends James Gordon-Cumming p.32, David Empson, pp.124–4, p.187, p.189, p.271, pp.274–5, p.300, p.318, p.356, Michael LoCicero, p.134, Andrew Thornton p298, p317, Tim Thurlow pp.8–9, Bob Smethurst, p.204, p.206, p.230, and Helen Charlesworth p.162, for permission to use a number of their privately-owned images.

Index

A NOTE ON THE AUTHOR

Richard van Emden has interviewed more than 270 veterans of the Great War and has written seventeen books on the subject including *The Trench* and *The Last Fighting Tommy*, both of which were top ten bestsellers. He has also worked on more than a dozen television programmes on the Great War, including the award-winning *Roses of No Man's Land*, *Britain's Boy Soldiers*, *A Poem for Harry*, *War Horse: the Real Story*, *Teenage Tommies* with Fergal Keane and most recently, *Hidden Histories: WW1's Forgotten Photographs*. He lives in London.

———